DATE DUE

6 1979

ROUSSEAU'S POLITICAL PHILOSOPHY

An Interpretation from Within

ROUSSEAU'S POLITICAL PHILOSOPHY

An Interpretation from Within

by STEPHEN ELLENBURG

Cornell University Press

ITHACA AND LONDON

320.5092
R864e
1976

First published 1976 by Cornell University Press.
Published in the United Kingdom by Cornell University Press Ltd., 2-4 Brook Street, London W1Y 1AA.

International Standard Book Number 0-8014-0960-8
Library of Congress Catalog Card Number 75-30481
Printed in the United States of America by York Composition Co., Inc.
Librarians: Library of Congress cataloging information appears on the last page of the book.

Acknowledgments

A fellowship from the National Endowment for the Humanities, supplemental grants from the Faculty Grants Committee of Mount Holyoke College, and a leave of absence from Mount Holyoke College enabled me to write this book. Shana R. Conron toiled to make my first draft intelligible. Without the extraordinary help later provided by Arthur R. Gold and Richard Johnson this book could not have been completed or published. Kurt Baum, John W. Chapman, Judith Ellenburg, Laura Fendrich, Philip Green, George Kateb, Susan J. Koch, Gerhard Loewenberg, William S. McFeely, Marion M. Smiley, and Margot S. Trout reacted or objected to parts or all of the various drafts. Marguerite S. Averill and Mary W. Shaughnessy typed and retyped manuscripts with good cheer. Lisa M. Perreault helped check proof. To all I am grateful.

Permission to quote from translations of Rousseau's writings has been kindly granted by St. Martin's Press, Inc., for *Jean-Jacques Rousseau: The First and Second Discourses*, edited by Roger D. Masters and translated by Roger D. and Judith R. Masters (New York, 1964); and by A. D. Peters and Co. Ltd., for *The Social Contract: Jean-Jacques Rousseau*, translated by Maurice Cranston (Baltimore, Penguin Books, 1968).

STEPHEN ELLENBURG

South Hadley, Massachusetts

Contents

7

Abbreviations

Annales   *Annales de la Société Jean-Jacques Rousseau.* 37 vols. 1905——.

CC   *Correspondence complète de Jean Jacques Rousseau.* Ed. R. A. Leigh. 21 vols. Geneva: Institut et Musée Voltaire; Madison: The University of Wisconsin Press; Banbury, Oxfordshire: The Voltaire Foundation, 1965——.

CG   *Correspondance générale de J.-J. Rousseau.* Ed. Théophile Dufour and P.-P. Plan. 20 vols. Paris: Armand Colin, 1924–1934.

H   *Oeuvres complètes de J.-J. Rousseau.* 13 vols. Paris: Hachette, 1865–1873.

P   Jean Jacques Rousseau, *Oeuvres complètes.* Ed. Bernard Gagnebin and Marcel Raymond. 4 vols. Paris: Bibliothèque de la Pléiade, Gallimard, 1959——.

Whenever possible, I cite CC and P.

ROUSSEAU'S POLITICAL PHILOSOPHY

An Interpretation from Within

CHAPTER 1

Introduction

Besieged by accusations of chaotic inconsistency and fanciful paradox during his lifetime, Jean-Jacques Rousseau repeatedly insisted upon the unity of his political writings. His
"principal works" are, he claimed, "inseparable and together
form a single whole."[1] In his *Letter to Beaumont*—Beaumont
was the Archbishop of Paris who had denounced *Emile* in a
pastoral letter—Rousseau expressed surprise at the official attacks from Paris and Geneva that greeted the publication of
Emile. The same ideas, Rousseau asserted, had appeared earlier
in the *Discourse on Inequality*, the *Letter to d'Alembert on
the Theater*, and *La Nouvelle Héloïse*: "I wrote on diverse
subjects, but always with the same principles; always the same
teaching, the same belief, the same maxims, and, if you prefer,
the same opinions."[2] Comparable declarations of consistency
are numerous.[3]

1. *Letters to Malesherbes* (Jan. 1762; P, I, 1136). The three "principal
works" are the *Discourse on the Sciences and Arts*, the *Discourse on
Inequality*, and *Emile*. Perhaps Rousseau excluded the *Social Contract*
because of his reluctance to mention writings before publication. His
judgments were also a bit fickle, except for unwavering pride in *Emile*
and reservations about the *Discourse on the Sciences and Arts*—after
the publication of the *Discourse on Inequality*—and *La Nouvelle
Héloïse*. Translations are my own, except where indicated.
2. *Letter to Beaumont* (Mar. 1763; P, IV, 928); see also *ibid.*, pp. 950–
951, where Rousseau explained that he assumes earlier works in order
to avoid repetition.
3. *Rousseau juge de Jean-Jacques* (P, I, 694–696, 930–933, 940–941);
Confessions (P, I, 406–407); *Jugement sur la polysynodie* (P, III, 645n).

Further evidence of Rousseau's tenacious determination to be consistent comes from his summoning his reader's indulgence while he prepares clarifications and from his inviting the reader to seek elaborations of a point at issue in earlier writings. Rousseau's discussion of "legitimate government" in the *Social Contract* begins with warnings of the delicacy of the subject and the difficulties of making oneself clear to the unattentive. His arguments that the power of rightful punishment belongs to a sovereign citizenry but cannot be exercised by this sovereign, and that a citizen is simultaneously a subject, are accompanied by pleas for the reader's patience, assurances of his own consistency, and complaints about the awkwardness of the conventional terminology available to him.[4] While discussing in *Emile* the inclinations of infants and children, Emile's choice of an occupation, and the import of Sophie's coquetry, Rousseau refers his reader to the *Discourse on Inequality* for a fuller treatment of the gradual appearance and development of man's sensibility, of the significance of an economic division of labor, and of the nature of jealousy.[5] His denunciation of the contemporary Genevan constitution in the *Letters from the Mountain* is accompanied by invitations to examine the arguments defending a true "separation of powers" in the *Social Contract*.[6] His proposal for a partial restoration of the ancient Polish constitution includes references to the principles of a true republic in the *Social Contract*.[7]

I believe that Rousseau's political writings do in fact contain an indigenous unity of intention, argument, and understanding, if not always a consistency of idiom and terminology. The writings abound with paradoxes, which the reader must accept and explain. But accusations of overall contradiction and inconsistency are superficial. In charting the course of

4. *Social Contract* (P, III, 395, 377, 373n).
5. *Emile* (P, IV, 556n, 466–467, 796).
6. *Letters from the Mountain* (P, III, 770–771).
7. *Government of Poland* (P, III, 975–982).

Rousseau's ideas, I find that Rousseau's political writings echo and reecho within each other; there is no shift of direction in successive writings. The *Discourse on Inequality* is an early tracing whose contours state and prepare the essence of his thought. Although I examine in separate chapters the *Discourse on Inequality*, the *Social Contract*, and *Emile*, I ignore chronology and enlist aspects of these and other writings to establish and sustain my argument.

This study has four parts. The three chapters of Part One provide the groundwork for my interpretation. Here I argue the unchanging structure of Rousseau's political thought by contrasting his ideas with that liberal individualist mode of thought first comprehensively expounded by Locke. I call "nonindividualist," not "collectivist," the related ideas out of which all of Rousseau's writings are constructed. The second chapter of Part One concerns the "form" of the *Discourse on Inequality*, specifically Rousseau's understanding of the significance of society and historicity. The third chapter introduces his nonindividualist notion of the "general" and the "particular," a subject I return to in Part Three.

Nonindividualism, however, provides only the framework of Rousseau's thought. In Part Two I discuss Rousseau's zealous imperative involving the absolute, unqualified individual liberty that comes with literal self-government. This radical political egalitarianism gives focus to his vision and animates all his writings; it accounts for the relentless momentum of his ideas and occasions his essential paradoxes. The ideas discussed in Part Three are the inevitable result of those discussed in Part One and Part Two: Rousseau's conception of a virtuous citizenry brings together nonindividualism and radical egalitarianism. A passionate unity and discipline of common life, which involves adherence to the general will of civic virtue embodied in every citizen (Part Three), is the essential means for the "perfect independence" of citizens (Part Two), all of whom are the mutually dependent creatures of a determinate common life (Part One). In the two concluding chapters (Part Four) I apply this interpretation to Rousseau's companion writings published in 1762, the *Social Contract* and *Emile*. These two works, the capstone of Rousseau's political philosophy, are fictive demonstrations that absolute liberty for social men is conceivable and feasible. These imaginary *histoires* of self-governing citizens also demonstrate, by way of contrast, our own irreparable enslavement. The *Social Contract* and *Emile* are eulogies to an unrecorded past by a lawgiver of the pen.

I employ the contrast with liberal individualism in Part One because I agree with Hume: "Everything in this world is judged of by comparison."[8] More specifically, the contrast with liberalism exposes the enduring structure of Rousseau's writings, and permits one to get inside Rousseau's philosophy in an orderly manner and without fortuitous or extraneous impositions. The nonindividualist structure of Rousseau's political philosophy and the implications of the contrast between Rousseau's philosophy and liberalism are also the basis for my own disagreement with many interpretations of his philosophy. These interpretations assert related contradictions concerning individualism and collectivism; or conscience, will, reason, and passion; or the abstract and the concrete; or natural liberty, moral freedom, and civil liberty; or Rousseau the moralist and Rousseau the political theorist; or Rousseau the celebrant of spontaneity within familial society, of the rustic simplicity of Swiss cantons, and of a Spartan discipline of civic virtue; or Rousseau the apologist of natural license and of authoritarianism. I find that none of these familiar accusations of contradiction is warranted.

One of the essential aspects of Rousseau's nonindividualism is his attentiveness to circumstantial variations of time and

8. David Hume, *A Treatise of Human Nature*, 2 vols. (London, 1911), II, 46.

space. The "placing" and therefore the appreciation of single writings, and many puzzling, seemingly contradictory requirements in Rousseau's thought, can be grasped only in their appropriate historical and social contexts, or with reference to what Rousseau calls the *rapports* and *moeurs* of a determinate common life. Similarly, Rousseau's nonindividualism compels one to consider inherently political those writings and ideas slighted by interpretations of Rousseau's philosophy which mistakenly distinguish politics from moral, social, religious, economic, and educational matters. Rousseau is first and foremost a political philosopher, a philosopher who sees as indistinguishable moral commitment and political integrity.

Liberalism, here, serves merely as an analytical device, not a villain, and is most definitely not the subject of this study. No doubt the tone of the comparison betrays my own hesitations about liberalism. Some of us are undeniably grateful to the liberal tradition, among others, for its support of civil liberties. And I do not want inadvertently to endorse those frenetic choruses of our own day which repudiate or are mindlessly nonchalant about "bourgeois" liberties. My quarrel with liberalism is not over general values, but with the philosophical assumptions upon which these values are, inadequately, understood and defended by liberals: the individualist assumptions of natural rights and utilitarian doctrines, as well as the parallel assumptions defining a so-called free market economy. I think the liberal mode of thought errs descriptively and that its related assumptions, so attractive to common sense, are, in Whitehead's phrase, fallacies of misplaced concreteness: an individual is not a self-made man; a society is not a numerical aggregation of discrete individuals and interest groups that mechanically collide and bargain as separate units; a general interest or common good, however realized or thwarted, is not a resultant sum of the private interests of separate units; the subject matter of politics is not exhausted by considerations of the form of government and the extent of government intervention in a private sector; and individual liberty, which does include the reciprocal right of fellow citizens to be left alone, is not equatable with aloneness. If ancient and postliberal political theories find their point of departure in what citizens, because of a shared past, are and may become in common and what they disclose through public action, then liberalism simply is not a true political theory. Socrates, considering the opportunity to evade his sentence, is reminded by the Laws of Athens that we "gave you life in the first place"; and Aristotle argues that an isolated man who does not "share in the benefits of political association" must be "either a beast or a god," must be "either a poor sort of being, or a being higher than man."[9] Such an understanding of politics was commonplace in the history of political philosophy until liberal theorists reified the "private citizen" and the interest group. Such understandings of common life presage some of the interrelated ideas forming the nonindividualist structure of Rousseau's philosophy, ideas more fundamental and pervasive than some undeniably illiberal considerations intrinsic to Rousseau's thought.

Current judgments and understandings of events are also inhibited by the unacknowledged legacy of traditional liberalism. The causes of contemporary political dilemmas are certainly not to be located in our political concepts. Nevertheless, superficial, sterile, and usually specious antinomies derived from liberalism dominate our political discourse and define our most recent science of politics. Minority rights or majority rule, individual liberty or public order, conflict or consensus, liberty or obedience, liberty or equality, self-reliance or paternalism, and selfishness or altruism are variations on liberalism's pervasive distinction of the individual versus society or of individualism versus collectivism. Our science of politics is conceptually muddled and descriptively inaccurate because it is the unwitting heir of liberal fallacies. This confusion may also be

9. Plato *Crito* 50d (trans. Hugh Tredennick); Aristotle *Politics* 1253a (trans. Ernest Barker).

seen from several fashionable preoccupations: a preoccupation with governmental institutions (or, to use current labels, with a political system, its boundaries, and those problems of boundary determination reminiscent of liberal theorists' difficulties in distinguishing public from private sectors); a preoccupation with struggles for power or pluralistic group interests that presume to explain the policy making process; and, awkwardly, a preoccupation with recently discovered private governments and political culture. Our empirical science of politics, which purports to describe how discrete units and separate interests are processed, stalled, or rejected by a political system, presents a picture not unlike the limited resource of a crowded divided highway along which self-propelled, anonymous automobiles travel toward no articulated destination. The separate, interchangeable, disposable, and unanchored parts, which together merely occupy a circumscribed environment, are competing or compatible demands of varying strengths. These demands may collide, or they may enter or be denied access to the processing machinery labeled the political system.

Consideration of these aspects of current political discourse is beyond my intention here. The implications of traditional liberalism are pursued in Part One no further than required for appreciation of Rousseau's contrasting view. And although a contagious "either/or" habit of thought is characteristic of Rousseau's own philosophy, Rousseau and liberalism do not exhaust the possibilities: many political theorists would straddle or be out of range of this contrast.

In Part Two I try to establish how Rousseau conceived absolute liberty—liberty itself, not specified liberties—as the very purpose of politics. I characterize this radically egalitarian imperative as anarchism, even though Rousseau called himself a republican, or very rarely a democrat, employed the word *anarchy* to refer only to the slavery and disorder of the modern state, and was apt to fasten onto the principle of natural goodness, rather than natural liberty or equality, as the basis of his political thought. The term *anarchism* is appropriate. Natural goodness, itself an eighteenth-century cliché, became for Rousseau the absence of a natural inclination to command or obey other men. And by the anarchistic imperative within Rousseau's thought I mean that, for Rousseau, the absolute liberty of literal self-government was the only alternative to the slavery of dependence upon another's will. Rousseau could conceive no middle ground between liberty and slavery. He denounced every arrangement, official and unofficial, in which some rule others who obey. He found every expression of inequality, every division between governors and governed, a denial of liberty and therefore slavery, for both ruler and ruled. Unlike Harrington, Sidney, and Montesquieu, Rousseau was a "republican" hostile to more than absolute monarchy.

My purpose in employing the term *anarchism*, which, like *liberalism*, is a nineteenth-century term covering a variety of political theories, is not to deprive Rousseau's thought of its intractable density and complexity. I do not wish to reduce Rousseau to a label or to the two labels, nonindividualism and anarchism. The term *anarchism* serves rather to locate and relate those crucial movements, in his nonindividualist philosophy, which constitute the very rhythm of his intelligence. The term *anarchism* is also helpful because it avoids confusion between my interpretation and those which detect a Kantian conception of moral freedom or perfectibility at the center of Rousseau's thought. And it is neither surprising nor contradictory that Rousseau's anarchistic imperative of absolute, "negative" liberty yields a vision of a united and disciplined citizenry obedient to rules but not rulers. As I discuss in Part Three, when nonindividualism is reconciled with anarchism, the final mark of Rousseau's anarchistic imperative is his relentless repudiation of political dismemberment and civic distraction.

The interpretation which I have briefly sketched eschews three "sources" frequently employed as approaches to Rousseau's political philosophy. Rousseau's psychological make-up and his life; his borrowings from contemporaneous and ancient theorists; and, retrospectively, the putative effects of Rousseau's ideas upon subsequent political theory and action.

A psychological study of Rousseau would offer perhaps the most seductive approach to Rousseau's philosophy, if only because of the fascination of Rousseau's life and character. Rousseau did insist on occasion that his formal political writings and life are inseparable, that to understand his ideas one must understand him. He offered his autobiographical writings as political documents, interpreted the events of his unusual life as illustrative of perennial political questions, and occasionally attempted in his daily habits to exemplify his thought.[10] Moreover, there is ample testimony to Rousseau's anarchistic imperative in his letters and autobiographical writings, with their lectures on man's right to unmediated liberty, the political ambiguities of gratitude and friendship and courtesy, the humiliation involved in signing letters "Your obedient servant," and the enslaving character of every form of foreign direction. But my elucidation of Rousseau's radically egalitarian imperative does not use these writings. In any case, the correspondence between Rousseau's life and political thought is far from clear. Often denying that he was or in contemporary times could become a virtuous citizen, Rousseau claimed that he remained a naturally good man uniquely entitled to the solitude necessary for reverie, writing, copying music, botanizing, making lace, and wandering about the countryside.[11] Yet the

---

10. Preface to *Narcisse* (P, II, 961, 973–974); *Letter to Beaumont*, pp. 962–965; *Rousseau juge de Jean-Jacques*, pp. 686–690, 695–697, 739–741, 755–759, 764–772; *Rêveries* (P, I, 1013). Yet in *Rousseau juge de Jean-Jacques*, Rousseau justified his life and writings in separate "dialogues," a distinction he insisted upon in both the *Letter to Lecat*, defending the *Discourse on the Sciences and Arts* (P, III, 97–102), and in *Letters from the Mountain*, pp. 790–794.

11. *Moral Letters* (P, IV, 1102–1103); *Rousseau juge de Jean-Jacques*,

vision of a virtuous citizenry unites Rousseau's nonindividualism and anarchism. Although he always claimed to speak for a common interest that transcends contemporary sectarianism, Rousseau believed that the occupation of a writer, including that of a philosopher, is not virtuous or useful. And he frequently distinguished personal preferences from judgments of political right; for example, the satisfaction he derived from attending and writing for the dramatic theater did not warrant the establishment of a theater in Geneva.

A further difficulty with a psychological approach is that it speciously equates the fundamental with the lower depths. From this perspective Rousseau's political ideas tend to become unrelated effusions of a personality, mere incidental illustrations for a different intellectual endeavor. Rousseau's *Emile* will become, as he occasionally suggested, an expiation for his shabby treatment of his own children.[12] It will become a writing about familial and moral duties and private education that, except for a brief coda, is of little intrinsic concern to the critic of Rousseau's political thought. Similarly, his fulminations against divisive particular societies of doctors, priests, philosophes, accountants, lawyers, and magistrates become evocations of his chronic maladies and recurrent political exile, just as his hymns to the sincere and simple egalitarianism of a golden age are read as nostalgia for an idealized youth or the resentment of a clumsy, shy outcast.

Indeed, one who is convinced of the autonomy, integrity, and importance of Rousseau's political philosophy might occasionally regret that, unlike Kant, Rousseau led an eventful,

---

pp. 812–830, 847–852, 859–860, 864–867, 873–874, 913; *Letters to Malesherbes*, pp. 1131–1133, 1137.

12. Letter to Mme Dupin (Dec. 11, 1760; CC, VII, 352); letter to Mme de Luxembourg (June 12, 1761; CC, IX, 15). See also *Emile*, pp. 262–263; *Confessions*, pp. 594–595. Rousseau suggested a similar atonement with *La Nouvelle Héloise*. Letter to M. de Saint-Germain (Feb. 26, 1770; CG, XIX, 242–243).

carefully chronicled life. Although personality and thought are sometimes incompatible, one often thinks that aspects of Rousseau's personality are best illuminated in his formal political writings, that the moral dilemmas of his life are prefigured in the demands of his philosophy. In any case and however inadvertently, to approach Rousseau's philosophy as disguised self-portraiture, as an incessant dramatization of his life, or as a series of passionate outbursts serving inner needs is to dismiss it preemptively or to demean it as a philosophy.

A second quite different approach traces Rousseau's intellectual debts, especially to ancient theorists. Rousseau's comprehension of classical texts and etymology was sometimes vivid; he preferred some ancient theorists and, in his own eccentric version, some ancient political societies to those of his own day. And Rousseau's understanding of citizenship and common life, unique in modern thought until the advent of socialist and socialist-anarchist theorists, suggest ancient philosophy. Nevertheless, a genealogical approach may stress aspects of earlier traditions that are not fundamental to Rousseau's own thought. Even though this approach notes both similarities and dissimilarities between Rousseau and ancient theorists, it still fails to establish the coherent meaning of Rousseau's own ideas, the integrity of single writings and his entire political theory. For example, the historical evolution of the species Rousseau described in the *Discourse on Inequality*, although not the significance he found in a differentiation between agriculture and metallurgy within this evolution, resembles that in Lucretius' *On the Nature of Things*. This observation, however, obscures the importance to Rousseau of historical periodicity and of economic specialization. It also obscures the intimate relationship of the *Discourse on Inequality* to both the *Social Contract* and *Emile*. A similar difficulty arises from what is often taken to be Rousseau's unacknowledged borrowings from contemporaries.

One cumulative but largely unstated conclusion of my argument is that Rousseau often failed to discover a vocabulary adequate to his ideas, a language for the expression of his thought. Many of the bare, conventional idioms of political philosophy, especially those of his contemporaries, are misleading: *state of nature, social contract, natural law* or *natural right, state, constitution, law, general will, republic, education* and *government* are examples. Every interpretation of Rousseau's thought should heed his advice to Mme d'Epinay: "Learn my vocabulary better, my good friend, if you want us to understand each other. Believe me, my terms rarely have their usual meaning."[13] Aspects of Rousseau's thought are apt to become more obscure if one merely catalogues the similarities and dissimilarities between Rousseau and other theorists, for Burke's observation about *Emile* is no less true of Rousseau's other writings: "To know what the received notions are upon any subject, is to know with certainty what those of Rousseau are not."[14] One needs to appreciate only the obstinate intensity and extraordinary originality of Rousseau's philosophy to accept the comment on genealogy by another student of Rousseau: "To determine a writer's sources is in the last resort, and by definition, to determine what he himself is not. It is more difficult to determine what he himself actually is, and it is not enough simply to subtract, as it were, his sources from himself."[15]

An interpretation that begins with classical theories of natural justice will slight much that is fundamental to Rousseau's thought, unless additional arguments are improvised. Although there are some correspondences, including misleading corre-

13. Letter to Mme d'Epinay (Mar. 12, 1756; CC, III, 296). See also *Fragments on the State of Nature* (P, III, 475) and *Fragments on Moeurs* (P, III, 558-559).

14. Quoted in Annie Marion Osborn, *Rousseau and Burke: A Study of the Idea of Liberty in Eighteenth Century Thought* (1940; reprint ed., New York, 1964), p. 119.

15. Jean Guéhenno, *Jean-Jacques Rousseau*, trans. John and Doreen Weightman, 2 vols. (London, 1966), I, 292.

spondences of terminology, Rousseau departed significantly from classical thought. He rejected the germinal notion of ancient thought that man is by nature a political being, that intelligence or reason or speech defines the essential character of man. Ancient understandings of virtue (and of kinds of virtue that transcend civic duty and political membership) do not correspond to Rousseau's idea of an essential but instrumental civic virtue that dissolves distinctions between society and polity, because Rousseau included, among the duties of virtuous citizens, both useful manual labor and participation in public celebrations of civic piety. And Rousseau's demand for literal self-government is incompatible with ancient (and contemporary) theories of distributive justice and proportionate equality. Herodotus' notion of Athenian democracy or isonomy notwithstanding, ancient citizens, in both theory and fact, constitute an exclusive group whose members rule and in turn are ruled by one another. Rousseau's virtuous citizens, in contrast, are radically equal or self-governing in the sense that all men are citizens and that no citizen ever rules or is ruled by another. Rousseau correctly claimed to be starting from scratch.[16] To interpret him as a modern classicist may drain ancient theory of much of its intrinsic meaning or exhibit more concern for the fate of ancient arguments and preoccupations among modern theorists than for his own political philosophy.

Rousseau is undoubtedly, if vaguely, representative of turbulent times for, as Trotsky remarked, landscape painters do not flourish in the Sahara. But those who have lined up behind barricades chanting Rousseauist slogans or have withdrawn from the modern state into solitude are awkward arbiters, whether initial or final, of his thought. My rejection of this third, retrospective source neither disputes nor affirms that Rousseau's ideas have had the effects attributed to them. Yet

16. *Letter to Beaumont,* pp. 967–969; *Moral Letters,* pp. 1087–1091; letter to Franquières (Jan. 15, 1769; P, IV, 1134–1136; 1139–1140); *Rousseau juge de Jean-Jacques,* pp. 728, 933–934.

the implications of the assumption that political theory and practice are inseparable, that traditional political theory is either an ideological guide to action or inaction, or a series of mistaken, emotive grunts of an unscientific character, do not square with essentials of Rousseau's philosophy. Even when, assuming the guise of a kind of remote patriot reformer, Rousseau advised Poles, Corsicans, and Genevans, his palliative, restorative proposals were consciously impractical. They recalled an irretrievable past. And the *Social Contract* and *Emile*, companion demonstrations that his principles of political right are feasible, cannot serve as manuals of remedial action for modern slaves. Whether or not one believes theory is sullied when associated with praxis, Rousseau's thought remains an uncompromising and pessimistic indictment of the self-destructive slavery and viciousness permanently embedded in the very fabric of contemporary life. Rousseau was concerned not with how mutually dependent parts might become a united whole but rather with how a political whole historically became and was obliged to remain diffuse. This same pessimism characterizes Rousseau's other fundamental ideas; and perhaps there is something noble about a radical egalitarian who never prophesied with comforting glee a revolutionary leap into the future kingdom of freedom, or justified an attempt to repeal the imperfect, or argued that the next, or most recent, revolution must be defended as mankind's last.

These three sorceries can shed light on Rousseau's political philosophy. But when the permanent structure and rhythm of Rousseau's philosophy are at stake, none of these approaches is a satisfactory point of departure and, especially, of return. None can demonstrate the unity of his thought for none can explain complexities and essential paradoxes intrinsic to his thought. Were Rousseau's "inaccurate" and "unfair" dismissals of Aristotle, Grotius, Pufendorf, Hobbes, Locke, Montesquieu, Condillac, and Helvétius merely gratuitous? or libelous? or ignorant? or a puerile refusal to acknowledge intellectual debto? Why, in view of Rousseau's reliance upon patriotic fervor and national unity, does his proposal for a partial restoration of the ancient Polish constitution begin by welcoming that loss of Polish territory and inhabitants occasioned by foreign partition? Why did he recommend that the Polish people further strengthen their nation with additional, voluntary contractions? Why did Rousseau hold such ancient, or dated, ideas of women with reference to politics? How does one reconcile arguments about law and a rule of law, about personal economic property, and about different modes of education? Why, in view of his insistence upon personal liberty, did Rousseau often endorse intolerance and censorship of various sorts, defend corvées, and condemn as unmitigated slavery the eighteenth-century English constitution and representative government? Both toleration and inventive entrepreneurship in the sciences and arts were subscribed to by every anglophile French theorist of the eighteenth century, and there was no more hated symbol of the discredited *ancien régime* than corvées. How, indeed, is a revolutionary zeal for liberty consistent with Rousseau's fears of imminent revolutions whose proffered defense, he recognized, would be liberty? Why did Rousseau assert that, in a true republic of self-governing citizens, the form of legitimate government and also the magistrates may be changed daily while denying enslaved men a right of resistance against governments of contemporary societies? How is a sensitivity to the hallowed texture of historical time and space compatible with a proclaimed disdain for facts and considerations of abstract political right? And, if an interpretation is to encompass Rousseau's thought, rather than merely to cite it, how can an appreciation of each of these curiosities be related to an appreciation of the others?

The stubborn wrinkles and creases of the final version of the *Social Contract* invite an interpretation from within. Why did Rousseau ascribe the foundation of a free society to both a social contract and a lawgiver? How can naturally free and equal men, when "totally alienated" and "forced to be free," lose nothing, gain much, "still obey themselves alone," and "remain as free as before"? How can there be limits to popular sovereignty? Why are all rulers of other men enslaved to those whom they thereby enslave? Why must the establishment of "legitimate government" be a comically complicated, noncontractual "complex act"? Why, in view of his argument that legitimate government tends to usurp popular sovereignty, did Rousseau reject mixed government and yet require a separation of legislative and executive powers? Is the rejection of representative government consistent with the rejection of direct democracy in favor of elective aristocracy? Why must "true law" be general in both its object and its source? Why are men who are convicted of breaking true laws punishable, with terrifying severity, as traitors, even when Rousseau conceded the inefficacy of punishment for both criminal and obedient citizen? These and other paradoxes of the *Social Contract* cannot be explained or even seriously encountered independently of the *Discourse on Inequality* and *Emile*. By simply repeating or ignoring these challenges to the integrity of Rousseau's political philosophy we fail to come to terms with the very meaning of that philosophy.

This book includes neither the critical appraisal which customarily concludes an interpretation of this sort nor an explicit, systematic refutation of contrasting interpretations. I would not have undertaken this study if I had thought everything worth saying had already been said. I believe, as perhaps other critics who have puzzled over Rousseau's political thought also believe, that more nonsense has been written about Rousseau than about any other major political theorist. On the other hand, many interpretations of Rousseau deserve sustained and careful examination. Such examination, however, would unnecessarily lengthen this study and blur its character. For the benefit of readers interested in pursuing similar and contrasting interpretations, I record in footnotes major agreements and disagreements regarding specific points and general arguments. Regrettably but unavoidably, these references are sometimes taken out of their larger contexts.

But to speak of agreements and disagreements is misleading. An attempt to understand both troublesome single passages and complete writings invites consideration of the entire scope and unity of Rousseau's philosophy. Rousseau's thought, however, is not a riddle that requires the discovery either of a key for unlocking all perplexities or of a formula of irrefutable scientific exactitude, after which scholars are permitted to move on to other subjects. A political philosopher as intricate, important, and occasionally exasperating as Rousseau must always occasion contrasting interpretations, if only because there are alternative approaches to his thought. For both provocation and recognition of the complexities of Rousseau's thought, I am as indebted to interpretations with which I cannot agree as to those with which I do.

That contrasting interpretations can scarcely cancel each other does not imply that the basis for understanding Rousseau is subjective taste or an initiation into esoteric doctrines and unspoken intentions. And an interpretation which argues or denies a fundamental unity to Rousseau's philosophy must be capable of encompassing all of his political writings. As I mentioned, Rousseau often lacked a terminology that has the clarity and concreteness his ideas required. In making his points he sometimes fell back upon rhetoric, irony, the unrecorded facts of an ancient past, "unfair" rejections of others' views, and historical myth, this last a kind of speculative narrative which reveals the origin or inevitable consequences of a political arrangement. And, once again, the specific social and historical referents of his ideas must be kept in mind, especially as these *rapports* of common life shift or evolve in a single writing.

The difficulty of sustained generalizing about Rousseau's ideas makes it especially tempting to document assertions with apparently conclusive citations. To argue, as is frequently argued, that Rousseau's thought, or a portion of his thought, is Lockeian in character, one might cite Rousseau's defense against the burning by Genevan authorities of the *Social Contract:* Rousseau claimed that Locke's philosophy had been based on "exactly the same principles" as his own.[17] But moving beyond citation by developing and sustaining this argument proves impossible. We can at least read, reread, and reflect upon the texts. Of course, not even an attentiveness to scope assures completeness or eliminates interpretative judgment and inference, as Rousseau recognized when he proscribed modern historians from Emile's curriculum. Hence I conclude this study with chapters on the *Social Contract* and *Emile.*

These two chapters of Part Four are also a kind of epilogue intended to substitute for the customary critical appraisal. There are several reasons for this substitution. I admit to a congenital dislike for summaries or Benthamite totals, and I find wearisome those conclusive but elusive exhortations in which one idea of a major political philosopher is arbitrarily singled out for applause and another for a spanking. I would not have been able to attempt this kind of study if I were unsympathetic to what I take to be the major burdens of Rousseau's political thought. Like ancient theorists Rousseau appreciated that politics concerns matters of substantive value and purpose which are public or common to "equal" citizens. His idea of citizenship is inseparable from individual liberty and public action. It means direct participation in and responsibility for the affairs of common life. It means more than occasional, secret balloting for representatives by certified and solitary residents in the

17. *Letters from the Mountain*, p. 812. Ancient and modern theorists are discussed throughout the *Social Contract* but Locke is never mentioned. More important, Rousseau repeatedly veiled and softened his ideas by invoking Locke or by employing Lockeian phrases in a misleading manner.

shrouded anonymity of voting booths. I also share Rousseau's views that true citizenship and the modern state are incompatible and that no ruler of others is self-governing, because he rules others. And like any reasonably alert observer of twentieth-century politics, I recognize the precariousness in inegalitarian forms of common life. In short, I am mesmerized by Rousseau's *Discourse on Inequality,* and not only because I find his other political writings scarcely comprehensible independently of it.

These bald sympathies for Rousseau's nonindividualism and anarchism do not preclude dissent. Because the intention behind this work is homage to a major political theorist rather than his posthumous trial, I include, and do not excuse, the sometimes repugnant and sometimes foolish implications of nonindividualism and anarchism. But my main reason for omitting a conclusive critical appraisal is respect for the complexities of perennial questions raised sharply by Rousseau. I recognize that a true and fair appraisal, grounded in Rousseau's philosophy, might itself be an original, comprehensive work of political theory. Rousseau deserves no less.

For a conclusion to this study of the unity of Rosseau's political thought, I can now offer only this introduction. Perhaps the study itself is a preliminary critical appraisal. As Henry James said: "To criticise is to appreciate, to appropriate, to take intellectual possession, to establish in fine a relation with the criticised thing and make it one's own."[18]

18. Henry James, *The Art of the Novel: Critical Prefaces,* ed. Richard P. Blackmur (New York, 1934), p. 155.

PART ONE

THE ARTIFICIAL
INDIVIDUAL

CHAPTER 2

Rousseau and the
Liberal Tradition

Questions about the shape and circumstances of personal liberty dominate Jean-Jacques Rousseau's political thought, as they do that of the traditional liberal philosophers with whom Rousseau is often but mistakenly lumped. Moreover, Rousseau advocated absolute liberty or literal self-government so insistently that he equated all instances of external rule, whether governmental or not, with slavery. Ignorance of this anarchistic imperative animating his thought makes his ideas a tangle of arbitrary assertions and robs them of their moral urgency.

Rousseau's understanding of individual liberty and the circumstances of its realization is also grounded in a philosophical orientation radically different from that upon which classical liberal thought is based, different in premises and in structure. Rousseau's rejection of the liberal mode of thought is the subject of these next three chapters.

The Liberal Individualist Mode of Thought

Liberalism posits the existence of a discrete individual either with private interests or with rights claimed independent of common life. The individual is either naturally endowed with rights and interests or acquires them unaided. The claim and exercise of these rights and interests originate neither in sustained, cohesive social involvement nor in mutual recognition of shared experience, even though others may be identically endowed or identically successful in their private acquisitions. The individual is literally self-made; he exclusively possesses himself because he owes no debts to others.

According to early liberal philosophy, individuals forfeit a portion of their self-exclusiveness to fabricate a political environment in which to secure private interests. Individuals make, but are not made by, political society: aside from gaining personal security by instituting government, individuals undergo no change by their deliberate aggregation. Society remains a numerical aggregation. Political society is merely a sum of separate, preexistent parts that join together and resign and rejoin. When individuals obey and disobey identical magistrates and an identical positive law, they still share nothing but their officially recognized private interests. Liberal philosophy begins with and retains the part at the expense of the whole; political society in liberal theory betrays no more solidarity and continuity than a supervised neighborhood bingo game.

Liberty, then, is a private remnant, the sphere of exclusiveness retained by each individual. Whatever is not surrendered to the public sphere of governmental management remains private and nonpolitical. Liberal philosophers contradict themselves and quarrel with each other about where to draw the line, but all proceed from the distinction between two mutually exclusive spheres of life. The scope of the political extends only to governmental action and to those who seek to influence or capture government. Politics is the relationship between private individuals, who obey, disobey, petition, and vote, and representative public men, who legislate and enforce positive law. All other relationships, whether temporary or not, are private contracts and therefore free; education, religion, economic and family affairs are nonpolitical considerations in an aggregation of private solitudes.

Liberal theorists dispute questions involving legitimacy and desirability, but they always consider governmental action to be intervention. It is an intrusion into that remnant private sector of individual freedom that announces the presence of authoritative political direction in a once fluid realm. Each individual is free when left alone within his private sphere; and liberty, preserved only by public inaction, can never be enhanced, much less created, by what must be considered external encroachment. Hence liberal thought always drifts toward laissez faire. Limited government assures security but must not tamper with individual spontaneity, self-reliance, and initiative. Correspondingly, liberal theorists emphasize the punitive and regulatory aspects of positive law, especially the appropriateness of punishments to crimes and the efficacy, usually doubtful, of governmental means to nonpublic ends.

Of course, individuals in a political aggregation may also form smaller voluntary aggregations of a private, nonpolitical character. Liberal theorists often assume these interest groups and private institutions to be the constituent units of society. Independent groups do collide, cooperate, and bargain like discrete individuals. But these groups do not and cannot constitute a cohesive society of engaged and mutually dependent parts. Liberal society, whether composed of individuals, interest groups, or private institutions, is always an aggregation. Although deliberate actions by individuals and groups may yield arrangements based upon similarities of role, talent, interest, merit, and the like, a pattern of cohesive social engagement is inconceivable. No engaged classes, orders, or estates appear in the liberal notion of society, no groups which originate in and are perpetuated by their inescapable indebtedness, whether cooperative or competitive, to other groups. Indeed the threat to individual liberty for the liberal theorist is precisely such isolated but concentrated organization, whether a sovereign power, the uniformity of opinion, an economic monopoly, or the privileged opportunities of a semiofficial aristocracy and clergy. What preserves the original competitive motion of society both assures and constitutes individual

liberty—a condition of noninterference permitting self-involvement and voluntary contracts among separate parts. Liberal
theorists forever recommend dispersing crowds, splintering
mass opinion, mixing government, and busting trusts. These
devices will either prevent or fragment official and informal
concentrations of power that threaten the naturally fluid motion of self-contained parts. Problems of majority rule and
minority rights, of order and liberty, are perennial dilemmas,
because liberal philosophers conceive of liberty as the self-
exclusiveness of private individuals.

Liberal philosophy cannot convey an abiding and authentic
sense of history, of historical periodicity or revolutionary
change. If it looks at history at all, it sees temporary discon-
tinuities, with periods of reform or revolutionary disturbance
defined by the replacement of government magistrates or
changes in the form of government: interregnums but not
transitions. A gradual or revolutionary social transformation,
resulting in a different life in common and including the dis-
appearance and emergence of mutually dependent groups, is
beyond the liberal view. Thus a succession of temporal events
is basically continuous; qualitative change is unusual and difficult, if not illusory; and neither progress nor decline is measured in the social character of citizens or the quality of common life. The emergence of new types of men, heralding and
responding to changed conditions of common life and to different kinds of social dependence, is inconceivable; the passions and interests of an individual are permanent because the
part is always prior to the whole, and the whole is a numerical
aggregate. Liberal theorists write history, but historicity is not
essential to their political ideas.

When political society is considered to be a formless aggregation, the general interest or the common good is merely a
sum of the interests of each partner or a majority will. If the
interests of groups conflict, the general interest is the product

of this conflict, provided that competitive advantages of monopoly and privileged access are not too serious. Making due allowance for the preservation of minority rights and of the competitive fluidity of society, liberal theorists display an irresistible predilection toward defining the general interest in terms of mere process or efficient method: the common good is not a condition of common life, comprising also the good of dependent parts, but is either the process of competitive exchange or the result of the sheer forcefulness of the interests of separate parts. The term *common good* is in fact a misnomer, because discrete individuals cannot accurately be said to share a common life. In the familiar aphorism of liberal philosophy, the endorsement of which accompanies both reservations about and commitments to representative democracy, the individual is the best judge of his interests. But this assertion is tautological. The anchoring of liberalism to the idea of a private individual assures that each individual can be the only judge of his interest because each must be the sole originator and custodian of his interests. The individual remains a private proprietor of both himself and all that he acquires.

The Example of Locke

Students of Locke's philosophy are often troubled by discrepancies arising from the empirical sensationalism of his *Essay concerning Human Understanding* and the qualified rationalist doctrine of natural rights asserted in his *Second Treatise of Civil Government*. Efforts to reconcile those doctrines often rely upon Locke's distinction in the *Essay* between an "innate idea" and a "law of nature," the latter a dictate of "right reason" acquired "by the use and due application of [our] natural faculties." For our purposes the affinity is significant: empiricist and rationalist varieties of traditional liberalism exhibit the same individualist mode of thought. The individual of the *Essay* "furnishes" the "empty cabinet" of his mind with sensations and ideas.[1] The individual of *Of Civil Government* acquires furniture.

Locke argued that man, unaided, initiates the establishment of his own private intellectual and moral consciousness: through passive sensation (the impression of external objects upon the mind) and active reflection (the "perception of the operations of our own mind within us"), and then through the memory of subjective responses of pleasure and pain, man defines himself. Anticipating somewhat Helvétius and Bentham, Locke asserted that "things . . . are good or evil, only in reference to pleasure or pain. That we call *good*, which is apt to cause or increase pleasure, or diminish pain in us; or else to procure or preserve us the possession of any other good or absence of evil. And, on the contrary, we name that *evil* which is apt to produce or increase any pain, or diminish any pleasure in us: or else to procure us any evil, or deprive us of any good."[2] This individual's experience of sensations is duplicated in Locke's defense of a natural right of property in *Of Civil Government*, for private property originates in an individual's exclusive possession of his own body and his unique comprehension of his bodily needs.

In Locke's *Essay*, passions such as love and desire, joy and sorrow, are remembered conditions of private feeling. Envy and anger, Locke cautioned, are unusual because they are not caused by pleasure and pain "simply in themselves." These passions have "in them some mixed considerations of ourselves and others."[3] But the active respondent nonetheless remains self-contained. Other men who contribute to the accumulation of passions of envy and anger merely constitute a portion of that same environment, completely separate and external to

1. John Locke, *An Essay concerning Human Understanding*, abridged and ed. Raymond Wilburn (London, 1947), bk. 1, chaps. 3, 2.

2. *Ibid.*, bk. 2, chaps. 1, 20.

3. *Ibid.*, bk. 2, chap. 20.

the discrete individual, which is the source of his initial sensations. This distinction between individual and society permits an individual to become related to other individuals only when he extends his consciousness to include them, only through his awareness or recollection of the pleasures and pains they either inspire in him or which he imagines them to be privately duplicating. The individual is left, as he had begun, alone and unaided, sharing nothing with other individuals except similar capacities for exclusively private responses to an alien environment.

In his political philosophy, Locke located the self-contained individual in a state of nature that precedes the institution of representative government. Each individual can obtain knowledge of "right reason." Right reason, which is natural law, restrains the appetites and actions of each rational individual and guarantees the exercise of those natural rights of life, liberty, and property inherent in each man. Natural law preserves peaceful isolation and noninterference among men: "The state of nature has a law of nature to govern it which obliges every one; and reason, which is that law, teaches all mankind who will but consult it that, being all equal and independent, no one ought to harm another in his life, health, liberty, or possessions." Locke further specified this individualism when defending the private right to acquire and possess property. The exercise of this right does not depend upon the consent or even the acknowledgment of other individuals; it is rather an extension of one's natural right to life, which has no effect upon other men. The individual remains his own man, the "master of himself and proprietor of his own person and the actions or labor of it." Because of his "necessity of subsisting," each individual, by mixing his labor and investing his human industry in unconquered nature, acquires legitimate title to property. Such property has been "joined" to that property each private individual already owns as the owner of himself; it has become a "part of him," an extension of the self to which he already holds exclusive title.[4] The source and justification of property is the individual's exclusive possession of his body and its strength. The responsibility for avoiding starvation and the sensation of hunger propel an individual to private accumulation.

Indeed, because the forcefulness of appetite figures so prominently in this justification of private ownership, or because individuals have roughly identical natural appetites and capacities, Locke argued differently when justifying unequal distribution of property: imperishable money, whose circulation rests upon tacit consent, permits accumulation and storage in excess of immediate need and use. But a chasm remains in Locke's argument, because men can satisfy natural bodily needs by working together, without each hungry and industrious first occupant claiming exclusive ownership and use of land.[5]

When Locke described both the motive and the means by which men depart from the state of nature to institute a public aggregation of private men presided over by representative government, he assumed a comparable individualism. Without uniform and certain public enforcement, natural law is inefficient; collisions among separate individuals occur. Because of the "corruption and viciousness of degenerate men" and the partiality of all individuals when they are judges in their own

4. *The Second Treatise of Civil Government*, in *Two Treatises of Government*, ed. Thomas I. Cook (New York, 1969), chaps. 2, 5.

5. *Ibid.*, chap. 5. Rousseau did not refer to Locke by name, but the notion of a natural or private right to property that he rejected was peculiarly Locke's: Rousseau dwelled on the fact that men's stomachs are approximately equal in size. I shall examine in Chapters 8 and 9 Rousseau's nonindividualist understanding of a reciprocal or civil right of fellow citizens to personal property. See *Discourse on Inequality* (P, III, 173–178); *Discourse on Political Economy* (P, III, 262–264, 269–278); *Social Contract* (P, III, 351–352, 364–367). In the first two instances Rousseau characteristically appeared to endorse Locke's view. And a similiar forcefulness, in this case one of numbers, underlies Locke's justification of majority rule: Rousseau asserted, as I shall also examine, that numerical strength alone commends a majority as such. See *Social Contract*, pp. 371–375, 440–441.

disputes, individuals decide to enhance their personal security by fabricating jointly a political society. Through a contract, individuals acting in concert delegate to others a portion of their natural patrimony, the power to execute the law of nature. A governmental superior, a certain and empowered "umpire," judges disputes, punishes the guilty, and receives appeals from the injured. The "end of political society and government," which is "the mutual preservation of the lives, liberties, and estates" of each, must be the separate but identical motive of each partner in the contract. Enforceable civil law, which now circumscribes a new public sector, serves as "guards and fences to the properties of all the members of the society"; each associate retains a portion of his self-exclusiveness, a secured "liberty to follow [his] own will in all things where that rule prescribes not."[6] Consent or political authorization, Locke added, is the only "true source" of legitimate "political authority." Rejecting in turn the force of the strongest, the right of conquest, and natural paternal authority as bases of legitimate political authority, Locke argued for "another rise of government, another original of political power," which understanding of politics he restricts to "the power of a magistrate over a subject" or "a right of making laws with penalties of death . . . for the regulating and preserving of property." The presence of an identical political authority becomes, like the private accumulation of property, a private extension of each partner: individuals "unite" their person to or "join into" a political society. The legislative power of civil government must also be nothing but the aggregative "joint power of every member of the society," Locke asserted in one of several elliptic arguments against Hobbes' theory of sovereignty. Because no individual has absolute power over himself in a state of nature, because a natural man cannot legitimately destroy himself or fall to pro-

6. *Of Civil Government*, chaps. 9, 6, 7, 4.

tect the exercise of his natural rights, governmental power accumulated from the voluntary contributions of separate parts cannot be absolute.[7]

Although the environment of individuals has changed with the security guaranteed by limited government, the individual himself is unaffected by this contract because governmental authority is merely the convenient mechanism of a numerical aggregation which assures the exercise of those private rights each individual possessed in a state of nature and retains in political society. Only through their simultaneous surrender of the power to execute the law of nature, only through obedience to identical governmental authority, do subjects constitute what Locke called "one coherent living body." But like all of Locke's other references to mutuality, community, incorporation, and the body politic, this phrase is curious because society is composed of unchanged "private men." Locke admitted that political society is without internal, cohesive engagement of its parts: private individuals must continue to consent expressly to the taking of their property; private men may appeal to some magistrates against the decisions of other magistrates in Locke's mixed government; when private individuals, temporarily assuming a "public" role, institute a representative legislative power, "the greater force" rules or "the act of the majority passes for the act of the whole." Indeed, "where the majority cannot conclude the rest, there they cannot act as one body, and consequently will be immediately dissolved again." Individuals remain "distinct persons still in reference to one another" even if, "in reference to the rest of mankind" outside the scope of their aggregation, Locke asserted that "they make one body."[8]

Locke's political society is precarious, for both individuals and majorities may be compelled to exercise their right of resistance. When arbitrary or despotic magistrates sever that

7. *Ibid.*, chaps. 1, 8, 7, 4, 11.
8. *Ibid.*, chaps. 19, 7, 18, 8.

"knot" which alone identifies a political society, this aggregation of individuals is reduced to a "confused multitude, without order or connexion." For Locke, revolutionary change
itself is only the replacement of unjust magistrates by the actions of a group of like-minded individuals. This must be the
case in an aggregation which is perpetually reratified, as it had
been initiated and might be dissolved, by the addition or subtraction of self-made parts. Men born within established political societies are not "natural subjects." The "law of right reason" requires that all mature individuals, as separate parts "and
not in a multitude together," must choose "what society they
will join themselves to, what commonwealth they will put
themselves under."[9] Locke's political society comes into being,
is governed, and perpetuates itself or is removed through the
addition and withdrawal of its parts.

Variations on Locke

Locke's ideas were enormously influential throughout the
eighteenth century, especially in France. Voltaire, who was
partly responsible for Locke's favorable reception in France,
began his essay on Locke in *Philosophical Letters* with the observation that there probably had never been a "wiser, more
orderly mind, or a logician more exact."[10] Condillac, who
altered some of Locke's formulations regarding the association
of sensations, proclaimed, "Immediately after Aristotle comes
Locke; for it is not necessary to count the other philosophers
who have written on the same subject."[11] He did not really
take Aristotle seriously, however; his individualist orientation
is something Aristotle rejected. In the *Treatise of Sensations*,

9. *Ibid.*, chaps. 19, 6, 8. See also *ibid.*, chaps. 17–18.
10. Voltaire, *Philosophical Letters*, trans. Ernest Dilworth (Indianapolis, 1961), letter 13.
11. Etienne Bonnot de Condillac, *Extrait raisonné du Traité des sensations*, ed. Georges Lyon (Paris, 1921), p. 32, quoted in Ernst Cassirer, *The Philosophy of the Enlightenment*, trans. Fritz C. A. Koelln
and James P. Pettegrove (Boston, 1955), p. 99n.

Condillac described the unaided self-definition of a single individual of rational understanding by using the idea of a marble statue and, initially, the single sensation of smell. By retaining and combining external sensations, the individual acquires memory and, later, imagination. The presence of passionate desires follows the reflective consciousness of pleasure and pain. Finally personality itself, the individual's sense of himself as the accumulated sum of his sensations, emerges when touch, the last sensation to develop, conclusively informs man of his separation from an environment of external objects.[12]

D'Alembert reproduced Locke's argument against innate ideas in his *Preliminary Discourse* to the *Encyclopedia* and asserted that the first dividend of the isolated mind's reception of sensations is the sense of the self's reality; man's second acquisition is the consciousness of the reality of external objects, which "tear us from the solitude that would otherwise be our lot."[13] Condorcet's *Sketch for a Historic Picture of the Progress of the Human Mind* begins with man's "ability to receive sensations," just as the more modest effort of Helvétius in *Of the Mind* begins with two passive faculties of the mind, sensation (the mind's receptivity to external impressions) and memory (retained but weakened sensations). Helvétius asserted that his own treatment of the individual's memory of pleasures and pains includes a relationship between the individual and society: an individual's sense of pleasure depends in part upon the standards of esteem he confronts in his social environment. No assumption of commonality is made here. The isolated individual merely searches outside his self-containedness for a separate confirmation of his own sense of pleasure. For whatever the social circumstances of the private accumulation of

12. Condillac, *Traité des sensations*, pts. 1–3, in *Oeuvres philosophiques de Condillac*, ed. Georges Le Roy, 3 vols. (Paris, 1947–1951), I.

13. Jean Le Rond d'Alembert, *Preliminary Discourse to the Encyclopedia of Diderot*, trans. Richard N. Schwab (Indianapolis, 1963), pp. 5–8.

sensations, what Helvétius called social "analogies" are distinct and external matters, in the same manner that the social environment contributing to the passions of envy and anger in Locke's *Essay* reinforce an individualist perspective.[14] The separate individual possesses himself alone and cannot share his origin and being with other men. His primary ideas form a series of private, passionate moods in which every moment is distinct and perhaps unique.

Jeremy Bentham's *An Introduction to the Principles of Morals and Legislation* opens with an almost word-for-word translation from Helvétius: "Nature has placed mankind under the governance of two sovereign masters, *pain* and *pleasure*. It is for them alone to point out what we ought to do, as well as to determine what we shall do. On the one hand the standard of right and wrong, on the other the chain of causes and effects, are fastened to their throne." His principle of utility, the greatest happiness of the greatest number, rests upon an "act of the mind," a "sentiment" of the private individual, or "the natural constitution of the human frame." Bentham classified thirty-two "circumstances" influencing the formation of the private sensibility; these are external environmental factors or peculiar disabilities of individuals which could threaten the accuracy of private calculations but not the self-containedness of the individual as he accumulates his personal inventory of pleasurable sensations.[15]

Although Bentham and other utilitarians rejected natural

14. Antoine-Nicolas de Condorcet, *Sketch for a Historical Picture of the Progress of the Human Mind*, trans. June Barraclough (New York, 1955), p. 3; Claude A. Helvétius, *De l'esprit* (Paris, 1843), discourse 1, chaps. 1, 3, 4; discourse 2. Because Rousseau did not distinguish the materialism of Helvétius, d'Holbach, and Condillac from Locke's dualistic notion that the mind is an independently active, nonmaterial substance, this variation is not discussed here.

15. Bentham, *An Introducton to the Principles of Morals and Legislation*, chaps. 1, 6, in *The Works of Jeremy Bentham*, ed. John Bowring, 11 vols. (Edinburgh, 1843), I. See Helvétius, *De l'esprit*, discourse 2, chap. 1.

law, the dictates of right reason, natural rights which devolve from a state of nature, and social or political contracts, these differences within the tradition of liberal thought do not alter its fundamental character: the individualism of both perspectives commands attention. Indeed, the empirical or utilitarian arguments and the theory of natural rights were effortlessly combined by liberal philosophers. D'Holbach's *Natural Politics* has a rationalist beginning, with Lockeian ideas of natural rights and the social contract, and concludes with a utilitarian defense of "the greatest happiness of the greatest number."[16] Diderot defended familiar dictates of right reason as the exclusive possession of each rational individual in the article *Natural Right* for the *Encyclopedia;* elsewhere, most inventively in his *Letters on the Blind* and *D'Alembert's Dream,* Diderot employed an empirical sensationalism.

The same concerns appeared among the French physiocrats who, except in their preoccupation with land and agriculture, were the precursors of liberal political economists in England. Mercier de la Rivière defended a kind of rational intuition supplemented by the "witness of the senses" so that each man, if he were merely to "examine himself," could discover the "natural laws" of political economy.[17] Adam Smith's conception of economic society is similarly individualist in both origin and operation. Rejecting "right reason" as a limiting natural law in economic exchange, Smith argued that "human wisdom" neither initiates nor controls an economic division of labor. A division of labor results from "a certain propensity in human nature . . . to truck, barter, and exchange one thing for another." Smith visualized a primeval economic market of

16. Kingsley Martin, *French Liberal Thought in the Eighteenth Century,* 3d ed., ed. J. P. Mayer (New York, 1963), pp. 187–188; Cassirer, *Philosophy of Enlightenment,* pp. 69–73. For a similar amalgamation, involving "private rights," "natural sensibility and personal interest," and a contractual "league," see Helvétius, *De l'esprit,* discourse 3, chap. 4.

17. Quoted in Martin, *French Liberal Thought,* p. 231.

deliberate, contractual aggregation "in a rude state of society" among three producers who respectively make bows and arrows, tend cattle, and build dwellings: "Without the disposition to truck, barter and exchange, every man must have procured to himself every necessity and conveniency of life which he wanted. All must have had the same duties to perform, and the same work to do and there could have been no such difference of employment as could alone give occasion to any great difference of talents." Regular exchanges of goods and money define an economic society, just as instituting and obeying governmental authority define Lockeian civil society. For Smith, individuals make markets to enhance the private interests that each owns alone. An individual is unchanged by this process, except in the extent of his personal profit and loss. The previous private encounter with nature, which establishes the first "natural price" of a commodity, is no less individualist than exchanges among separate producers. Natural prices follow from the investment of one's body; the individual's "labor [is] the first price, the original purchase" that is paid for the private possession of a product.[18] This too is reminiscent of Locke's individual accumulating private property by extending the labor of his body into the objects of nature when he senses hunger.

A substantial accumulation of private capital arises from a private individual's self-imposed restraint upon spending, not from relationships among mutually dependent creatures of a common life. He avoids immediate consumption in preference to the greater, long-term rewards of saving and reinvesting. Self-restraint, which Smith also called "a principle of human nature," is the abstinence theory of capital accumulation of the next generation of liberal political economists. For Smith, "the principle which prompts us to save is the desire of bettering our condition, a desire which, though generally calm and dis-

18. Adam Smith, *The Wealth of Nations*, 2 vols. (London, 1910), I, bk. 1, chaps. 2, 5, 6.

passionate, comes with us from the womb, and never leaves us till we go into the grave."[19] Locke had already described self-restraint in more general terms in the *Essay concerning Human Understanding*, where he discussed the cautious strategy of maximizing individual pleasures through the pursuit of "remoter absent good." The unhesitant satisfaction of immediate desires, Locke argued, arising from both the "ordinary necessities of our lives" (the "uneasinesses of hunger, thirst, heat, cold, weariness, with labor, and sleepiness") and the "fantastical uneasiness . . . which custom has made natural to us" (the "itch after honour, power, or riches"), may disrupt those private calculations necessary for long-term profits. But not always, because the mind has "a power to *suspend* the execution and satisfaction of any of its desires" and "is at liberty to consider the objects of them, examine them on all sides, and weigh them with others." These moments of self-involvement are not a "restraint or diminution of freedom" but "the very improvement and benefit of it." Through unmolested self-commitment, the individual discovers and utilizes his liberty to avoid the "misery and slavery" of indifferent or uninhibited passion and of having his will "under the determination of some other than himself." Like natural man's profitable self-discipline through "right reason" in *Of Civil Government*, "every man," in the *Essay*, "is put under a necessity, by his constitution as an intelligent being, to be determined in willing by his own thought and judgment what is best for him to do." Nor is only this individual the best judge of his own interests. "God himself," Locke added, "cannot choose what is not good; . . . God Almighty himself is under the necessity of being happy; and the more any intelligent being is so, the nearer is its approach to infinite perfection and happiness."[20]

---

19. *Ibid.*, bk. 2, chap. 3.
20. Locke, *Essay*, bk. 2, chap. 21. See also Helvétius, *De l'esprit*, discourse 1, chap. 4; discourse 3, chap. 4; Condillac, "Dissertation on Liberty," in *Oeuvres philosophiques*, I, 315–317.

Wherever he is first located, in a prepolitical state of nature or a premarket condition of natural prices, the discrete individual is always central to liberal philosophy. Liberalism enshrines the private citizen, the unindebted individual who finds other individuals merely useful or harmful to his intentions: one convicted of breaking the law and justly punished, as we say, has paid his debt to society. Liberalism makes aloneness a supreme political virtue and the freedom from politics a new political right. Rousseau and other exponents of the older traditions of political philosophy would find incomprehensible and self-contradictory this concept of the private citizen.

Rousseau's Nonindividualism

The essential unifying structure of Rousseau's political philosophy is nonindividualist. An individual is not permanently defined by self-containedness, nor does an individual define himself, whether by passive, unaided reception of sensations from outside, by the suspension of private desires, by a natural capacity for rational self-direction, or by the self-motivated accumulation of private property. To Rousseau, an "individual" is a socially dependent creature, deriving his identity from the cohesive, social involvement in which he originates and of which he remains an indivisible part. He is *of* or *through* society, not merely *in* or *with* society. He is an artificial individual. Social dependence itself, every form of social engagement among mutually dependent parts, is similarly artificial because presocial natural man is not naturally sociable and cannot deliberately initiate common life of even the crudest sort.

Rousseau did visualize a private individual as instinctively pursuing inclinations of a passionate, prerational character during a static, presocial condition of natural independence. But these natural inclinations are almost silenced in the gradual and periodic transformation of the private individual into a public person. This new public person owes his essential being not to assertive self-reliance but to organic relatedness, the common corporate life in which his being is embedded. His language, his virtue, his foresight and judgment all are made possible by a nonaggregative society unavailable to individuals in a pre-social state. Indeed, the very consciousness of self exhibited by this social man mirrors and is limited by the historical evolution of successive forms of social dependence. Thus the concepts "individual" and "society" are correlative realities. Artificial individuals are men indebted to one another, to their public life. And together, in unity or disorder, artificial individuals always remain a political whole, an entity of mutual indebtedness and organic connection.[21]

21. While identifying aspects of Rousseau's thought with the thought of Pufendorf, Grotius, Hobbes, and Locke, Derathé argues that Rousseau's uses of "organic" are only juridical metaphors, the "banal analogies" or "legal fictions" characteristic of the "individualism of the School of natural right." Rousseau's state "is only a plurality of individuals united by a convention." Robert Derathé, *Jean-Jacques Rousseau et la science politique de son temps* (Paris, 1950), esp. pp. 157–171, 236–239, 397–413. Citing Derathé's view with approval, Cobban notes that "Rousseau is too much a man of the eighteenth century to discard individualism" and that Rousseau's conception of a common good involves a sum of individual utilities. Alfred Cobban, *Rousseau and the Modern State*, 2d rev. ed. (London, 1964), p. 70. More recently, Masters has argued a "mechanistic conception of political life" in Rousseau. Rousseau's concept of a general will is a "construct of reason" used to explain the frictionless operation of an ideal society; and "organic" merely connotes the "conventional" status of political society itself. Roger D. Masters, *The Political Philosophy of Rousseau* (Princeton, 1968), pp. 285–293.

Two points should be stressed about Rousseau's use of the terms *organic* and *machine*. Rousseau recognized that *organic* is awkward because a body politic is not a "natural" or physical unit like the body of man. Nevertheless, the term *organic*, especially because Rousseau contrasted it with *aggregative*, does capture the nonmechanistic connectedness of fellow citizens. Second, the terms *organic body* and *machine* were not opposites to Rousseau, a consideration which Derathé takes into account. (See also Derathé's note to the *Discourse on Political Economy*, P, III, 1393–1394.) Thus, in describing his own bodily deterioration, Rousseau referred to "my poor machine." Rousseau also noted that man's capacity for choice or "free agency" distinguishes the "human machine" from the "ingenious machine" of other animals who cannot resist the demands of natural instinct. *Letters to Malesherbes* (Jan.

These inescapable social connections among artificial individuals—imitation, opposition, and cooperation—constitute a common, though often unstable, historical tradition. A temporal succession of different forms of social dependence constitutes qualitative, revolutionary change. New social groups, different patterns of mutual engagement among dependent men, as well as the changing moral and intellectual countenances of artificial individuals, fashion and reflect successive historical periods. Neither social unity nor civil war, the latter an organized discord of mutually dependent parts, is amorphous.

The men who, from one point of view, occasion this social transformation by inspiring another individual with objects of desire and by making possible a mutual consciousness of rights and duties—these men are not an alien intrusion or a separate duplication of one's being. Social transformation leaves men neither isolated from one another and unchanged nor free to determine their addition to or subtraction from a community. Common life in Rousseau transforms all members reciprocally and simultaneously: agent and recipient, creator and creature. Similarly, their common good is a shared condition of common life; it cannot be the quantitative result, a balance sheet of pluses and minuses, of the interests of discrete parts. In some historical periods of common life, the general interest will be unrelated or opposed to the outcome of a majority vote, to a

---

1762; P, I, 1137, 1138); *Confessions* (P, I, 409); *Discourse on Inequality*, p. 141. For this reason both the physical universe and a single society were organic "machines" to Rousseau: "When considering through the eye of philosophy the play of all the parts of this vast universe, it is soon apparent that the greatest beauty of each part which composes the universe does not reside in itself; and that it was not formed in order to remain alone and independent but in order to contribute with all the other parts toward the perfection of the entire machine. It is the same in the moral order. The vices and virtues of each man are not relative to himself alone. Their greatest relationship is with society, and it is their relationship to the moral order in general which constitutes their essence and their character." *Fragments on* Moeurs (P, III, 554).

sum of the socially acquired desires of artificial individuals. When Rousseau accepted majority determination of the common good, he grudgingly accepted a mere instrument, an unavoidable mechanism often imperfect and always misleading for declaring the common good of mutually dependent men.

An artificial individual does not move within mutually exclusive private and public spheres, nor does he assume and discard a variety of private and public roles. His creation does not delineate a limited public sector of governmental supervision. Instead of distinguishing between private and public Rousseau distinguished between particular and general, between the different circumferences of various societies—family, occupation, class, magistracy, legal or moral society—to which social men are simultaneously indebted. Each of these societies is public. All particular societies fall within the scope of the most comprehensive society of fellow citizens, the state. In Rousseau's view, then, there exist a number of concentric and overlapping circumferences of public life, some particular and, for all artificial creatures in their capacities as members of a determinate corporate whole, one general. Even the composite "inner life" of a single individual, however divided or complementary his loyalties and inclinations, is an echo of social transformation, of multiple memberships which are themselves distinguishable between particular and general.[22]

22. Rousseau did use the term *private*, but such uses were immediately preceded or followed by the more usual terminology of *particular* (and *general*). See *Social Contract*, pp. 357, 371, 373–374, 404, 429. When Rousseau used *privé* rather than *particulier*, it is translated "private." But "particular" is clearer because it connotes a socially derived preoccupation which is exclusive in character. And Rousseau's understanding of "private" and "general" can no more be identified with the liberal distinction between private and public sectors than can Aristotle's view that household considerations are nonpolitical matters of mere life which take place "in private" and do not directly concern the good life. Rousseau's nonindividualism also explains his "classical" use of the terms *state* and *constitution* to refer, respectively, to a specific society of citizens (or, more technically, to members in their inactive or non-

Artificial individuals first recognize themselves and are known to others by their inescapable dependence upon one another. Although they can and frequently do act selfishly, their desires are particular interests of a public character. Nor can the liberty of an artificial individual consist of his hoarding a remnant sector of private rights. Because of the common origin of these individuals, the liberty of one of them necessarily implies and affects the liberty of his fellow citizens: a creature of society is free, or not free, in his indivisible relationship with his fellow citizens, not in an impervious sphere of noninterference. And an artificial individual removes himself physically from common life at the risk of self-destruction. Flight is never a simple matter of self-preserving subtraction; exile often stimulates a heightened consciousness of social indebtedness.

For these reasons, all the social relations that define this new public creature are themselves political. Artificial individuals are immersed in political situations that exceed the scope of governmental direction and antedate its institution, because politics comprises the inescapable patterns of social engagement among mutually dependent parts, the ways in which each part is informed by the whole of which it is an indivisible member. In short, a political whole is greater than a "sum" of its dependent parts. And Rousseau's conception of common life is based upon the idea of the artificial individual, whose first reflective self-consciousness originates in those refractions of a sustained consciousness of others which signify the beginning of his social creation.

---

legislative capacity) and to the manner of common life which includes but goes beyond governmental institutions and civil laws. Both terms are used throughout this study in conformity with Rousseau's meanings.

CHAPTER 3

Social Dependence and
Historical Periodicity

Rousseau's *Discourse on the Origin and Foundations of Inequality among Men* is, on his own testimony, the "first complete development of his principles" and a work of "the greatest importance."[1] It is not, in spite of frequent interpretations to this effect, an individualist work. Although Rousseau located discrete individuals in a presocial state of natural independence and described in great detail individuals' accelerating pursuit of personal desires, he neither equated the former with the latter nor saw the latter as evolving from the former. Rousseau's acquisitive individuals are new, artificial men, transformed creatures indebted to common life for their identity. Their desires are particular, not private. Successive patterns of social engagement among new, public men are themselves an accidental replacement and finally a total repudiation of the natural state, not its natural development or extension. The conflict between rich and poor, for example, constitutes the fifth and penultimate stage of common life, and occurs long after men have surrendered their natural indolence. Class war is not an effect of private bodily needs, the personal growth of self-made men, voluntary social stratification, or the collisions of separate groups; rather, it is one form of cohesive social engagement. Rousseau's assumption that isolation and indepen-

1. *Confessions* (P, I, 388). I have used the translation of the *Discourse on Inequality* in *Jean-Jacques Rousseau: The First and Second Discourses*, ed. Roger D. Masters; trans. Roger D. and Judith R. Masters (New York, 1964), pp. 77–228.

dence are natural in no way, then, indicates a liberal individualist view; rather, it serves as the basis of his nonindividualist thought, which stresses the importance of social dependence and historical periodicity.[2]

Because the reputed "individualism" of the *Discourse on Inequality* is in fact the theoretical foundation of later, nonindividualist works, it is consistent with the *Discourse on Political Economy* (also published, in the *Encyclopedia,* in 1755) and with the *Social Contract* (on which Rousseau most likely began work in 1754). Nor is the liberal distinction between individualism and collectivism, a distinction many critics have found in Rousseau, indigenous to a political philosophy which consistently takes individual and society to be correlative realities.[3]

2. The ideas in the *Discourse on Inequality* had been anticipated three years earlier in what Rousseau asserted to be an unsatisfactory and abridged fashion in the *Discourse on the Sciences and Arts* and in his seven replies defending the earlier writing against some of its nearly seventy "refutations." For a discussion of themes which Rousseau in these replies began to call his "system" or his "sad but true system" (Préface d'une seconde lettre à Bordes [P, III, 105]), see Mario Einaudi, *The Early Rousseau* (Ithaca, N.Y., 1967), pp. 84–113. For Rousseau's elaborations upon the earlier *Discourse,* see George R. Havens, introduction, *Jean-Jacques Rousseau: Discours sur les sciences et les arts,* ed. George R. Havens (New York, 1946), pp. 34–61; Harry J. Benda, "Rousseau's Early Discourses," *Political Science* (Wellington, New Zealand), V (Sept. 1953), 13–20; VI (Mar. 1954), 17–27; Jack Howard Broome, *Rousseau: A Study of His Thought* (New York, 1963), pp. 26–33; and Antoine Adam, "De quelques sources de Rousseau dans la littérature philosophique, 1700–1750," in *Jean-Jacques Rousseau et son oeuvre: Problèmes et recherches* (Paris, 1964), pp. 125–132.

3. Vaughan claims that Rousseau's defense of "individual rights" in the *Discourse on Inequality* "suggested . . . a more extreme form of individualism than any previous writer had ventured to set forth." *The Political Writings of Jean Jacques Rousseau,* ed. C. E. Vaughan, 2 vols. (1915; reprint ed., Oxford, 1962), I, 14, 119. Vaughan also asserts fundamental contradictions between the "individualism" of early writings and the "collectivism" of later works, between the influence of Locke and the influence of Montesquieu: there is a constant "ill-veiled hostility" in Rousseau's writings between "two rival elements, the individual and the

Nature and Society

The discrete individual of the presocial state of nature, the subject of the first part of the *Discourse on Inequality*, is capable only of physical survival and an instinctive catering to the

community." Vaughan concedes that Rousseau's "collectivist" *Discourse on Political Economy* and *Social Contract* are barely distinguishable from the *Discourse on Inequality* in terms of dates of composition; but he argues that the early *Discourses* are the satires of a "moralist" and that only the latter works belong to "political" theory proper. *Ibid.*, pp. 1–5, 12–14, 38–41, 231, 235. For a similar view, see Derathé, *Rousseau et la science politique*, pp. 114–120, 236–239. Derathé sees Lockeian discipleship in the *Discourse on Inequality* and a Hobbesian "étatiste" character in later writings, but argues that these two positions are reconciled in Rousseau's notion of a general will of "conscience" or right reason. See also Ernst Cassirer, *The Question of Jean-Jacques Rousseau*, trans. and ed. Peter Gay (Bloomington, Ind., 1963), pp. 51–52; Martin, *French Liberal Thought*, pp. 197–208; and Cobban, *Rousseau and the Modern State*, pp. 141–142, 164–170. The last two interpretations find a "balance" between individual and community throughout Rousseau's thought. See also Leo Strauss, *Natural Right and History* (Chicago, 1953), pp. 253–255, 261, 290–294. Strauss locates the "substance of Rousseau's thought" in the "obvious tension between the return to the [ancient] city and the return to the state of nature." Rousseau "presents to his readers the confusing spectacle of a man who perpetually shifts back and forth between two diametrically opposed positions," namely "the rights of the individual or the rights of the heart against all restraint and authority" and "the complete submission of the individual to society or the state [which] favors the most rigorous moral or social discipline." An "insoluble conflict" between individual and society, or between freedom and civic virtue, is taken to permeate Rousseau's writings.

See also Georges Lapassade, "L'Oeuvre de J.-J. Rousseau: Structure et unité," *Revue de métaphysique et de morale*, LXI (July–Dec. 1956), 386–402, for an appreciation of Rousseau's substitution of social *rapports* for sensationalist psychology. (Lapassade, however, argues that for Rousseau society is corruption in its essence.) Bronislaw Baczko, "Rousseau et l'aliénation sociale," *Annales*, XXV (1959–62), 225–230, and Bertrand de Jouvenel, "Essai sur la politique de Rousseau," in *Du contrat social de Jean-Jacques Rousseau*, ed. Bertrand de Jouvenel (Geneva, 1947), pp. 39–40, 48–49, 54, also make this point. Interpretations which stress the variety among types and stages of common life are: Robert Derathé, "L'Unité de la pensée de Jean-Jacques Rousseau," in *Jean-Jacques Rousseau* (Neuchâtel, 1962), pp. 203–213; Gustave Lanson, "L'Unité de la pensée de Jean-Jacques Rousseau," *Annales*, VIII

immediate needs of his body. Personal development cannot occur and acquisitiveness cannot appear among self-contained individuals because of their isolation from one another. Correspondingly, the activities of men after their departure from the state of nature, the subject of the second part of the *Dis-*

(1912), 11–15; Henri Gouhier, "Nature et histoire dans la pensée de Rousseau," *Annales*, XXXIII (1953–55), 26–28; Léon Eméry, *Rousseau l'annonciateur* (Lyons, 1954), pp. 11–18, 21–23, 52–59, 67–68, 107–112, which recognizes the "organic" character of Rousseau's society; Emile Durkheim, "Le *Contrat social* de Rousseau," *Revue de métaphysique et de morale*, XXV (1918), 15–19, 21–23 and XXVI (1919), 129–132, 159–161; Jean Starobinski, "Aux origines de la pensée sociologique," *Les Temps modernes*, XVIII (Dec. 1962), 961–979; and Jean-Jacques Chevallier, "Jean-Jacques Rousseau ou l'absolutisme de la volonté générale," *Revue française de science politique*, III (Jan.–Mar. 1953), 6, 9–13, 18–19, 27–30. For Rousseau's qualification, sometimes obscure in the *Discourse*, that he condemns only "our" contemporary societies, see *Rousseau juge de Jean-Jacques* (P, I, 828); *Letters to Malesherbes* (Jan. 12, 1762; P, I, 1135); and *Letter to Beaumont* (Mar. 1763; P, IV, 966–967).

A "dialectical" discussion of the individualism-collectivism distinction is found in Einaudi, *Early Rousseau*, pp. 13–18, 42–43. Einaudi sees two "different ideal standards" in Rousseau's thought—not "contradictions" but "truth-giving tensions": the liberty and egoism of private man (*Emile*) and the discipline and collective action of public man (*Social Contract*). See also Henri Wallon, "*Emile; ou, de l'éducation*," *Europe* (Nov.–Dec. 1961), pp. 128–129, 135. Wallon argues a "constructive solution" in Rousseau's thought as *Emile* reconciles metaphysical and absolute individualism with the sovereign collectivity described in the *Social Contract*. A discussion of a "contractual" Rousseau, preoccupied with equality and individual liberties, and a "social" Rousseau, preoccupied with social cohesion and a common interest is found in Bernard Groethuysen, *J. J. Rousseau* (Paris, 1949), pp. 45–51, 91–99, 117–140, 156–159, 173–174, 326–329. For an examination of other interpretations, accompanied by a plea for "going beyond" individualism and collectivism, see Eric Weil, "J. J. Rousseau et sa politique," *Critique*, IX (Jan. 1952), 3–28. See also Basil Munteano, "Les 'contradictions' de J.-J. Rousseau: Leur sens expérimental," in *Jean Jacques Rousseau et son oeuvre*, pp. 95–111.

Earlier studies of Rousseau by Faguet, Lemaître, and Espinas also found fundamental contradictions between individualism and collectivism. See Lanson, "L'Unité de la pensée de Rousseau," pp. 1–5, 25. Burke too wavered between criticizing Rousseau for excessive individualism and criticizing him for excessive collectivism. See Osborn, *Rousseau and Burke*, pp. 12–16, 139–140, 153–155. Perhaps the distinction of being the first to miss the nonindividualist character of the *Discourse on Inequality*

course on Inequality, are the activities of artificial men occasioned by accidents which alone permitted common life.
Between these two conditions is an unbridgeable gap, "an
immense space": the public creature of social dependence replaces the private individual; six successive historical stages of
common life replace the barren, repetitive self-involvement of
presocial nature. To Rousseau the state of nature is defined by
the absence not of governmental institutions and positive law
but of society. And the gap between the inert individual of
the state of nature and the public creature is not bridged by
the idea of a contractual aggregation of unchanged parts.[4]

---

belongs to Charles Bonnet, a Genevan philosophe, who challenged the
logic of the *Discourse* in an anonymous letter to the *Mercure de France*
in October, 1755. Assuming man's natural "faculty of perfectibility"
(which Rousseau had conceded), Bonnet argued that everything consistent with man's faculties, including society itself, is thereby "natural."
See *Letter from M. Philopolis* (P, III, 1383–1386). See also Rousseau's
response, the *Letter to M. Philopolis* (P, III, 230–236).

4. *Discourse on Inequality* (P, III, 192). Because "original man" vanishes "by degrees" during the three "intermediary positions" (*ibid.*,
pp. 191–192) which follow the presocial state of nature, Rousseau
employed the phrases "pure state of nature" and "first state of nature"
(*ibid.*, pp. 147, 170, 216) to refer to man's presocial condition, and
"last stage of the state of nature" (*ibid.*, p. 164) to characterize the third
period of common life. Natural goodness and liberty are "annihilated"
(*ibid.*, p. 145) only during the fourth period of common life, when
amour-propre triumphs and common property is usurped: the artificial
individual who first seizes land and claims exclusive possession is "the
true founder of civil society" (*ibid.*, p. 164). To avoid confusion, the
phrases "state of nature" and "natural man" or "savage" are used here
to refer only to presocial independence and original man. One possibility of confusion arises from a later designation of the family as the
"oldest of all societies, and the only natural one." *Social Contract* (P,
III, 352). The family is "natural" in the sense that it first appears during
the second stage of common life and that the previous herd society is
temporary and does not permit a reciprocal recognition of rights and
duties. For a discussion of Rousseau's unusual use of the concept "state
of nature," and a slightly different periodization of subsequent social
life in the *Discourse on Inequality*, see Jean Starobinski, "Du *Discours
de l'inégalité* au *Contrat social*," in *Etudes sur le Contrat social de
Jean-Jacques Rousseau* (Paris, 1964), pp. 100–103; Jean Starobinski, "Rous-

Rousseau summarized his rejection of contemporary inequality by observing that "the spirit of society alone" introduces and permits inequality, unknown in "the original state of man." This primacy of social dependence is also seen in Rousseau's criticism of other philosophers' conceptions of the state of nature. These philosophers have failed to go backwards far enough in historical time to arrive at a conception of the original man in his natural condition. By ascribing ideas of justice, interest, property, and authority to natural man, they have mistakenly equated the natural, presocial man with the passionately active and assertive slaves of contemporary societies: "All of them . . . speaking continually of need, avarice, oppression, desires, and pride, have carried over to the state of nature ideas they had acquired in society: they spoke about savage man and they described civil man."

Rousseau's comparison of natural endowment with subsequent social acquisition and transformation dominates the *Discourse on Inequality*. His intention, he announced in the preface, is to ascertain and describe the "original state" of man dispersed in a state of nature, the savage as "nature formed him": "It is no light undertaking to separate what is original from what is artificial in the present nature of man." Because man is "altered in the bosom of society by a thousand continually renewed causes, by the acquisition of a mass of knowledge and errors, by changes that occurred in the constitution of bodies, and by the continual impact of the passions," man's natural attributes are scarcely recognizable today. To judge if the moral or political inequality of contemporary society is warranted by nature, then, one must distinguish "natural man" from the "man of man." And having traced the slow succession of intermediate stages of social dependence which concludes

---

seau et Buffon," in *Jean-Jacques Rousseau et son oeuvre*, pp. 135–146; and Jean Starobinski, introduction to the *Discourse on Inequality* (P, III, lv–lix, lxii–lxviii).

with contemporary common life, Rousseau claimed to have demonstrated to the attentive reader "how the soul and human passions of men, altering imperceptibly, change their nature so to speak; why our needs and our pleasures change their objects in the long run; why, original man vanishing by degrees, society no longer offers to the eyes of the wise man anything except an assemblage of artificial men and factitious passions which are the work of all these new relations and have no true foundation in nature."[5]

The private individual of a presocial state of nature is without rule or law. He exhibits two unconscious passions "anterior to reason" which constitute "the first and simplest operations of the human soul." He instinctively pursues his own physical welfare and self-preservation; and, from a natural aversion to seeing any other sensible being suffer pain or death, especially members of his species, he has a natural passion of pity, the compassion of commiseration. The two passions qualify one another, rendering man "naturally good" and the state of nature peaceful; natural man's love of self (*amour de soi*) is modulated by his natural pity for others except when his own preservation is at stake. Moreover, the very isolation of natural men precludes the development of maxims of right reason. The maxims of natural law are not natural but social acquisitions. Without a common language, with only an instinctive, inarticulate "cry of nature" on urgent occasions, natural man could not discover, pursue, or communicate precepts of right reason. A true binding natural law implies awareness on the

5. *Discourse on Inequality*, pp. 193, 132, 122–123, 192; *Confessions*, p. 388. Moreover, the difficulty of detecting natural man behind contemporary men explains Rousseau's attributing his understanding of natural man to introspection and self-portraiture. See *Rousseau juge de Jean-Jacques*, p. 936. For a discussion of the "extra-historical" character of Rousseau's state of nature, and how he uses the concept "to understand the historical man" and therefore himself as well, see Gouhier, "Nature et histoire," pp. 8–20. See also Groethuysen, *Rousseau*, pp. 18–22, 26–29, 35–42.

part of those who acknowledge it. It would have to speak directly to man through the voice of nature.[6]

As a matter of partisan convenience, according to Rousseau, other philosophers have presented the natural savage in the guise of an enlightened philosopher who follows "metaphysical" principles of "rational justice." In denying Locke's arguments for a natural right to property that original man could comprehend and respect, Rousseau claimed that whatever has proven useful to some social men cannot be assumed to have been within the unaided reach of isolated individuals in the state of nature. With no consciousness of personal belongings, natural man is incapable of reason and rational acquisition: "What progress could the human race make, scattered in the woods among the animals? And to what point could men mutually perfect and enlighten one another, who, having neither fixed domicile nor any need of one another, would perhaps meet hardly twice in their lives, without knowing or talking to each other." The development of the human understanding awaits the appearance of those passionate needs originating in social dependence, which transform a dull and gentle beast into an intelligent, acquisitive man: "It is by the activity [of the passions] that our reason is perfected; we seek to know only because we desire to have pleasure; and it is impossible to conceive why one who had neither desires nor fears would go

---

6. *Discourse on Inequality*, pp. 123–126, 156–157, 148–151. See also *Essay on the Origin of Languages* (H, I, 370–371, 373–375, 388–389). Rousseau defended the naturalness of pity by inference from observable facts involving the attitudes of mothers toward their children, an audience's reactions at the theater, and the behavior of animals. He also anticipated the obvious individualist rejoinder, the assertion of self-interest: "Even should it be true that commiseration is only a sentiment that puts us in the position of him who suffers—a sentiment that is obscure and strong in savage man, developed but weak in civilized man —what would this idea matter to the truth of what I say, except to give it more force? In fact, commiseration will be all the more energetic as the observing animal identifies himself more intimately with the suffering animal." *Discourse on Inequality*, p. 151.

to the trouble of reasoning." Moreover, once new men have acquired the reason of the philosopher, they often repudiate the natural passion of pity. This "first sentiment of humanity" is silenced in civilized men of mere reason. The man of mere reason has become self-interested. He puts his hands to his ears and argues briefly with himself in order to suppress the natural impulse of pity, when not acknowledging a murder taking place beneath his window.[7]

Without common life, Rousseau's natural man is permanently stuck in a self-enclosed, static existence. And he is indolent. Unlike Locke, Helvétius, and Condillac, Rousseau rejected the possibility that this individual could define himself through receiving sensations. Because of the absence of that common life which permits imagination, foresight, general ideas, memory, and language, there remains what Rousseau called a "gap" between passively experiencing sensations and consciously acquiring and creatively employing experience in the form of knowledge. While man remains isolated, injuries are not crimes to be remembered and punished but unique encounters which, when painful, are immediately repaired through flight or mechanical, instinctive revenge. A discrete individual can have no sense of a permanent self which can be threatened by others and would therefore have to be avenged.[8]

7. *Discourse on Inequality*, pp. 146, 156, 143.
8. *Ibid.*, pp. 144, 148–152, 157. Rousseau planned a refutation of Helvétius' *De l'esprit* after its publication in 1758 but fear of further embarrassing Helvétius, after the official condemnation of *De l'esprit*, led him to burn his notes. See *Letters from the Mountain* (P, III, 693). Rousseau's marginal notes in his copy of *De l'esprit* dispute Helvétius' equation of passive sensation with the active faculties of memory and judgment: "To perceive objects is to sense, but to perceive relationships is to judge." And judgment presupposes society in a way that for Rousseau nullifies Helvétius' system (P, IV, 1121–1130). Rousseau's letters to Mme d'Houdetot contain a more complete critique of liberal sensationalism. Stressing the inaccuracy of the senses, Rousseau employed the same terminology of his marginal notes on Helvétius, rejected specifically the self-made statue in Condillac's *Treatise of Sensations*, and complained about vain metaphysicians who confidently shuffle

The presocial desires of the natural savage, "the simple desires of nature," cannot exceed his physical needs: "The only goods he knows in the universe are nourishment, a female and repose." Food and sleep are easily obtained in a manner that perpetuates his static condition of natural isolation. "I see him," Rousseau added, "satisfying his hunger under an oak,

---

words to establish absurd systems. See *Moral Letters* (P, IV, 1087–1099). See as well Rousseau's early letter on the "gap" between mere instinct and human reason that Pope's great chain of being ignores. Letter to Conzié (Jan. 17, 1742; *CC*, I, 132–139). Rousseau also insisted that time and place contribute to the fashioning of that passionate disposition capable of simply perceiving and describing the countryside. See letter to M. de Luxembourg (Jan. 20, 1763; *CC*, XV, 48-51); *Rousseau juge de Jean-Jacques*, pp. 808–812, 821.

Sometimes Rousseau's references to sensationalist doctrine appear trivial. Saint-Preux is certain, after kissing Julie's equally charming and amiable cousin, that "sensations are nothing but what the heart makes them." Julie concurs. *La Nouvelle Héloïse* (P, II, 64, 138). On other occasions Rousseau's complaints capture the essence of his nonindividualism: sensationalism is merely "aggregative," not "organic." It cannot allow for the generation of "organized," "intelligent" beings, for a city like the Roman republic is composed of related men, not "pieces of wood." Letter to Franquières (Jan. 15, 1769; P, IV, 1140).

For a contrasting interpretation, which appreciates the historicity of Rousseau's *Discourse* in contrast to Condillac's "static" statue but sees Rousseau indebted to Condillac's individualism for his notion of natural man and the origin of language, see Jean Morel, "Recherches sur les sources du *Discours de l'inégalité*," *Annales*, V (1909), 143–160, 179–198. Although Durkheim grasps Rousseau's "unhistorical" use of the state of nature as a concept intended "to distinguish between the social elements and those inherent in the psychological make-up of the individual," he, too, argues Rousseau's sensationalism when he asserts that, for Rousseau, "society could only be a concretization of the characteristic properties of the nature of the individual." Emile Durkheim, *Montesquieu and Rousseau: Forerunners of Sociology*, trans. Ralph Manheim (Ann Arbor, 1960), pp. 66, 68, 83-84. Allers argues the centrality of the *Discourse on Inequality* for subsequent writings and denies that the individualist/collectivist distinction is applicable to Rousseau. He also finds a (Lockeian) dualism in Rousseau's notion of man's nature, involving sensationalism with reference to man's "physical" nature and "moral freedom" with reference to man's "moral" being; "political" questions are then subsidiary. See Ulrich S. Allers, "Rousseau's Second *Discourse*," *Review of Politics*, XX (Jan. 1958), 91–120.

quenching his thirst at the first stream, finding his bed at the foot of the same tree that furnished his meal; and therewith his needs are satisfied." Presocial man also seeks only "physical love," the blind desire which instinctively inclines the sexes to unite, with the unintended and unnoticed propagation of the species following. This is not the "moral love" of later social men whose new sentiments of the heart determine and fix a desire exclusively upon a particular woman. Physical love reveals nothing of the feelings of admiration, devotion, jealousy, and rivalry or the socially acquired ideas of beauty, merit, proportion, and fidelity. Every woman equally satisfies the desires of natural man; the sexes unite without design as accident, opportunity, and inclination permit. After physical gratification, they part with equal indifference, the man having no affection or even memory for the woman: "It is easy to see that the moral element of love is an artificial sentiment born of the usage of society."[9]

Similarly, the family has no place in Rousseau's presocial state of nature and cannot evolve from occasional physical couplings of natural savages. Rousseau explicitly rejected Locke's and Condillac's assigning of language and the family to the state of nature. There is no need or occasion for speech before society. And there is no sustained relationship between mother and child in the state of nature: "The mother nursed her children at first for her own need; then, habit having endeared them to her, she nourished them afterward for their need. As soon as they had the strength to seek their food, they did not delay in leaving the mother herself; and as there was practically no other way to find one another again than not to lose sight of each other, they were soon at a point of not even recognizing one another." This fragile and temporary relation-

9. *Discourse on Inequality*, pp. 143, 135, 157–159, 164. Physical love shows nothing of frenzy and conflict because the human sexes, unlike those of other animals, are equal numerically and are not periodic in their natural inclinations.

ship between mother and children supports only a static, vagabond life. Not even a trace of their esoteric language remains after mother and children have separated. Philosophers like Condillac, who argued that language begins in domestic intercourse between parents and children, in "reasoning about the state of nature, carry over to it ideas taken from society." Condillac ignored the "many thousands of centuries [which] would have been necessary to develop successively in the human mind the operations of which it was capable"; he "assumed what I question—namely a kind of society already established among the inventors of language."[10] Locke also "supposes what is in question" because he does not reach far enough back "beyond the centuries of society" in defending the idea of the natural family: "Although it may be advantageous to the human species for the union between man and woman to be permanent, it does not follow that it was thus established by nature; otherwise it would be necessary to say that nature also instituted civil society, the arts, commerce, and all that is claimed to be useful to men." The child in a state of nature, Rousseau continued, has greater need to express its desires to its mother through inarticulate sounds and gestures than she to the child. Utterances of the child remain as various and numerous as the children speaking them and are forgotten with the permanent separation of mother and child: "Although the organ of speech is natural to man, speech itself is nonetheless not natural to him."[11]

Natural men fear only the immediate moment of pain and

10. *Ibid.*, pp. 147, 146. Typically Rousseau backed into this criticism of Condillac. Condillac (*Essai sur l'origine des connoissances humaines*, pt. 2, chap. 1, in *Oeuvres philosophiques*, I) argued in individualist fashion, that language results spontaneously from "instinct" and the communicating of natural "interests" or "needs" to others. He imagined two children, wandering about in the desert after a deluge; their first simple sounds are "cries of passion," after which words, without the need of "reflection," follow.

11. *Discourse on Inequality*, pp. 215–218, 210.

hunger, not death, "because an animal will never know what it is to die; and knowledge of death and its terrors is one of the first acquisitions that man has made in moving away from the animal condition." As they had lived alone, natural men die of old age alone "without it being perceived that they cease to be and almost without perceiving it themselves." In the ceaseless, uneventful routine of presocial existence, life and death are without meaning. The presocial individual is permanently anonymous, especially to himself. Each moment, each chance event and each encounter of natural life is unique because no past is recalled and no future is summoned. The indolent savage has merely fragmentary experiences of food, a female, and, most frequently, sleep.[12]

Rousseau's conception of man's natural perfectibility provides the only possible connection between the self-contained individual of this presocial state of nature and the artificial individuals of later periods of social dependence. Natural man's "metaphysical and moral" character includes his ability to make discoveries and errors, to pursue virtue and vice, because he is endowed with a free will. Other beasts obey the commands of natural instinct unhesitatingly, but man is free to acquiesce in or resist the responses prescribed to him through his senses. And he is capable of becoming conscious of his freedom. This capacity to choose constitutes a "spirituality of his soul," completely inexplicable, Rousseau asserted, by laws of sensationalist association governing all animals. Underlying man's power to choose is his "faculty of self-perfection," a faculty which, "with the aid of circumstances, successively develops all the others, and resides among us as much in the species as in the individual."[13] But when new circumstances arise permitting the exercise of man's "potential" (or "virtual") faculties, they are, significantly, neither of natural man's making nor under his control. He had in "instinct alone, every-

12. *Ibid.*, pp. 143, 137, 140, 145.
13. *Ibid.*, pp. 141–142.

thing necessary for him to live in the state of nature; he has, in a cultivated reason, only what is necessary for him to live in society." The new circumstances are extraneous physical accidents which, enforcing closer and more regular physical contact, end the state of natural isolation by compelling men to self-recognition; only through recognition and comparison of themselves with others are men permitted self-recognition. These accidents initiate the gradual transformation that leads to the creation of new, artificial individuals; social engagement through cumulative historical periods of common life replaces the timeless self-involvement of the natural individual, whose will, although free, is necessarily uncreative.[14]

The accidental ties of "mutual dependence" and "reciprocal needs" are necessary for both perfection and degradation, for both the civic virtue which carries social man beyond natural goodness and the vice of aggressive vanity. Man's faculties "could never develop by themselves . . . [but] needed the chance combination of several foreign causes which might never have arisen and without which he would have remained eternally in his primitive condition." There remains, as a result, that unbridgeable gap between the presocial state of nature and subsequent social dependence: common life in all its forms is a transformation which natural savages can neither initiate nor comprehend. Rousseau called explicit attention to the fact that natural pity could not bring men into permanent social union. Indeed, the existence of natural pity removes the "necessity of introducing" into the state of nature a principle of natural "sociability," upon which contract theorists depended. When men are capable of calculating mutual advantages and intitiating voluntary agreements, they have already become the new creatures of earlier, less complex modes of social life. Before common life, isolated man achieves only an inert and faint self-consciousness by imitating and comparing himself with wild beasts. He imitates their industry to obtain food,

14. *Ibid.,* pp. 152, 159–160, 208.

and loses his fear of them by measuring his own skill and agility against their greater strength. But these limited comparisons only anticipate the later, enforced comparisons among social men, for man's natural isolation still precludes self-definition.[15]

Finally, the coarseness of some of natural man's senses exemplifies with almost sarcastic defiance Rousseau's rejection of liberal assumptions. Touch and taste, the natural faculties of softness and sensuality, must, Rousseau argued, remain gross and crude for isolated natural men, while sight, hearing, and smell, required for self-preservation, can become subtle.[16] Rousseau's repeated strictures against ascribing the vanity, passionate acquisitiveness, and reason of artificial men to presocial individuals, his denial that langauge and a family are natural to man, his insistence upon man's need of society if he is to be able to translate momentary sensations into that reflective judgment which exhibits his natural capacity of free agency—each of these positions testifies to Rousseau's nonindividualism. And all of these points, most specifically the inescapable crudity of two of man's natural senses so long as he is deprived of the fellowship of other men, testify to Rousseau's basic disagreement with traditional liberalism: an individual cannot be a self-made man. That a man can be educated does not mean that he first educates himself.

Stages of Common Life

After his accidental departure from natural isolation, man moves through six stages of common life; these are the stages

15. *Ibid.*, pp. 162, 126, 105–106. Rousseau's most sustained discussion of the accidental character of social dependence is in *Origin of Languages*, pp. 384–393. For further discussion of sociability and perfectibility in Rousseau's philosophy, see René Hubert, *Rousseau et l'Encyclopédie: Essai sur la formation des idées politiques de Rousseau (1742–1756)* (Paris, 1928), pp. 91–95; Gouhier, "Nature et histoire," pp. 17–19; and Jouvenel, "Essai," pp. 45–48.

16. *Discourse on Inequality*, p. 140.

by which artificial individuals and groups create each other. At first the transformation is progressive; then it is retrogressive. These transformations form a history of the human heart.[17] We shall return repeatedly to the sequence of six periods for "placing" and interpreting Rousseau's other writings.[18]

Man neither rationally nor naturally inclines toward sociability. Rousseau's speculations concerning "the different accidents that were able to perfect human reason while deteriorating the species [and] made a being evil while making him sociable" are only speculations. Something thwarted man's automatic acquisition of food. Trees grew higher, so that fruit was more difficult to obtain; or animal populations increased, forcing indolent savages to greater activity or to greater reliance upon "natural weapons." Increasing contact resulted and ultimately compelled self-recognition. Men confronted each other in the accident of repeated physical contiguity; then, and only then, did they acquire a faint consciousness of distinct membership in a species. For through these contacts, man began to form certain relational concepts: "These relationships that we express by the words large, small, strong, weak, fast, slow, fearful, bold, and other similar ideas, compared when necessary

17. *Letter to Beaumont*, p. 936. Here Rousseau compressed the *Discourse* into three epochs: presocial nature, a simple society of virtuous men, and later social men whose particular interests are opposed to the "public good."

18. Interpretations which note the importance of historicity in Rousseau's thought are: Bertrand de Jouvenel, "Rousseau the Pessimistic Evolutionist," *Yale French Studies*, XXVIII (Fall–Winter, 1961), 83–96, which finds Rousseau the "first great exponent of social evolution"; Derathé, *Rousseau et la science politique*, pp. 132–133; Eméry, *Rousseau l'annonciateur*, pp. 24–25, which argues that for Rousseau "man is no longer an invariable given, a being once and forever defined"; Gisèle Bretonneau, *Valeurs humaines de J.-J. Rousseau* (Paris, 1961), esp. pp. 26–33, 289–292; and Lionel Gossman, "Time and History in Rousseau," in *Studies on Voltaire and the Eighteenth Century*, ed. Theodore Besterman, vol. 30 (1964), pp. 311–349. Gossman also pursues Rousseau's "historical mode of analysis" into autobiographical writings and examines the "politics" of his musical theory.

and almost without thinking about it, finally produced in him some sort of reflection, or rather a mechanical prudence that indicated to him the precautions most necessary for his safety."[19] Man thereby lost the natural anonymity of isolated self-involvement and acquired an indelible sense of self. Individuality is authenticated only when men confirm and ratify each other, whether in combat or cooperation.

Mechanical prudence, a socially acquired necessity, more certain and much more rapid than any kind of reasoning, appears during temporary economic cooperation and occasional conflict. This, the first period of social dependence, requires only crude and imperfect languages. Men learn that the "love of well-being is the sole motive of human actions." They learn both reliance and distrust. Those who think themselves strong obtain their well-being by force; those comparatively weak try cleverness and cunning. For occasional "mutual undertakings," individuals united in herds or "some kind of free association that obligated no one and lasted only as long as the passing need that had formed it." For some "present and perceptible interest," men would trap a deer together, using a primitive discourse of inarticulate cries, gestures, and some imitative sounds which correspond to the natural languages of crows and monkeys. These simple tasks require nothing more permanent; the prerational character of their tasks permits nothing more binding. Through "multitudes of centuries" of such mutual undertakings, men acquire a "crude idea of mutual engagements." During this "epoch of a first revolution" they develop talent and a new spirit of industriousness. Men sleep less. They shape tools of hard, sharp stone for digging and for cutting branches; they fashion huts, and plaster them with mud.[20]

The second period shows a better organized and more per-

19. *Discourse on Inequality*, pp. 162, 165.
20. *Ibid*. pp. 165–167.

manent pattern of social dependence comprising established
though scattered families. Each man's hut is a limited physical
property, but he does not claim personal possession. When the
strong build huts, the weak choose to imitate rather than dis-
lodge the strong, but not because of conscious ideas of rightful
ownership. The safety of imitation is preferable to the risks of
battle. Two emotions, which arise from living together in small
dwellings, represent the finest sentiments of humanity—conjugal love and paternal affection: "Each family becomes a
little society all the better united because reciprocal affection
and freedom were its only bonds." Each family develops its
own mode of discourse. Sexual differentiation develops. Women,
becoming increasingly sedentary, remain indoors while men
hunt for sustenance. Families occasionally cooperate with each
other against wild beasts, and men lose much of their natural
strength. Further, the simple wants and easy comfort of familial solitude create a burden of leisure, which is now spent idly.
Later leisure will inspire desire for conveniences that, mistakenly, seem to fulfill natural needs.[21]

A small society, a unified, self-conscious "nation" whose
members begin to become hostages to their vain desires, marks
the third period. To explain the advent of this society and a
common language, Rousseau posited another *deus ex machina:*
floods and earthquakes force some families to live more closely
together, perhaps at first on small island refuges. Such families
form a "particular nation" unified by "[*moeurs*] and character,
not by regulations and laws, but by the same kind of life and
foods and by the common influence of climate." Each nation
has a new solidarity and density. Men who once had wandered
in herds, or away from their respective families, now stay at
home. But, paradoxically, this comparative solidarity brings the
first sign of the destructive discord of vain passions and predatory egotism. Hints of vanity had appeared toward the end of

21. *Ibid.,* pp. 167–168.

the second period of social dependence but could not then be indulged. Now, however, men who pursue particular interests receive public esteem. Membership within a national community engenders ideas of invidious preference upon which subsequent acquisition of economic property and the development of reason partially depend.

When national communities are young, men gather in front of huts for festivals of singing and dancing. Later, competitive attitudes of merit and beauty appear. Natural pity is weakened, and so is man's capacity to discern his true needs. Even affection within families begins to wither. This third period thus invites social dismemberment: "Each one began to look at the others and to want to be looked at himself, and public esteem had a value. The one who sang or danced the best, the handsomest, the strongest, the most adroit, or the most eloquent became the most highly considered; and that was the first step toward inequality and, at the same time, toward vice." The "first duties of civility" and the first expressions of insincerity, disrespect, and cruelty appear simultaneously. The artificial individual, who earlier had seen himself only as a cooperative and peaceful member of a herd and then a family, acquires a clear sense of himself as property: a distinctive, deserving personality to be measured by others. Public acknowledgment, whether applause, disrespect, or rivalry, becomes the social basis for a number of aggressive interests. Common life weakens as men direct each other to perceive and pursue their personal advancement. For the first time injuries become personal outrages or crimes deserving of punishment, for men take swift and terrible vengeance when they do not receive the public consideration to which they think themselves entitled.[22]

During this sketch of national societies, Rousseau paused briefly to recall his description in the first part of the *Discourse on Inequality* of the origin of aggressive vanity. There, he

22. *Ibid.,* pp. 168–172.

argued the primacy of social dependence by demonstrating the long history of common life between the era of the calm, disinterested individual of the presocial state and that of the acquisitive, self-interested creatures of later forms of social dependence. Rousseau's explicit adversary was Hobbes, who assumed, according to Rousseau, that man is destructively acquisitive by nature. Hobbes "correctly" saw that natural man is a stranger to all ideas of virtue and is not restrained by right reason. But, argued Rousseau, natural pity tempers natural love of self (*amour de soi*), a feeling distinct from socially engendered self-love (*amour-propre*). Moreover, the natural desire for self-preservation, though uninhibited by virtuous principles, occurs in a condition of isolation, and cannot be prejudicial to others. Therefore, the state of nature is a condition of peace, not war. Hobbes' error was to include "in the savage man's care for self-preservation the need to satisfy a multitude of passions which are the product of society and which have made laws necessary." Hobbes assumed that natural man is strong yet still dependent upon the will of others; this is self-contradictory. The desire even to oppress depends upon a sense of competitive personal identity, which in turn demands acknowledgment from fellow men: "The same cause that prevents savages from using their reason, as our jurists claim, prevents them at the same time from abusing their faculties." Because natural men "had no kind of commerce among themselves; since they consequently knew neither vanity, nor consideration, nor esteem, nor contempt; since they did not have the slightest idea of thine and mine, nor any true idea of justice," war must be a condition of society.[23]

23. *Ibid.*, pp. 136, 153–155, 157, 219–220. Rousseau also rejected the contrasting assumption of Cumberland and Pufendorf that natural man is timid and fearful. For further criticisms of the "absurd" and "revolting" system of the "sophist" Hobbes, see *Fragments on the State of War* (P, III, 601–616). Here too Rousseau's arguments are nonindividualist: the successful Hobbesian warrior, seizing all property and killing

For those like Hobbes who ignored the social transformations and the immense historical distances that separate the benign "stupidity of brutes" from the "fatal ingenuity of civilized man," Rousseau invoked "the axiom of the wise Locke": *"Where there is no property, there is no injury."*[24] Rousseau's use of Locke is characteristically misleading because Rousseau cannot have meant by "property" the private ownership of land. Artificial individuals of the third period do not yet understand rightful possession, even of their familial mud huts. And both the accumulation of land and the conscious claim to rightful possession occur in the next historical period and have nothing to do with the needs of the body, the natural rights of private individuals, or the exclusive claims of industrious first occupants. Rather, "property" here refers to a firm but socially acquired consciousness of self: "As soon as men had begun to appreciate one another, and the idea of consideration was formed in their minds, each one claimed a right to it, and it was no longer possible to be disrespectful toward anyone with impunity."[25] To Locke and other liberal individualist theorists, this property in oneself is either given or the result of unaided self-definition.

Without other men, according to Rousseau, natural man remained "naturally good" but beyond, or before, good and

---

all competitors, has no one to acknowledge his triumphs. For a contrasting interpretation which sees a Hobbesian "psychology" of social struggle in Rousseau's social man, see Derathé, *Rousseau et la science politique*, pp. 108–112. For a discussion of Rousseau's "relative" understanding of *amour-propre*, as well as the view that the division of labor and economic inequality are basic to his understanding of historical decline, see Iring Fetscher, "Rousseau's Concept of Freedom in the Light of His Philosophy of History," in *Liberty* (*Nomos IV*), Yearbook for the American Society for Political and Legal Philosophy, ed. Carl J. Friedrich (New York, 1962), pp. 29–56.

24. *Discourse on Inequality*, p. 170. Locke's maxim, which he offered as an example of a self-evident proposition, reads: "Where there is no property there is no injustice." *Essay*, bk. 4, chap. 3.

25. *Discourse on Inequality*, p. 170. See also *ibid.*, pp. 167, 172–173.

evil: "Men . . . not having among themselves any kind of moral relationship or known duties, could be neither good nor evil, and had neither vices nor virtues." Only when judged retrospectively in a "physical sense," Rousseau explained, can the words *virtue* and *vice* be applied to the natural passions contributing to or inhibiting self-preservation. In this sense the most virtuous man is the natural man "who least resists the simple impulses of nature." The vanities of later men united in national communities, in contrast, are the new emotions of artificial individuals; common life makes possible passions that drive men to distinguish themselves *from* the conditions of common life. These new individuals, only somewhat outside the society of which they are creatures, signified to Rousseau the decline of common life, rather than, as for liberal theorists, the distinction between the private individual and public society.[26]

Men in the third historical period acquire vanity; they become self-conscious moral arbiters who suffer, judge, and avenge personal injuries. Natural pity can no longer regulate relationships. Nevertheless, the earliest national communities, when families are economically self-sufficient and men gather before huts for common festivals, are the happiest, most stable of epochs.[27]

The "extraordinary circumstances of some volcano which, by throwing up metallic materials in fusion," gave observers "the idea of imitating natural operations," initiates the fourth period. The simple men of national societies could hardly dig and smelt ore without a prior notion of the result or its possible use. The art of metallurgy, suggested by the volcanic eruption, invites joint labor with iron tools. Men stumble upon

26. *Ibid.*, p. 152. For a more extensive treatment of natural *amour de soi*, the innocuous "pride" of early, simple men, and the self-destructive *amour-propre* of late social men, see *Rousseau juge de Jean-Jacques*, pp. 669–673, 686–687, 805–807.

27. *Discourse on Inequality*, pp. 170–171.

the apparent advantages of accumulating an economic surplus. Industrious and acquisitive because of earlier social transformations, no longer content with gathering fruits or fishing and hunting for daily needs, and already beginning on their own to use sharpened stones and pointed sticks to cultivate vegetables and roots, men now accept immediate loss in order to reap greater future gain. With equal foresight they develop the arts of husbandry. A division of labor (which owes nothing to a natural "trucking disposition") combines with possession of economic property in a new pattern of social engagement. The claims by the few to personal ownership of economic property are a "new kind of right." The strongest, the most skillful, and the most ingenious assert a "right to property, different from the one which results from natural law." Striving for public consideration and influence, rather than the satisfaction of bodily needs, a few obtain illegitimate title to portions of the common land on which they labor.

Initially, exchanges between farmers and tool makers and the arts of husbandry and metallurgy dominate this fourth period. Other economic arts and refinements of language follow. Men rank themselves on the basis of wit, beauty, skill, and, especially, the extent of property ownership and the power to serve or injure others. This period witnesses the self-destructive fulfillment of man's natural capacity for "self-perfection." It includes "faculties developed, memory and imagination in play, vanity aroused, reason rendered active, and the mind having almost reached the limit of the perfection of which it is susceptible." Because wit and wealth attract public consideration, destitute men begin to affect them. The civilized individual is a hypocrite, opaque to himself and others. "To be and to seem to be became two altogether different things; and from this distinction came conspicuous ostentation, deceptive cunning, and all the vices that follow from them. . . . Finally, consuming ambition, the fervor to raise one's relative fortune less out of true need than in order to place oneself above others, inspires in all men a base inclination to harm each other, a secret jealousy all the more dangerous because, in order to strike its blow in greater safety, it often assumes the mask of benevolence." The period that permits a division of labor forever destroys simplicity.[28]

This era is so explosive that Rousseau needs imagine no convenient accident to account for the transition to the fifth period. Conflicts between first occupants and the strongest lead to permanent, endemic violence and eventually to organized war between rich and poor classes. Usurpation, plunder, suppression, and mutual enslavement by rich and poor result from unbridled vanity which, in making men "avaricious, ambitious and evil," suppresses all traces of natural pity. But the contending classes constitute an organic, if unstable, form of social dependence. Their struggle is internecine, with opponents defined and motivated by their oppressive rivalry. The conflict of rich and poor is not a shapeless conflict between separate groups with private interests. It is not an external collision between discrete parts, some industrious and self-reliant, others unlucky and insufficiently self-assertive. The very existence of either group is inconceivable without the other. The rich are rich because the poor are poor, and vice versa. As heirs to a historical series of social transformations, each class in turn educates the other in the vanity and cruelty of which their conflict is but an expression. This fifth stage of social dependence is what Hobbes mistakenly called the natural condition of mankind, for "nascent society" has yielded "the most horrible state of war."[29]

28. *Ibid.*, pp. 171–175.

29. *Ibid.*, p. 176. Rousseau asserted this organic connection between rich and poor in two defenses of the *Discourse on the Sciences and Arts*. See *Observations* and *Last Response* (P, III, 49–51, 79–80). In the latter: "Luxury feeds a hundred poor in our cities and the death of a hundred thousand of the poor in the countryside. . . . We need sauces in our kitchens; therefore many sick people have no soup. We need

Individuals are now rational creatures capable of pursuing particular interests with deceiving calculation and brutal foresight. The state of war is not permitted to endure in an unrestrained, permanently violent fashion. All men reflect upon the overwhelming calamities of unbridled conflict. The wealthy suffer most; they risk property as well as life. As Rousseau described the outcome, a rich man, "pressed by necessity, finally conceived the most deliberate project that ever entered the human mind. It was to use in his favor the very forces of those who attacked him, to make his defenders out of his adversaries, inspire them with other maxims, and give them other institutions which were as favorable to him as natural right is unfavorable." Asserting that there can be no safety in riches or poverty, he "seduced" the poor into agreeing to the establishment of representative political authority. Equal positive law, to which all men must conform, may make amends for the caprices of fortune, the man of property cunningly asserted. The weak will be protected from oppression, the ambitious will be restrained, and every man will be secure

---

wine on our tables; therefore the peasant drinks only water. We need powder for our wigs; therefore many poor have no bread." See also *Fragments on Luxury, Commerce, and the Arts* (P, III, 521–523); *Moral Letters*, p. 1089. Sven Stelling-Michaud, "Rousseau et l'injustice sociale," in *Jean-Jacques Rousseau*, pp. 177–178, discusses this connectedness between rich and poor and sees, in contrast to this study, a reformist or revolutionary optimism in Rousseau's diagnosis of contemporary life in common. See also Lucio Colletti, *From Rousseau to Lenin: Studies in Ideology and Society*, trans. John Merrington and Judith White (London, 1972), pp. 143–216. A discussion of Rousseau's early ideas on economic inequality and social distance is Jean Starobinski, "Tout le mal vient de l'inégalité," *Europe* (Nov.-Dec. 1961), pp. 135–147. Economic inequality is taken to be the root cause of man's decline by Gouhier, "Nature et histoire," pp. 25–26; Martin, *French Liberal Thought*, pp. 197–201; and Einaudi, *Early Rousseau*, pp. 19–21, 63, 80–82, 128–129, 143, 150, 191–201, 224–233. An alternative view is Jouvenel, "Rousseau the Pessimistic Evolutionist," p. 95. Jouvenel argues that historical decline could not be "remedied by a social policy of equal shares" because economic inequality merely reflects a pervasive climate of invidious "consideration" or "esteem."

in the possession of his property. It was a clever swindle, and "all ran to meet their chains" at his proposal. Thus, new fetters are imposed upon the poor, new powers are given the rich, and all mankind, for the benefit of a few ambitious men, is subject to perpetual labor and misery. The natural law of pity survives only in infrequent peaceful relationships among societies, under the name of the law of nations, as a tacit convention to facilitate economic exchange.

Rousseau distinguished three minor periods within this sixth stage, which brings the historical evolution of common life up to contemporary times. During the first, common authority is instituted by social contract to protect the property of the wealthy. This requires no regular form of government. Witnesses to a dispute judge it according to a few specific rules. Difficulties then lead men to entrust public authority to particular persons by means of a political contract, the form varying with the extent and mode of unsanctioned inequality. This permanent magistracy is supposed to remedy the effects of the "law of the strongest," but inevitably becomes unbridled despotic power. When magistrates usurp power by encouraging social dissension, the exercise of governmental power becomes a rule of undisguised naked force. Men of wealth, rank, power, and personal merit, exhibiting the relative qualities "by which men form an estimate of each other in society," use legal means to oppress others. Wealth rules. Property is enthroned: "Wealth is the last [quality] to which they are all reduced in the end because, being the most immediately useful to well-being and the easiest to communicate, it is easily used to buy all the rest." Contemporary life in common is legalized warfare. The few who are wealthy and powerful and the many who are poor and weak are fellow prisoners: "If one sees a handful of powerful and rich men at the height of grandeur and fortune, while the crowd grovels in obscurity and misery, it is because the former prize the things they enjoy only insofar as the others are deprived of them; and because, without changing their status, they would cease to be happy if the people ceased to be miserable."[30]

Contemporary men are not the heirs but the repudiation of original men. They are vain and predatory as a cumulative result of the several historical transformations.

30. *Discourse on Inequality*, pp. 177–189.

CHAPTER 4

The Undecided Self
and the Divided Self

Not all liberal philosophers initially located the discrete individual in Locke's pregovernmental state of nature or in Adam Smith's premarket "rude state of society," but the unrepentant individualism of liberal theory does not require these conventions. The philosophers' discussions of genius and interest provide two related, persistent variations on the theme of the individual indebted to neither common life nor historical past. These concepts reveal by contrast Rousseau's conception of common life and of the new, composite personality of the artificial individual.

Liberalism: Genius and Interest

Liberal theory has long been preoccupied with genius, which it defines as a separate person's unaided capacity for invention; this includes the ability to define himself and to fashion deliberately the language he uses. Locke, Helvétius, Condillac, d'Alembert, and Bentham all described a process of unaided self-education. To Locke, internal reflection and memory—the repetition, comparison, and union of simple ideas that the mind has "stored"—permit each individual to "invent" or "frame" more complex ideas. A man acquires an idea of God through his mental labor. Reflecting upon his accumulated memorial inventory, and especially his memory of himself, he stretches the simple ideas of "existence, knowledge, power, and pleasure" to the point of infinitude and conceives an "eternal, omniscient, omnipotent, infinitely wise and happy being."[1]

Locke argued that simple words are "outward marks of our internal ideas." The child, with a temporarily limited capacity for reflection, is nevertheless capable of significant utterance.[2] From this it is a small jump to Condorcet's applause in the *Sketch* for "certain men of genius, humanity's eternal benefactors, whose name and country are for ever buried in oblivion," who, by recognizing the possibility for unlimited combinations in a small number of words, invented language.[3] D'Alembert's *Preliminary Discourse* asserts that it is "feeling which creates": reconciling and combining sensations is the natural creativity of the intellect.[4] Original inventiveness of this sort assumes an integral, creative, acquisitive self that is its consciousness. "*Self* is that conscious thinking thing," according to Locke, "which is sensible or conscious of pleasure and pain, capable of happiness or misery, and so is concerned for itself, as far as that consciousness extends."[5] Self-definition, whether uniting oneself to property and a political society or inventing complex ideas and language, depends upon and reflects men's aboriginal self-containedness. D'Alembert observed that "our first reflective ideas must be concerned with ourselves, that is to say, must concern that thinking principle which constitutes our nature and which is in no way distinct from ourselves."[6]

Liberal theorists from Locke to Mill were fascinated by the genius not only of the individual in acquiring basic faculties but of exceptional individuals as well. Large portions of Helvétius' *Of the Mind* concern public reception of the inventions and legislative innovations of those with unusual delicacy

---

1. Locke, *Essay*, bk. 2, chap. 2; bk. 3, chap. 6. See also *ibid.*, bk. 2, chap. 12.
2. *Ibid.*, bk. 2, chap. 11.
3. Condorcet, *Sketch*, p. 7.
4. D'Alembert, *Preliminary Discourse*, pp. 26–34, 39–51, 60, 75.
5. Locke, *Essay*, bk. 2, chap. 17.
6. D'Alembert, *Preliminary Discourse*, p. 8.

of senses, extent of memory, and capacity for attention.[7] Turgot postulated a fundamental drive of human nature to innovate, to bring into being ever newer and more beneficial combinations of sensations. Assuming a fixed ratio between the births of geniuses and ordinary natalites, Turgot welcomed population increase.[8] Voltaire in his *Age of Louis XIV*, Diderot in *Rameau's Nephew*, and Condorcet, whose eighth "stage" of the human mind in the *Sketch* begins with the invention of the printing press, attributed historical change to the reception of new ideas and to the effects of inventions, both useful and aesthetic, in the arts and sciences.

Voltaire was especially concerned with original discovery. He heralded smallpox inoculation in his *Philosophical Letters* as a symbol of a new, confident, and enlightened age. In the *Essai sur les moeurs*, he was also attentive to the inventions of artisans and mechanics: the first use of eyeglasses; the development of windmills; the replacement of porcelain by earthenware; the spreading use of window glass, mirrors, tower clocks, and precision scientific instruments like the compass; new roofing techniques and modern fireplaces; candles, knives, and forks. Voltaire mentioned these as rivals to Greek inventiveness in arts and letters.

Behind this celebration of genius is the goal of liberating mankind from the crushing burdens of historical tradition. Diderot's article, *Encyclopedia*, for the fifth volume of the *Encyclopedia*, distinguishes two cultivators of the sciences: the man of genius who increases the fund of knowledge and "the writers of texts" who present discoveries in an understandable, ordered scheme for public enlightenment. Both contributions encourage the substitution of autonomous reason for authority and social tradition. With its convenient index of cross refer-

7. Helvétius, *De l'esprit*, discourse 2, chaps. 19, 20; discourse 3, chaps. 1–4, 30; discourse 4, chap. 1.

8. Frank E. Manuel, *The Prophets of Paris* (Cambridge, Mass., 1962), pp. 17–18, 49–51.

ences, the *Encyclopedia* is organized according to the faculties —reason, memory, and imagination—essential to the inventive mind. The three columns listing the articles are headed philosophy, history, and poetry. A large number of articles concern original inventions and discoveries, especially in useful trades and technology. Diderot interviewed craftsmen and served temporary apprenticeships in workshops and on farms. The *Encyclopedia* contains detailed descriptions of mechanical processes and eleven volumes of engraved illustrations concerning these processes.[9]

Bentham was almost a caricature of the deepest concerns and metaphors of liberalism. Tirelessly campaigning for reforms in penal, constitutional, and civil law and in Parliamentary and church government, Bentham thought his discovery of the principle of utility as a "logic of the will" made him comparable to Aristotle. Sometimes he called himself a second Lavoisier, giving morals a scientific nomenclature and foundation; sometimes, a modern Archimedes. He visualized "morals reformed, health preserved, industry invigorated, instruction diffused, public burdens lightened" if the Panoptican prison design, a "simple idea in architecture," were applied to the construction of new factories, mental institutions, hospitals, and schools.[10] Bentham's hostility to the historical sensibility of Blackstone and Savigny betrays the agony of the inventor, the man with an unending supply of experimental gadgetry. Tasks are immediate, technical matters. There is no problem that cannot be mastered simply by applying the principle of utility, which frees the mind from bondage to "ancient customs" and

9. See René Hubert, *Les Sciences sociales dans l'Encyclopédie* (Paris, 1923), pt. 2, chap. 7.

10. Bentham, preface to *Morals and Legislation*, p. iv; *Of Nomography*, chap. 7, in *Works*, III. See also A. V. Dicey, *Lectures on the Relation of Law and the Constitution during the Nineteenth Century*, 2d ed. (London, 1948), p. 131; Elie Halévy, *A History of the English People in the Nineteenth Century*, trans. E. I. Watkin and D. A. Barker, 6 vols. (New York, 1961), I, 585.

superstitions. One might "open an *Historical School, à la mode de l'Allemagne*," Bentham wrote in 1830 while defending a new plan of Parliamentary reform for France; "Der Heer Savigny, in Germany—could furnish admirable masters. . . . To the army and the navy of a country, substitute, for example, a history of the wars waged by that same country, . . . To an order on the cook for dinner, substitute a fair copy of the housekeeper's book, as kept for and during the appropriate series of years."[11] Mill tempered the Benthamite celebration of egoism, but *On Liberty* still suggests the liberal view of genius. Private liberty, obtained exclusively outside of and in opposition to society ("collective mediocrity") and historical tradition ("the despotism of custom"), is synonymous with "individual spontaneity," "genius and eccentricity," and "originality in thought and action."[12] An individual is either inventive or he follows the oppressive crowd in unthinking obedience to the past.

Some individuals possess genius, but all have exclusively private interests to protect, pursue, and expand, assertive desires carried like suitcases. As in Mandeville's *Fable of the Bees*, liberal theorists reduced moral and political experience to self-interest. That some individuals are selfish, others unselfish, does not change the picture. Nor does it matter whether the individual achieves happiness through self-restraint or self-indulgence. Both of these qualities depend on the fiction of the separate self. Further, liberals used the metaphor of good economic calculation to describe the benefits of moral planning. For Locke, what counts in moral action is precise calculation: "Judging is, as it were, balancing an account, and determining on which side the odds lie. If therefore either side be huddled up in haste, and several of the sums that should have gone into

11. Bentham, *To His Fellow–Citizens of France, On Houses of Peers and Senates*, sect. 3, in *Works*, IV.
12. John Stuart Mill, *On Liberty*, chap. 3, in *Utilitarianism, Liberty, and Representative Government* (London, 1910).

the reckoning be overlooked and left out, this precipitancy causes as wrong a judgment as if it were a perfect ignorance. . . . To check this precipitancy, our understanding and reason were given us."[13] The moral dilemmas of the individual in liberal theory are always grounded in the idea of an undecided self that must tally short-range losses against long-range profits.

Bentham also emphasized private arithmetic and foresight. He composed an elaborate balance sheet of pleasures and pains, credits and debits, with a complicated system of double-entry bookkeeping to facilitate doing one's sums.[14] In heralding a "realistic" school of political analysis which reduces politics to pluralistic interests, Bentham asserted that we must accept the "practical principle" of what is rather than the "theoretical principle" of what ought to be. The "self-preference principle" is constant and universal.[15] The individual is an accountant who constantly calculates a momentary balance sheet of interests against his inventory. Similarly, Helvétius argued that the passions of avarice, pride, and friendship are "natural pleasures." Because of pride, we desire the esteem of others. Friendship is merely the form that our desire for esteem takes, for we give esteem in order to receive it. The greater the feeling of esteem the more lively the sensation of friendship.[16]

Bentham rejected the principle of "asceticism" as an alternative to the "self-preference" principle: "The principle of asceticism never was, nor ever can be, consistently pursued by any living creature. Let but one tenth part of the inhabitants of this earth pursue it consistently, and in a day's time they will have turned it into a hell."[17] This is precisely the point. Bentham's rejection confirms the liberal fixation upon the interests of the discrete individual rather than qualifying it, be-

13. Locke, *Essay*, bk. 2, chap. 21.
14. But to be useful, a numerical scheme must itself be simple. See "Specimens of Bentham's Conversation," in *Works*, X, 562.
15. Bentham, introduction to *Constitutional Code*, in *Works*, IX.
16. Helvétius, *De l'esprit*, discourse 1, chaps. 1, 4; discourse 2, chaps. 1–3, 15, 19; discourse 3, chaps. 10–11, 13–14.
17. Bentham, *Morals and Legislation*, chap. 2.

cause, to the liberals, only two exhaustive possibilities for judgment and action are conceivable, the rational, systematic calculation of pleasure and the rational, systematic calculation of pain or ascetic self-denial. Adam Smith observed that in spite of the necessity of contractual "mutual help" in a civilized society, "it is not from benevolence of the butcher, the brewer or the baker that we expect our dinner but from their regard to their own interest."[18] Mill, taking a more "spiritual" tack, was impatient with earlier utilitarian defenses of "selfish egoism" and "selfish indifference" to others.[19] But the idea of "nobility of character" that Mill defended is equally a matter of private interest: "As between his own happiness and that of others, [the doctrine of] utilitarianism requires him to be strictly impartial as a disinterested and benevolent spectator."[20] In making his personal calculations, the liberal individual is always a spectator of other, equally self-contained individuals.

Bentham saw the advantage of temporary "asceticism" for the accumulation of personal fortunes. An individual may "sacrifice" immediate pleasures in anticipation of larger or more enduring future pleasures. With this understanding of interest, the alternatives of self-interest and asceticism become identical; the distinction between the accumulation of pleasures and the ascetic pursuit of pain dissolves. Self-denial and saintliness are merely the self-interested calculations of the very foresighted. "If a hermit or monk imposes on himself the law of silence, flogs himself every night, lives on pulse and water, sleeps on straw, offers to God his wickedness and ignorance," Helvétius observed, "he hopes by virtue of his mortification to make a fortune in heaven."[21] Self-interest is indeed unavoidable, because the self is taken to be a separate entity.

18. Smith, *Wealth of Nations,* bk. 1, chap. 2.
19. John Stuart Mill, *On Bentham & Coleridge* (New York, 1962), pp. 61–75.
20. Mill, *Utilitarianism,* chap. 2.
21. Helvétius, *De l'homme,* sect. 4, chap. 20, in *Oeuvres complètes d'Helvétius,* 3 vols. (Paris, 1818), II.

The liberal conception of the common good is, of necessity, in Bentham's words, "the sum of the interests of the several members who compose it." He added, "It is in vain to talk of the interests of the community, without understanding what is the interest of the individual." And so Bentham distinguished the "public interest," as an individual's numerical "share . . . in the happiness and well-being of the whole community," from the "private interest" of an individual, which is his numerical "share . . . in the well-being of some portion of the community less than the major part."[22] This formula was echoed or duplicated by other liberal theorists. Beccaria, whose ideas of crime and punishment had influenced Bentham, rejected the arbitrary character of many customary laws: "Never have they been dictated by a dispassionate student of human nature who might, by bringing the actions of a multitude of men into focus, consider them from this single point of view: the *greatest happiness shared by the greatest number*."[23] Helvétius, asserting that the moral universe is subject to the laws of interest just as the physical universe is governed by the laws of motion, concluded that the principle of moral action is "the interest of the public, that is to say, of the greatest number." Laws must be drafted upon "the principle of the utility of the public, that is to say, the greatest number of men subject to the same form of government."[24] Condorcet, noting aggregative "ties of interest and duty" among separate men, argued that "the progress of the human mind" in each generation comes down to arithmetic: "This progress is subject to the same general laws that can be observed in the development of the faculties of the individual, and it is indeed no

22. Bentham, *Morals and Legislation*, chap. 1; *The Book of Fallacies*, pt. 5, chap. 3, in *Works*, II.
23. Cesare Beccaria, *On Crimes and Punishments*, trans. Henry Paolucci (Indianapolis, 1963), p. 8.
24. Helvétius, *De l'esprit*, discourse 2, chap. 17. See also *ibid.*, discourse 2, chaps. 1, 2, 15, 24; discourse 3, chap. 4.

more than the sum of that development realized in a large number of individuals joined together in society."[25] Mercier de la Rivière proclaimed that without government intervention individuals would be free to pursue their private interests and contribute to a greater total of happiness: "Each of us by force of this full and entire liberty, and pricked by desire of enjoyment, is occupied, according to his state, in varying, multiplying, perfecting the objects of enjoyment which must be shared among us, and thus increase the sum of the common happiness."[26]

Often, however, because of the burden of custom, this sum cannot be a matter of automatic or immediate addition. Liberals employed three methods to aggregate the interests of individuals.[27] The first involves the fusion of interests: individuals, sensitive to the hardships of other individuals, exercise self-restraint or moral sympathy for others. Shaftesbury and Francis Hutcheson, and, at moments, Adam Smith, Diderot, and Bentham employed this approach. A second method, the positing of a natural identity of interests, assumes harmony among interests and promotes unrestrained pursuit of self-interest to the category of a moral duty. Smith's "invisible hand" in the *Wealth of Nations*, Mandeville in *Fable of the Bees*, and Helvétius in *Of the Mind* illustrate this method. So do Hartley and Priestley. A third method is the artificial identification of interests. This relies upon legislative direction, educational incentive, and an enlightened system of legal rewards and punishments. Helvétius flirted with this method, but the major representative here is Bentham with his repertory of legal and architectural reforms. But whether the aggregative process is subtraction, addition, or multiplication, liberal theorists are preoccupied with private interests.

25. Condorcet, *Sketch*, pp. 3–4.
26. Quoted in Martin, *French Liberal Thought*, p. 234.
27. Elie Halévy, *The Growth of Philosophic Radicalism*, trans. Mary Morris (Boston, 1955), pp. 13–20.

A conception of society as numerical aggregation accompanies each method of acquiring an accurate sum. Bentham angrily dismissed all references to organic societies. Expressions like "body politic" are misleading metaphors which encourage "false and extravagant ideas," he asserted: "An analogy, founded solely on this metaphor, has furnished a foundation for pretended arguments, and poetry has invaded the dominion of reason." Because individuals and interests are fundamental, "the community is a fictitious *body*, composed of the individual persons who are considered as constituting as it were its *members*."[28] For Helvétius, "a nation is only a collection of the citizens of which it is composed."[29]

The sense of social cohesiveness, and with it social power of an informal or nongovernmental character, is strong in Mill's writings. And Mill's early impatience with Bentham for having ignored the necessity for a "philosophy of national character" and "national culture," and his extraordinary generosity in *On Coleridge*, are not typical of liberal thought.[30] But these considerations do not alter Mill's individualism. The antithesis he used is the emblem of the liberal mode of thought. On the one hand there is society, on the other the individual. As the one encroaches, the other steadily resists. He began *On Liberty* with the subject of "Civil, or Social Liberty: the nature and limits of the power which can be legitimately exercised *by* society *over* the individual." It is necessary to establish a "fitting adjustment between individual independence and social control"; thus, "spontaneity and individuality" or "self-development" are opposed by the "social principle," by "compulsion and control, whether the means used be physical force in the form of legal penalties, or the moral coercion of public

28. Bentham, *An Essay on Political Tactics*, chap. 1, in *Works*, II; *Morals and Legislation*, chap. 1.
29. Helvétius, *De l'esprit*, discourse 2, chap. 17.
30. Mill, *On Bentham & Coleridge*, pp. 64, 73, 82, 121–122.

opinion."[31] Mill's understanding of this irreconcilable conflict is a variation of the usual liberal view of the conflict between private and public sectors, between individualism and collectivism, minority rights and majority rule, self-reliance and paternalism, spontaneity and regulation. Any action by one individual in relation to another is bound to be interference.

Mill's phobia on the "moral coercion of public opinion" is characteristic of the liberal fear of monopolistic concentrations which threaten the natural, self-perpetuating fluidity of society. As Locke required a mixed government for private individuals to enjoy freedom from external interference, and as Smith required a competitive economic market for the contractual exchange of goods by self-interested individuals, so, for Mill, opinions must be permitted to compete in a free intellectual marketplace devoid of the stagnating uniformity that results from public intolerance and governmental interference. Such sensitivity to monopoly again does not qualify, but rather confirms, the liberal conception of common life. The liberal condemns a selfish, self-constituted monopoly as an "unnatural" privilege, as an external offense to a "society" composed of discrete parts.

Bentham ridiculed the sanctuaries of "partial, separate and sinister interests," that "spirit of corporation" he found in the land-owning aristocracy, the established church and, late in his life, the unreformed Parliament and the monarchy. Such inheritances, sanctioned by law, deprive society of its fluidity and diminish individual opportunity: "If the laws do not oppose [equality]—if they do not maintain monopolies—if they do not restrain trade and its exchanges—if they do not permit entails—large properties will be seen, without effort, without revolutions, without shock, to subdivide themselves by little and little."[32] As in Mill, each individual is the best, because the

31. Mill, *On Liberty*, chaps. 1, 3 (emphasis added).
32. Bentham, *Plan of Parliamentary Reform*, sect. 3, in *Works*, III;

only, judge of his private interests. The Laws against usurious rates of interest, Bentham argued, create monopolies which interfere with the liberty of each individual to calculate and pursue his interests in the money market: "No man of ripe years and of sound mind, acting freely, and with his eyes open, ought to be hindered, with a view to his advantage, from making such bargain, in the way of obtaining money, as he thinks fit: nor (what is a necessary consequence) anybody hindered from supplying him, upon any terms he thinks proper to accede to."[33] While Mill's specific judgments of invasive circumstances are seldom identical with Bentham's, his intentions, his conception of a desirable society, and his fear of monopoly, are. Mill applauded Coleridge "for having vindicated against Bentham and Adam Smith and the whole eighteenth century, the principle of an endowed class [the "clerisy"] for the cultivation of learning, and for diffusing its results among the community."[34] But as late as 1869 he opposed financial support of education by government because it would constitute "a mere contrivance for molding people to be exactly like one another"; it would produce "a despotism of the mind, leading by natural tendency to one over the body."[35] He agreed with Coleridge that the ownership of land is in some sense a public trust requiring careful government regulation.[36] In prefaces to successive editions of his *Principles of Political Economy*, he gradually permitted increasing government action to restore competitive opportunity in the industrial economy. But government action is always intervention.

Adam Smith envisoned three interest groups: land, labor,

Principles of the Civil Code, pt. 1, chap. 12, in *Works*, I. See also Halévy, *Growth of Philosophic Radicalism*, pp. 254–263.

33. Bentham, *Defense of Usury*, letter 1, in *Works*, III (emphasis removed).

34. Mill, *On Bentham & Coleridge*, p. 26.

35. Mill, *On Liberty*, chap. 5.

36. Mill, *On Bentham & Coleridge*, pp. 158–160.

and capital. Each group is temporary and voluntary; its basis is man's natural "trucking disposition." The members of the group do not share a history. Society is only the market mechanism of which they are the separable parts, and they are themselves mechanisms with separate parts. The total aggregation, if monopolies and government do not intervene, is an "obvious and simple system of natural liberty." Indeed, there is less social cohesiveness among Smith's three "classes" than among the eighteen groups of laborers that the division of labor requires in the making of pins.[37] (At least these groups share a common economic enterprise beyond maximization of private profits, although their economic cooperation also originates in private individuals' economic interests.) Such disengagement among social groups, and within a single group, is also apparent in the "wages fund" theory of Ricardo and Nassau Senior. Borrowing Smith's tripartite division, they argued that the poverty of laborers is attributable to the excessive numbers of laborers competing for their share of the fund of wages available to laborers as a group. The sum is too small for the number of interests in which it must be subdivided. This doctrine would not be refuted for the benefit of orthodox liberal economists until the 1869 edition of Mill's *Principles of Political Economy*.[38]

The Genius of Common Life: General and Particular

Rousseau's individual is not by nature inventive. Nor can he pursue an expanding repertory of private interests. What liberalism took for granted and never questioned, the individual's motive to self-improvement, Rousseau explained historically as

37. Smith, *Wealth of Nations*, bk. 1, chaps. 6, 8–11; bk. 4, chap. 9. Smith's laissez faire argument exempts the Navigation Acts and some "public works" for which available "private" capital is inadequate or the likelihood of "private" profits uninspiring.

38. Halévy, *History of the English People*, I, 572–577, and Halévy, *Growth of Philosophic Radicalism*, pp. 318–325, 331–333, 356–358.

the result of an evolving pattern of common life. Infrequent encounters among "dispersed individuals" of presocial nature are confined to gestures and inarticulate cries until social "passions" or "moral needs" permit and require language: "This leads me to think that if the only needs we ever experienced were physical, we should most likely never have been able to speak; we would fully express our meanings by the language of gesture alone." Natural societies of beavers, ants, or bees, "which live and work in common," have natural languages. But man cannot speak until "he has some means of contact with his fellow men, by means of which one can act and the other can sense."[39] Because of the absence of common life, the existence of natural man retains the static timelessness of a permanent infancy: "All knowledge that requires reflection, all knowledge acquired only by the linking of ideas and perfected only successively, seems to be altogether beyond the reach of savage man for want of commmunication with his fellow man—that is to say, for want of the instrument which is used for that communication and for want of the needs which make it necessary."[40] For Rousseau, the earliest common speech, the "first social institution," has nothing to do with rational intentions or adaptive techniques. It is an emotional response to the accidental opportunities afforded by common life, and it comes from "the tongues of poets" rather than "the tongues of geometers." "All the passions tend to bring people back together again, but the necessity of seeking a livelihood

39. *Origin of Languages* (H, I, 370, 372–374). I have used the translation, *Jean-Jacques Rousseau: Essay on the Origin of Languages*, trans. John H. Moran in *On the Origin of Language* (New York, 1966), pp. 1–74.

40. *Discourse on Inequality* (P, III, 199). See also *ibid.*, pp. 146–149, 210. For a discussion of the complexities about causality, in Rousseau's understanding of the relationship between speech and society, and of Rousseau's criticisms of Condillac, see Paul Léon, "Rousseau et les fondements de l'état moderne," *Archives de philosophie du droit et de sociologie juridique*, III–IV (1934), 200–205.

forces them apart. It is neither hunger nor thirst but love, hatred, pity, anger, which drew from them the first words."[41]

Genius, then, is not the exceptional natural capacity of an individual. Rather, it is located in and defines the character of a specific historical society. Because moral or political passions, intellect, and reason are themselves social acquisitions, the standards by which these are judged vary in different societies. Rousseau's persistent and extraordinary sensitivity to the intrinsic importance of national variety and temporal variation is a corollary of his conceptions of organic social dependence and historical periodicity.

Rousseau apologized for "forgetting times and places" in the *Discourse on Inequality*. As his subject "concerns man in general" and he has "the human race for an audience," he must "try to use a language that suits all nations." Nevertheless, this historical record of "the life of the species" exhibits a consistent concern for social "genius." Differences in climate affect the hairiness of the skin, the use of animal skins for clothing, and the original industriousness of people. Differences of soil affect the initial manner of living together in herds. In forests the first social men fashion bows and arrows for hunting while at the sea and along river banks hooks are used for fishing. The events of the last historical period confirm the cumulative effects of a distinctive common past: "The various forms of government derive their origin from the greater or lesser differences to be found among individuals at the moment of institution." The succession of six historical periods itself acknowledges fundamental variety in patterns of common life. Except for the two natural passions of pity and self-preservation, "human nature" changes in response to developing conditions.

A long footnote in the *Discourse on Inequality* virtually demands the creation of a new discipline—comparative cultural

---

41. *Origin of Languages*, pp. 370, 373–374.

anthropology. Noting that "the whole earth is covered by nations of which we know only the names—yet we dabble in judging the human race," Rousseau invited capable observers of foreign men and *moeurs*, and "not stones and plants," to journey and report upon the distinctive societies of the world. A voyage to the crude societies of the Carribean islands and Florida is "the most important voyage of all and the one that must be undertaken with the greatest care." Sailors and soldiers, merchants, and missionaries, the usual travelers, are prejudiced observers who report what is already known: "Those true features that distinguish nations and strike eyes made to see have almost always escaped theirs." Until better reports are made, Europeans, familiar with only contemporary European *moeurs*, will persist in the "fine adage of ethics, so often repeated by the philosophical rabble: That men are everywhere the same; that as they have the same passions and the same vices everywhere, it is rather useless to characterize different peoples—which is about as well reasoned as if one were to say it is impossible to distinguish Peter from James, because they both have a nose, a mouth, and eyes."[42] One never recognizes oneself until one has a sustained consciousness of others.

For similar reasons, Rousseau organized his *Essay on the Origin of Languages* around variations of time and place involving forms of language, writing, scripts, literary inflections, and the emotional powers of speech. Rousseau's *Letter to d'Alembert* partly defends the absence of a theater in contemporary Geneva on the basis that the "genius" of Genevan society—austere republicanism—clashes with a frivolous dramatic theater. Differing habits of common life make for diverse standards of taste, pleasure, and moral worth: "At London a

42. *Discourse on Inequality*, pp. 133, 140, 143–144, 165, 186, 212–214. See also *Last Response* (P, III, 76, 90–91). For Rousseau's use of travelers' reports on primitive societies, see Daniel Mornet, *Rousseau: l'Homme et l'oeuvre* (Paris, 1950), pp. 39–43. See also Claude Lévi-Strauss, "Jean-Jacques Rousseau, fondateur des sciences de l'homme," in *Jean-Jacques Rousseau*, pp. 239–243.

drama is interesting when it causes the French to be hated; at Tunis, the noble passion would be piracy; at Messina, a delicious revenge; at Goa, the honor of burning Jews."[43] Correspondingly, Rousseau's infrequent discussions of individual genius are appropriately inconclusive and cautious. Saint-Preux in *La Nouvelle Héloise* asserts that genius cannot be the work of nature because it would imply natural inequality, a contradiction in terms. Julie largely ignores his observation, but notes that discerning a true talent is hazardous since childhood inclination is apt to be equivocal and imitative. True genius is not restless or active; apparent genius, noisy and combative, reflects the desire for public distinction.[44] And Rousseau can see the "genius" and "character" of Emile only after completing his educational task.[45]

Heroic lawgivers figure importantly in Rousseau's writings, but not as "geniuses." Their work is neither invention nor original discovery. In drafting fundamental laws, the lawgiver is an "architect" constructing from preordained materials and sites. He must gauge for population and economic resources, the strength of neighboring states, terrain, soil, climate and, especially, the peculiar *rapports*, the social customs or the "public opinion," of a people. He must not ignore the "chief object" of a people, the moral or political purpose shared by

43. *J.-J. Rousseau: Lettre à M. d'Alembert sur les spectacles*, ed. M. Fuchs (Lille, 1948), pp. 21–36. I have used the translation in *Politics and the Arts: Letter to M. d'Alembert on the Theater*, by Jean-Jacques Rousseau, trans. and ed. Allan Bloom (Glencoe, Ill., 1960). Page references are to the French edition.

44. *La Nouvelle Héloise* (P, II, 536–538, 563–568). See also "Genius" and "Taste," in *Dictionary of Music* (H, VII, 125, 128–129); *Emile* (P, IV, 324–325, 429, 474–475), and the preliminary version of *Emile*, the *Favre Manuscript* (P, IV, 99, 112–113, 167–168).

45. *Emile*, p. 266. For discussion of how Rousseau's ideas of national taste relate to the creative artist, see Broome, *Rousseau*, pp. 186–196. For the special indebtedness of men of letters to the *moeurs* of common life, see *Rêveries* (P, I, 1015–1016); preface to *Narcisse* (P, II, 967–968); and *Last Response*, pp. 73–74.

fellow creatures of a common life: for Jews and Arabs, religion; for Athenians, literature; commerce for Carthage and
Tyre, shipping at Rhodes, war at Sparta, and at Rome civic
virtue. Nor must a lawgiver attempt to change the laws of an
established people or to rehabilitate civil laws and institutions
already abolished or lapsed.[46] Before beginning his work as
patriot adviser to Corsicans, Rousseau requested "indispensable" information about their common life: physical circumstances and commercial conditions, political history, number
and location of towns, occupations and amusements of citizens,
fiscal and judicial machinery of government, relationships of
laity and clergy—everthing about the "national character" of
Corsicans.[47]

Rousseau constantly referred to community, fellowship,
fatherland (patrie), body politic, organic society, social body,
and social confederation.[48] Even in the legalized war between
the rich and the poor of contemporary societies, contending
parts constitute a cohesive if unstable whole with an "unshakeable base." The parts of a society neither clash, cooperate, nor
bargain as discrete units: "As nothing is less stable among men
than those external relationships which chance produces more
often than wisdom, and which are called weakness or power,
wealth or poverty, human establishments appear at first glance
to be founded on piles of quicksand. It is only by examining

46. *Discourse on Political Economy* (P, III, 250); *Social Contract*
(P, III, 384–393). See also *Fragments on Sparta and Rome* (P, III, 538–
542). I have used the translation in *The Social Contract: Jean-Jacques
Rousseau*, trans. Maurice Cranston (Baltimore, 1968).

47. See Rousseau's letters to Mathieu Buttafoco, a Corsican patriot and
soldier, in Vaughan, ed., *Political Writings*, II, 356–365. For Buttafoco's
first letter soliciting Rousseau's advice, see letter from Buttafoco (Aug.
31, 1764; CC, XXI, 85–88).

48. The term *fatherland* has an understandably unpleasant ring to
contemporary ears. This translation of *patrie* is unavoidable, however.
Rousseau frequently distinguished true citizenship within a "fatherland"
from a more casual or merely residential kind of politics of a "country"
or *pays*.

them closely, it is only after removing the dust and sand that surround the edifice, that one perceives the unshakeable base upon which it is built, and that one learns to respect its foundations."[49] Contemporary struggles between rich and poor are fratricidal.[50]

Thus, for Rousseau, the "body politic, taken individually, may be considered as an organized, living body, similar to man's." Rousseau pursued this analogy: the "sovereign power represents the head; the laws and the customs are the brain"; the judges and magistrates are the "organs" of the brain; "commerce, industry and agriculture are the mouth and stomach which prepare the common subsistence; public funds are the blood; a prudent *economy*, working like the heart, distributes nutriment and life throughout the body; the citizens are the body and the members, which make the machine live, move, and work." Because Rousseau condemned as slavery every division which differentiates a ruled part from a ruling part, and because the body politic is an artificial, not a natural unity, the traditional organic metaphor was a bit clumsy in his hands. But his intent was clear; and the term *body politic* was neither a misleading poetry to Rousseau, as it was to Bentham, nor a casual personification, nor a legal fiction. A political society is a unity of mutually dependent parts, a corporate whole, not an aggregation of unchanged partners.

Like a natural body, a body politic has its own "life." Its life is "the *self* common to the whole [*le* moi *commun au tout*], the reciprocal sensibility and internal correspondence of all its

49. *Discourse on Inequality*, pp. 126–127.
50. Rousseau's contrast between non-European peoples' wars and wars among European states made the same point. Wars involving barbarian tribes, Asian states, or African states are prepolitical or "private" encounters because the antagonists do not share a common past. European states, in contrast, have a lingering or "imperfect social bond" (the legacies of Roman law, Christianity, a European priesthood, similar *moeurs*, and frequent commerce), and their wars are thereby more ferocious. See *Perpetual Peace* (P, III, 565–574).

parts." Its common self is a "will," a given "general will" comprising the social identity shared by all mutually dependent members of a determinate common life. The general will is their political or moral genius; it provides their "rule of justice and injustice." The general will is their reciprocal public sentiment which has as its end the good of the whole and its indivisible parts: where there is no common or general will, there is no political society.[51] The members of the state, the organically related parts of the body politic, are artificial individuals in their capacities as citizens, for all social men are simultaneously and permanently indebted to their most comprehensive common life, or to one another, for their creation. Each member, in his new social definition as citizen of the whole, has an identical, single will. A political society, then, is a determinate moral person, whose life consists of the union of its members. The general will each citizen shares and exhibits is the emblem of an artificial individual's new, common existence.[52]

51. *Discourse on Political Economy*, pp. 244–245. There are two intimations of the concept of a general will in the *Discourse on Inequality*, pp. 184–185, 202.

52. *Social Contract*, pp. 361–362, 363, 372, 437. The term *general will* is used by earlier and contemporaneous philosophers. See Charles W. Hendel, *Jean-Jacques Rousseau: Moralist*, 2d ed., 2 vols. (New York, 1962) I, 100–112; Jouvenel, "Essai," pp. 105–120. Both critics note that Rousseau repudiated a single general will as the "dictates of right reason" for the entire species. Jouvenel, especially, focuses on Rousseau's sense of the "moral" or "psychological" reality of a general will and how this differs from the "logical," "juridical," or "theological" fiction of Fontenelle, Malebranche, Hobbes, Bayle, and Diderot: Rousseau's general will is the "common sensibility" of fellow citizens. Their bond is one of "affection," not "reason." See also Arthur M. Wilson, "The Development and Scope of Diderot's Political Thought," in *Studies on Voltaire and the Eighteenth Century*, vol. 27 (1963), pp. 1876–1877.

An alternative, individualist view takes Rousseau's general will as timeless and universal right reason. See Cobban, *Rousseau and the Modern State*, pp. 91–98, which interprets the general will as a "rational ideal"; Lester G. Crocker, "The Relation of Rousseau's Second *Discours* and the *Contrat social*," *Romanic Review*, LI (Feb. 1960), 38–39, which argues that Rousseau's general will is a "rational" will of all men, a

Other "particular societies," which are also responsible for creating the political countenance of their members, are also organic groups. Every instance of social dependence, from an often temporary family to a larger social class, is a moral or legal being contained within or "subordinate" to the comprehensive state. The exclusive members of each particular society similarly exhibit a lesser general will, a particular will, which seeks their shared or common good: "These societies which everybody perceives, because they have an external and authorized form, are not the only ones that actually exist within the state; all men united by a common interest compose as many

---

"hypothetical" or "metaphysical" postulate that does not refer to or describe empirical reality; Hans Barth, "Volonté générale et volonté particulière," in *Rousseau et la philosophie politique,* Annales de philosophie politique, vol. 5 (1965), pp. 38–48, which equates Rousseau's understanding with Diderot's notion of natural reason and argues that Rousseau's general will is a preexisting, divinely implanted will for justice, a "moral absolute" that is a "sort of incarnation of divine justice"; and Stanley Hoffmann, "Du *Contrat social,* ou le mirage de la volonté générale," *Revue internationale d'histoire politique et constitutionnelle,* n.s. IV (Oct.–Dec. 1954), 293–295. Hoffmann recognizes the civic determinateness of Rousseau's concept, but he argues that Rousseau's general will is esentially a "rational" will, a fusion of man's will, reason, and moral sense or "good will." This last interpretation specifically invokes Kant, whose interpretation of Rousseau's thought was indeed the first "rationalist" one.

As a term Rousseau's *general will* can obscure his nonindividualist meaning, for the word *will* suggests the natural ego of a deliberative individual or Locke's "power of mind" (*Essay,* bk. 2, chap. 21). But this difficulty would also apply to an artificial individual's "particular wills," which are also social in origin. Moreover, an artificial individual is free not to make a general will but to declare a general will; and in so doing he chooses from among competing artificial inclinations or "desires" or "intentions." See *Favre Manuscript,* p. 88; *Moral Letters* (P, IV, 1106). See also William Pickles, "The Notion of Time in Rousseau's Political Thought," in *Hobbes and Rousseau: A Collection of Critical Essays,* ed. Maurice Cranston and Richard S. Peters (Garden City, N.Y., 1972), pp. 393–395. Of course, the word *will* carries one unmistakable advantage for an anarchist: the general will of a sovereign citizenry would seem to be necessarily indivisible and unrepresentable.

others, either permanent or transitory, whose strength is not less real because it is less apparent."[53]

A single artificial individual is thus a creature or member of many concentric and overlapping circles of public life. He is a "composite" self, indebted to and often divided by different loyalties and duties.[54] A single magistrate, for example, automatically has at least three "essentially different" inclinations and loyalties, or, as Rousseau called them, "wills," of increasing generality. Each of these wills is public, the result of transformations of nature's private individual into society's public man. First is "the will which belongs to the individual and tends toward his personal advantage." This particular will is his self-love (*amour-propre*), that property in oneself which social comparison originates and public esteem sustains. Second is the will common to magistrates, a corporate will which is general in relation to the society of magistrates but particular in relation to that entire citizenry of which the magistracy is a part. Third is the will common to all citizens. A magistrate's socially acquired identity includes the "self common to the whole," the general will of the entire political society.[55] If this magistrate is also a father, a farmer, and a man of wealth, then, because of these instances of social indebtedness, more numerous, passionate demands tug within him: the welfare and preservation of his family, the common good of the society of farmers, the corporate interests of the rich. These artificial loyalties always represent a "particular will" from the standpoint of the entire body politic because their membership is exclusive. Only the corporate will of the entire society, that

53. *Discourse on Political Economy*, pp. 245–246.

54. Rousseau noted that social men "are not precisely speaking doubles but composites" because cumulative changes in natural man create a new being: "The man of society is not merely natural man behind a mask." *Favre Manuscript*, p. 57. However, Rousseau viewed himself as an exception to this principle. See Marcel Raymond, "J.-J. Rousseau: Deux aspects de sa vie intérieure," *Annales*, XXIX (1941–42), 5–57.

55. *Social Contract*, pp. 400–401.

general will of the whole exhibited by all members, can constitute the good of the whole: "The will of these particular societies has always two relations; for the members of the society, it is a general will; for the greater society, it is a particular will which is often right in the first respect and vicious as to the second. One may be a devout priest, or a brave soldier, or a zealous patrician, and a bad citizen. A public decision may be advantageous to the small community but very pernicious for the greater society."[56]

Furthermore, each state has its own general will. Each general will reflects a history and has geographical limits. Rousseau's attention to circumstantial variety contrasts with Diderot's individualist conception of a single general will identical with the timeless and universal "natural reason" of mankind. In his *Encyclopedia* article *Natural Right*, Diderot maintained that all men are naturally endowed with an "interior sentiment" of rational direction. As a result mankind constitutes in principle a "general society," a natural cosmopolis of self-defined individuals restrained by natural law; and if animals were able to communicate among themselves, comprehend the language of men, and contribute their votes to a general assembly, then this general society would include animals as well.[57] Rousseau's first version of the *Social Contract*, the *Geneva Manuscript*, begins with several objections to Diderot's conception of a

---

56. *Discourse on Political Economy*, p. 246.

57. Diderot's article is reprinted in Vaughan, ed., *Political Writings*, I, 429–433. In addition to the previously cited interpretations by Hendel and Jouvenel, see Hubert, *Rousseau et l'Encyclopédie*, pp. 31–49, 120–121, which examines, in Rousseau's point by point response to Diderot in the *Geneva Manuscript*, his concern with the "nature of the social bond." See also Léon, "Rousseau et les fondements de l'état moderne," pp. 213–231. For the general intellectual character of Rousseau and Diderot's early relationship, see Antoine Adam, "Rousseau et Diderot," *Revue des sciences humaines*, n.s. LIII (Jan.–Mar. 1949), 21–34; George R. Havens, "Diderot, Rousseau, and the *Discours sur l'inégalité*," in *Diderot Studies*, ed. Otis Fellows and Gita May, vol. 3 (1961), pp. 219–262.

single, universal general will among all sensitive beings. A self-contained individual has no obligatory motive for just action, even if he were somehow capable of appreciating and communicating the demands of rational justice. There are no provisions or institutions for avoiding errors. But most important, man can consult an "interior sentiment" of duty or "conscience" only when this sentiment has been "formed" by those "habits of judging and feeling" made possible by social membership: "We conceive a general society [of mankind] after our [experience of] particular societies; the establishment of little republics makes us dream of a greater one; and we only begin to become men after having been citizens." The "social bond" of the "human species" is either a "chimera" or a mere "collective idea" because the species is not in fact a "moral being having, with a sentiment of common existence which gives it individuality and constitutes it as one, a universal motivating force which makes each part act for an end which is general and relative to the whole."[58]

These arguments duplicate Rousseau's criticism in the *Discourse on Inequality* of philosophers who attribute reason to the presocial individual: there could be no consensus of mankind because mankind does not constitute a single natural society. There are many dissimilar general wills among various political societies, and lesser general wills of particular societies within a single state. A general will can aim at the well-being and security only of those who share a determinate common life. Therefore a general will, "unerring with reference to all citizens, may be erroneous for foreigners; and the reason for this is clear: the will of the state, although general in relation to its members, . . . becomes a particular and individual will" for foreigners.[59] Diderot's general will is a natural law of reason which self-contained individuals are understood to consult

58. *Geneva Manuscript* (P, III, 283–287).
59. *Discourse on Political Economy*, p. 245.

from time to time in their various roles as man, citizen, subject, and father. Rousseau's general will *is* citizenship; it emanates from and supports the relationships to which artificial individuals are indebted for their creation.[60] It is difficult to know one's general will, and citizens are often moved by the particular or partial will of lesser societies. But for artificial individuals the general will is given. It is "unchanging" and "indestructible," unless the common life of fellow citizens completely disintegrates.[61] Under these circumstances members would be overtly at war or even begin to revert to their original anonymity which was always without moral bonds or political obligations.[62]

If there is conflict between particular wills and the general will for the artificial individual, then a political society, even under the best of circumstances, can never become a completely harmonious whole: "The citizens may call themselves members of the state, but they can never be united to it as closely as the members are to the [human] body. It is impossible to prevent each of them from having an individual and separate existence, by virtue of which each is self-sufficient in his own maintenance. The nerves [of the corporate body] are less sensitive, the muscles are less powerful, the ligaments are looser; the smallest accident can shatter its unity."[63] But this "individual and separate existence" is not a remnant of self-exclusiveness from a presocial state of nature. The divided self may have many separate desires, but none corresponds to the private calculations of a discrete individual; this is so whether or not the desires conform to his general will, whether or not they echo the natural passions of pity and self-preservation.

60. Diderot, *Natural Right*, p. 432; *Geneva Manuscript*, pp. 286–287.
61. *Social Contract*, pp. 437–439.
62. *Discourse on Political Economy*, pp. 246–247; *Social Contract*, pp. 424–425.
63. *Fragments on the State of War*, p. 606. See also *ibid.*, pp. 603–605; *Geneva Manuscript*, pp. 296–297.

Each desire corresponds to the particular will of one of the groups to which each citizen belongs, or to the general will of the citizenry. All are social creations.[64]

Even that personal vanity which seeks property and wealth is a public will. It is not Adam Smith's "desire of bettering our condition . . . which . . . comes with us from the womb and never leaves us till we go into the grave." Vanity for Rousseau has a profound sociological importance. Vanity is the inner dimension of an artificial, organic relation: "the vanity of appearing opulent" to others, the desire of the rich to distinguish themselves from the poor. The vain are "seduced" by objects of luxury and fashion, amusement and idleness "which strike all eyes, and can less be hidden, as their whole purpose is to be seen; these objects would be useless if not seen." Contemporary men, who "would a hundred times sooner . . . die of hunger than of shame,"[65] indicate the distance artificial individuals have traveled from early forms of common life, indeed, from the presocial state of nature itself: "Feelings that make men restless, foresighted, and active arise only in society. To do nothing is the primary and the strongest passion of [natural] man after that of self-preservation."[66] What is true of man's selfishness is equally true of his aggressiveness: "Man is by nature peaceful and timid; at the least sign of

64. *Discourse on Political Economy*, pp. 246–247; *Social Contract*, p. 438. For an appreciation of the way particular interests are not spontaneous because they are occasioned by society, see Pierre Burgelin, *La Philosophie de l'existence de J.-J. Rousseau* (Paris, 1952), pp. 251–255. Contemporary man lives simultaneously in a state of nature and society only in the sense that he is a member of both a European state and European society. See *Fragments on the State of Nature*, pp. 479–480; *Perpetual Peace*, p. 564; and *Fragments on the State of War*, p. 610.

65. *Discourse on Political Economy*, pp. 276–277. See also *Discourse on Inequality*, p. 189.

66. *Origin of Languages*, p. 388n. See also *Discourse on Inequality*, p. 192.

danger, his first instinct is to flee; he acquires boldness only by experience and habit. Honor, interest, prejudice, vengeance—all the passions which made him able to face death and peril—are far from him in the state of nature."[67]

The general is always the condition of the particular. Historically the earliest acquired "interests" of social men are a shared love of their common life and a reciprocated interest in self-defense. Invidious, predatory interest is a later social corruption of the desire for public distinction.[68] Political theorists misunderstand the origin and exaggerate the significance of "interest": more fundamental is "the love of distinction," a "stronger, more general" passion, which "makes use of interest as a means of satisfying itself."[69]

One might expect that a philosopher unable to conceive "private interest" in the liberal sense would ignore the element of conflict in society. But when the individual is himself a public creature, when even the most pernicious and self-destructive interests echo the habits of judging and feeling of common life, then a conflict of competing public identities or loyalties is intense. The struggle of general and particular "wills," of a self divided between simultaneous inclinations toward civic duty and particular desires, is especially ferocious among men of contemporary societies. The "avid heirs and often his own children" secretly hope for the death of a man of wealth. The wreck of a ship at sea is good news to some merchant. A "debtor of bad faith" would wish to see a firm and the papers it contains destroyed by fire. A people rejoices in the disasters of its neighbors. "But what is still more dangerous is that public calamities are awaited and hoped for by a mul-

67. *Fragments on the State of War*, p. 601. See also *Rousseau juge de Jean-Jacques* (P, I, 846–847).

68. Preface to *Narcisse*, pp. 969n–970n.

69. *Fragments on Honor and Virtue* (P, III, 502). See also *La Nouvelle Héloïse*, p. 491.

titude of individuals. Some want illnesses, others death, others war, others famine. I have seen atrocious men weep with sadness at the probability of a fertile year; and the great and deadly fire of London, which cost the life or goods of so many unfortunates, perhaps made the fortune of more than ten thousand people."[70] In a corrupt society, public life remains a dilemma of divisiveness, a torment of self-contradictions; and the contradictions are not the sort that, as liberal theorists would have it, can be reconciled or balanced in the way an undecided man assigns arithmetic weights to separate interests by calculating short and long-term profits.

When citizens, out of preference for particular wills of subordinate societies, persistently ignore their general will, common life declines into violent discord. Looking upon the moral person which constitutes the state as "a mere rational entity (since it is not a man)," they regard what they owe the common cause as a "gratuitous contribution." By seeking to enjoy the legal rights deriving from citizenship while ignoring its corresponding duties, they will their destruction.[71] When such citizens vote as particular men seeking to realize partial, particular interests, the result is a momentary "will of all," which bears no resemblance to the "indestructible," "unchanging" general will.[72] But even when men vote as virtuous citizens, attempting to declare what the common good of the whole requires, a fabricated will of all closely approximates but is not identical with the given general will. Every political society, like every social group of whatever circumference, exhibits a characteristic moral or political "genius" which represents the common good of its individual members: the

70. *Discourse on Inequality*, pp. 202–203.
71. *Social Contract*, p. 363. See also *Fragments on the State of War*, p. 608.
72. *Social Contract*, pp. 371–372, 437–439. See also *Discourse on Political Economy*, pp. 245–247.

general will remains "the self common to the whole," whatever the momentary declaration of its members.[73]

The concept of a general will and its relationship to public opinion present many problems, among them Rousseau's insistence that a continuing discrepancy between the general will and a will of all constitutes enslavement. But Rousseau's problems and "solutions" never involve the characteristic arithmetic of liberal theorists—the Benthamite calculus, the dilemmas of majority rule and minority rights, the various methods of achieving a satisfactory public sum from an aggregate of private integers, and the like. Nor do the complications in Rousseau's concept of the general will result, as some have argued, from a sudden shift to "collectivism" in the *Discourse on Political Economy* and subsequent writings. Rather, because of the nonindividualism pervading all Rousseau's works, the question of "individual" welfare can never be distinguished from the welfare of the whole: "It must not be believed that a man can injure or cut his arm, without the pain being conveyed to his head; and it is no less credible that the general will would consent that one member of the state, whomever he might be, should wound or destroy another, than it is that the fingers of a man in his reason would scratch out his eyes. . . . Is the preservation of a single citizen any less the common cause than that of the entire state?" When one's society is the "common mother of her citizens," one's own happiness is not a private warehouse of agreeable sensations.[74]

73. For a contrasting view, which sees the general will as the aggregative result of a deliberative process, so that the common good is a sum of preexisting individual goods, see Glen O. Allen, "*La Volonté de tous and la volonté générale*: A Distinction and Its Significance," *Ethics*, LXXI–LXXII (July, 1961), 263–275. A short, vigorous statement of the general will's given character is Simone Pétrement, "Rousseau et la liberté," *Le Contrat social*, VI (Nov.–Dec. 1962), 340–342.

74. *Discourse on Political Economy*, pp. 256, 258. As I noted, Rousseau said the general will provides a "rule of justice and injustice" for a specific society. And he repeatedly designated "just" both a citizen who

There are many shorthand references to the fundamental differences in substance and metaphor between Rousseau and the liberal theorists. The individual of Locke's philosophy, it will be recalled, is endowed with a natural right to property and legitimately acquires private property in response to natural bodily needs: one does not require the testimony of other men to confirm one's hunger. Rousseau's private individual, the natural presocial man of the *Discourse on Inequality*, drinks or does not drink each time he passes a stream. The new man created by society, the artificial individual of common life, claims and takes personal possession of something only when he is driven by invidious competition for public esteem, only when he observes other artificial individuals doing the same: "This idea of property, depending on many prior ideas which could only have arisen successively, was not con-

---

follows his general will and a society of such citizens. But his meaning is obscured if the concept of the general will is identified with classical or contemporary theories of distributive justice and proportionate equality. (Hence my temporarily equivocal notion of a general will of civic duty or of a general will for the common good. I specify in subsequent chapters the implications of citizens' adherence to their general will—radical equality or absolute "negative" liberty.) Theories of distributive justice assume men's distinct, conflicting, and often irreconcilable interests and claims. When benefits and burdens are distributed in a just manner, gains by some individuals spell losses to others, even when interests are considered impartially and liberties are allocated equally to all individuals. For these reasons "justice" is characteristic of Rousseau's "will of all"; and a true republic of self-governing citizens paradoxically transcends considerations of distributive justice, except in cases of criminal disobedience. For views which identify Rousseau's general will with distributive justice, see George Kateb, "Aspects of Rousseau's Political Thought," *Political Science Quarterly*, LXXVI (1961), 519-534; John Plamenatz, *Man and Society: A Critical Examination of Some Important Social and Political Theories from Machiavelli to Marx*, 2 vols. (London, 1963), I, 388-391, 406-409, 411-418; Raymond Polin, *La Politique de la solitude: Essai sur la philosophie de Jean-Jacques Rousseau* (Paris, 1971), pp. 75-134; John Hall, *Rousseau: An Introduction to His Political Philosophy* (London, 1973), pp. 126-137, 140-148, and *passim*.

ceived all at once in the human mind."[75] His act of appropriation is a public act, even when its end is self-aggrandizement.

Nearly two centuries after Locke, and in spite of his own understanding of social conformity, John Stuart Mill argued in his *Logic* that the actions and passions of men "in a state of society" are "obedient to the laws of individual human nature. Men are not, when brought together, converted into another kind of substance with different properties, as hydrogen and oxygen are different from water, . . . Human beings in society have no properties but those which are derived from, and may be resolved into, the laws of the nature of individual man."[76] Rousseau, too, employed metaphors from chemistry. But he used these metaphors to convey the contrasting notion that social man is qualitatively different from presocial man, that determinate societies of fellow citizens constitute a new chemical compound. Hence, once again, Rousseau rejected Diderot's idea of a single society of the species guided by a single general will of natural reason: "If the general society existed anywhere except in the systems of philosophes, it would be . . . a moral being which had qualities peculiar to it, and distinct from those particular beings who compose it, somewhat like the chemical compounds which have properties unlike those of the mixtures of which they are composed." And if such a universal society existed, the "public good or the public misfortune would be not merely the sum of particular benefits and particular misfortunes, as in a simple aggregation, but would rest in the bond which unites them; it would be greater than this sum; and in so far as the public good depended upon the happiness of individuals, the public good would be the source of their happiness."[77]

75. *Discourse on Inequality*, p. 164.
76. *A System of Logic, Ratiocinative and Inductive*, bk. 5, chap. 5, in *John Stuart Mill's Philosophy of Scientific Method*, ed. Ernest Nagel (New York, 1950).
77. *Geneva Manuscript*, p. 284. See also *Emile*, p. 530.

Rousseau observed in *Emile* that "society must be studied through individuals, and individuals through society; those who treat politics and morals separately will never understand anything about either."[78] Questions of politics and morals are indeed indistinguishable within Rousseau's philosophy because he conceived the natural or essential dignity of man to be liberty, because the destiny of mutually dependent individuals must be a perfect independence of the will of one another, an absolute liberty of literal self-government. This anarchism or radical egalitarianism is the source of the abrasiveness of Rousseau's political thought.

78. *Emile*, p. 524.

PART TWO

THE FREE
INDIVIDUAL

CHAPTER 5

Liberty or Slavery

Many modern theorists defended a conception of men's natural liberty and equality. As a result, few of them accepted classic arguments that political authority should be obeyed because some political hierarchies are just or because some men are naturally superior. Although definitions of legitimate resistance to unjust rule have always existed, the modern abandonment of these classic bases of obedience has made the obligation to obey a central rather than a peripheral problem.

Few critics have doubted that Rousseau shared these concerns of modern orthodoxy, but few have recognized that Rousseau went more deeply than other modern theorists into the problem of liberty, and that he repudiated their solutions. The hollow formulas of popular sovereignty and consent, meant to contradict claims of corporate privileges or monarchical divine right, merely nibble at the edge of Rousseau's concern and only alert us to Rousseau's more fundamental, more radical demand. Some critics have held that Rousseau subscribed to Kantian principles of moral freedom or autonomy, "positive" liberty, or perfectibility. But these interpretations obscure a very different radical egalitarianism; and no moralist aspect of Rousseau's philosophy can be separated from alternative political phases or levels or writings.[1]

1. Theorists of "moral freedom" locate liberty in the reason or deliberation of a single agent who avoids bondage to ignoble, appetitive desires. In this interpretation of Rousseau, a single individual is free when he is master of himself or autonomous, for he then obeys self-imposed moral

The persistent requirement within Rousseau's political thought is absolute "negative" liberty for all men: each man must be completely independent of the will of every other. The only legitimate direction is unmediated self-direction, for one man is never entitled to command another, nor is one ever

laws; politics is a derivative of ethical concerns. Moral freedom is also compatible with and perhaps requires a division of society into governors and governed.

Cassirer especially reads back into Rousseau what inspired Kant. He discusses Rousseau's "ethical conception of personality," the notion that men are entitled to "legal and moral equality" in a protected "realm of freedom." Rousseau believed in man's "capacity for self-determination" and a future "victory of reason" over "merely physical wants and . . . passions." He assigned an "ethical task" to politics but "subordinated politics to this ethical imperative" by requiring an "overcoming and elimination of all arbitrariness, the submission to a strict and inviolable law which the individual erects over himself." Rousseau's free individual does not suffer any "shadow of caprice or arbitrariness" from his rulers; and he is "under an obligation which he himself recognizes as valid and necessary, and to which he therefore assents for its own sake as well as for his own." Thus, in Cassirer's view, Rousseau was concerned with the distribution of property only "insofar as the inequality of property endangers the moral equality of subjects under the law." For equal subjects can obtain "real freedom, which consists in tying all men to the law"; they can become "individuals in the higher sense—autonomous personalities." Cassirer, *The Question of Rousseau*, pp. 56, 82, 104, 66–67, 62, 60, 55. For Kant's view of Rousseau, see Ernst Cassirer, *Rousseau, Kant, and Goethe: Two Essays*, trans. James Gutmann, Paul Oskar Kristeller, and John Herman Randall, Jr. (New York, 1963), pp. 1–24, 43–60. Cassirer also argues for Rousseau's optimism and constitutionalism in this study (pp. 25–35), as well as in his *Philosophy of Enlightenment*, pp. 262–264.

For similar interpretations of Rousseau's thought, see Franz Haymann, "La Loi naturelle dans la philosophie politique de J.-J. Rousseau," *Annales*, XXX (1943–45), 65–110; Jean Wahl, "La Bipolarité de Rousseau," *Annales*, XXXIII (1953–55), 49–55, which distinguishes the moral freedom of man in *Emile* and *La Nouvelle Héloise* from that of the "denatured" citizen in the *Social Contract;* Masters, *Political Philosophy of Rousseau*, pp. 53, 69–72, 125, 147–151, 197–198, 233, 152–154, 165n, which argues that Rousseau retreated from the idea of liberty to that of perfectibility and which distinguishes natural, civil, and moral liberty in his thought; Ernest Hunter Wright, *The Meaning of Rousseau* (1929; reprint ed., New York, 1963), pp. 26–29, 95n, which discusses the three

obligated to obey another. Men cannot delegate their liberty to others either in whole or in part. A man's natural power of self-legislation cannot be legitimately represented by others in any circumstances. Rousseau's theory is quite literally one of popular sovereignty or self-government: he required literal

---

"great forms of liberty" in Rousseau's thought but focuses upon "civil" rather than "moral" or "natural" liberty; John W. Chapman, *Rousseau— Totalitarian or Liberal?* (New York, 1956), pp. 5–41, 58–73; and Robert Derathé, *Le Rationalisme de J.-J. Rousseau* (Paris, 1948), pp. 84–135, 151–174, 181–191, which accepts Cassirer's view but argues that Rousseau is a "moralist" of "sentiment," not "law." See also Plamenatz, *Man and Society*, I, 371–373, 380–385, 409–412, 440–441; Polin, *La Politique de la solitude*, pp. 70–74, 99–100, 102–105, 149–159, 166–173; David Cameron, *The Social Thought of Rousseau and Burke* (London, 1973), pp. 95–102, 105–106, 143–151. For contrasting interpretations which approach Rousseau's radical position about liberty, see Durkheim, "Le *Contrat social* de Rousseau," pp. 130–132, 159–161; Leo Strauss, "On the Intention of Rousseau," *Social Research*, XIV (Dec. 1947), 456–457, 480; and Jouvenel, "Essai," pp. 15–20, 94–104. Jouvenel stresses Rousseau's "moralist" critique of formal government. See also Chevallier, "Rousseau ou l'absolutisme de la volonté générale," pp. 5–30, which sees how, because of the "sacred character" of the social bond, the true citizen remains independent of the will of others because he obeys only his general will. Chevallier, however, identifies this situation with limited government. For three articles in a single collection which argue the importance of liberty in Rousseau's thought, largely with reference to the institutional arrangements described in the *Social Contract*, see François Gilliard, "Etat de nature et liberté dans la pensée de J.-J. Rousseau," in *Etudes sur le Contrat social*, pp. 111–118; Jacques Dehaussey, "La Dialectique de la souveraine liberté dans le *Contrat social*," pp. 119–141, which stresses the enslaving effect of particular societies and particular wills; and Jean de Soto, "La Liberté et ses garanties," pp. 227–252, which shows how Rousseau's egalitarianism implies that a master of other men is not free, but sees a kind of "paternalism" in what is taken to be a permanent lawgiver. Also, Bernard Groethuysen, "La Liberté selon Rousseau," *La NEF*, IV (Aug. 1947), 3–17, which grasps how liberty for Rousseau cannot be a matter of competing private and public sectors because the "citizen is always a citizen, our existence in the civil state is always relative, always *en rapport* with the whole" (p. 14); and Hoffmann, "Du *Contrat social*," pp. 289–293, 296–298. Hoffmann argues a "synthesis" or "fusion," not a Lockeian "partition," of liberty and authority in Rousseau's thought, so that the "liberty of the citizen and the authority of the state" are compatible.

self-government, direct and permanent self-legislation in all aspects of common life. Expressed consent and voluntary submission cannot justify any arrangement involving men who rule and others who are ruled. This insistent demand for absolute liberty permeates and animates Rousseau's philosophy. It explains the problems he saw, the manner in which he saw them, and the often curious "solutions" he offered. It forms the very rhythm of his intelligence.

Of any political arrangement, governmental and nongovernmental, Rousseau asked a single question: does it distinguish between ruler and ruled? If it does, there is slavery, for such men depend upon the will of one another. And slavery is always a state of war, even when disguised by legality, peaceful civility, and mutual flattery. Now, when the writings of a political theorist argue that every exercise of political authority by some men over other men is incompatible with liberty and constitutes slavery, and that there is no alternative to liberty except slavery, and that those who rule are themselves enslaved because they rule others, then the reader is in the intellectual company of an anarchist.

Rousseau's conviction that man's dignity is liberty creates a paradox. New, artificial individuals must preserve the old natural condition of masterlessness and political equality: men's liberty is not a matter of moment, scope, degree, or numerical extent. A return to the state of presocial independence is neither conceivable nor desirable; but Rousseau never relinquished the egalitarianism of man's natural condition in his understanding and judgment of social men. A society always defines the thoughts and actions of artificial individuals; yet social men subject to external or superior political direction are enslaved.

Many passages in Rousseau's writings, especially if examined in isolation, appear to justify political authority for some men: magistracy must be based upon consent, not force, or government must be limited and nonarbitrary, or magistrates must act for the benefit of those they govern. Sometimes Rousseau simply could not sustain the imperative of his anarchism. He bluffed. He played verbal tricks. Ultimately we shall have to examine his bluffs and tricks, for they confirm his insistence upon absolute liberty. In general, however, the magistrates who form "legitimate government" in the *Social Contract* do not govern or command subjects. And the existence of this legitimate government was precisely intended to prevent division of the body politic between governor and governed.

In contemporary society, Rousseau saw no prospect of regaining absolute liberty. He suggested palliatives to stem a decline into even more brutal slavery; constitutionalism or limited political authority was preferable to a tumultuous rule of naked, unbridled violence. But so long as men are dependent upon the will of others they are enslaved. At each point in the evolution of society, men are either free or not free. Rousseau was not intrinsically interested in how the exercise of political power can be just, benevolent, representative, limited, nonarbitrary, officially promulgated, in conformity with fundamental law, and the like. The basic problem of common life is neither the origin, the character, nor the abuse of political rule; authoritative direction by any men is itself an abuse under every circumstance. Anarchism also explains Rousseau's frequent assertions that rulers are enslaved to the slaves whom they would command: rulers are dependent upon the will of the governed to obey or disobey.

Traces of Rousseau's radically egalitarian demand are to be found in strange, unsuspected places. Sometimes Rousseau endorsed corvées. Sometimes he praised sumptuary laws. In general he advocated a united, disciplined common life that few readers find bearable, much less liberating. But his occasional endorsements of corvées and sumptuary laws provide only further, indirect evidence of his unremitting egalitarian imperative, understandable only in light of his pervasive demand for absolute liberty. The alternatives to corvées and sumptuary laws he rejected as slavery.

Thus, there is another paradox in Rousseau's insistence upon absolute liberty: absolutely free men must obey. But they obey only rules, never rulers. Free men obey only impersonal laws which inhere in common life and civil laws made by themselves in legislative assemblies. Such obedience on the part of indivisible members of a determinate common life is necessary to preserve the moral or political equality of presocial nature. Only such obedience assures that no member of the corporate whole obeys or commands another. Free individuals are self-governing subjects, for only the members of a corporate whole, as a whole, simultaneously command and obey themselves.

This demand for literal self-government deprives every contemporary regime of the slightest legitimacy: the life of modern men is, in Rousseau's judgment, slavery. Yet Rousseau also commented frequently on the horrors and futility of revolution and never justified revolutionary disobedience. That united and disciplined common life which assures literal self-government is in the irretrievable past. Further authoritative direction, even in the name of liberty, cannot restore the liberty of men who are already the victims of masters. As the sequence of historical periods in the *Discourse on Inequality* suggests, further revolutionary change after an initial transfer of liberty to others only deepens and renders more violent the enslavement of later social men.

Liberty and Legalism

Rousseau's discussions of law and the rule of law best reveal his anarchism. Some critics have interpreted Rousseau's treatment of law as a familiar defense of constitutionalism, the responsible exercise of political authority limited by both fundamental law and popular consent.[2] Rousseau welcomed law in the dedication to the *Discourse on Inequality* as an "honorable, . . . salutary and gentle yoke" which "the proudest heads bear with all the more docility because they are suited to bear no other." Other writings resound with hymns to law. He advised Polish citizens to repeal unenforced civil laws so that laws would not fall into disuse: "All abuses which are not forbidden remain inconsequential; but anyone who utters the word 'law' in a free state is invoking that before which every citizen, including first of all the king, should tremble. In short, suffer anything to happen rather than to weaken the force of law; for once its power has been exhausted, the state is lost beyond redemption." In *Constitutional Project for Corsica*, he argued that "a government without laws cannot be a good government." He frequently warned of the danger of a magistrate's placing himself above the law. When this occurs the magistrate is a "master" and "tyrant" over a people forced to obey his will. People who consent to a temporary exercise of government power independent of the law set a dangerous precedent which will be seized by the unscrupulous: "At bottom, as all social engagements are reciprocal by their nature, it is impossible to place oneself above the law without renouncing its advantages; and no one owes anything to someone who claims he has no obligations to others." The very possibility

2. In addition to Cassirer's moral freedom interpretation, see Wright, *Meaning of Rousseau*, pp. 74, 79, 82n, 88–91, 97–112; Osborn, *Rousseau and Burke*, pp. 128–139, 213–217; Groethuysen, *Rousseau*, pp. 111–114, 116–174, 189–201; Carl J. Friedrich, "Law and Dictatorship in the *Contrat social*," in *Rousseau et la philosophie politique*, pp. 77–79; Hendel, *Rousseau*, I, 16–17, 63, 90–91, 112–120, 140–156, 164–171, 177–183; II, 163–164, 195–201; and Masters, *Political Philosophy of Rousseau*, pp. 188–195, 269–276, 311, 335–340. For an argument that Rousseau was no mere constitutionalist, see Marshall Berman, *The Politics of Authenticity: Radical Individualism and the Emergence of Modern Society* (New York, 1972), pp. 119–123.

of society would seem to require universal and equal obligation to legal authorities.[3]

Other passages, however, are inconsistent with constitutionalism. In the *Discourse on Inequality*, enforceable laws are established through a social contract during the last historical period. This contract "authorizes" the rich to continue their oppression of the poor and to keep property unjustly seized. Later, magistracy, established through a political contract, exercises representative political authority limited by law, an oppression of the weak by the powerful. Then a third change announces arbitrary, unrestrained, rule of violence. These later developments complete that master and slave arrangement "which is the last degree of inequality and the limit to which all the others finally lead." Rousseau added that the "vices that make social institutions necessary are the same ones that make their abuse inevitable": there is a historical "necessity" in this progress of inequality. Furthermore, the oppression contributed by the first two developments is both legal and voluntary, in the sense that no man exercises political rule from above or beyond the laws to which all men have agreed to submit. This initial establishment of limited authority under law had been an easy swindle because corrupt men "had too many disputes to straighten out among themselves to be able to do without arbiters, and too much avarice and ambition to be able to do without masters for long. All ran to meet their chains thinking they secured their freedom. . . . Even the wise saw the necessity of resolving to sacrifice one part of

3. *Discourse on Inequality* (P, III, 112); *Government of Poland* (P, III, 1002–1003); *Constitutional Project for Corsica* (P, III, 901); *Social Contract* (P, III, 422); *Discourse on Political Economy* (P, III, 249). See also *Letters from the Mountain* (P, III, 811–812); *Fragments on the State of War* (P, III, 610); and the fragments pertaining to the *Letter to Beaumont* (P, IV, 1013–1014). For *Government of Poland* and *Constitutional Project for Corsica* I have used the translations in *Rousseau: Political Writings*, trans. and ed. Frederick Watkins (Edinburgh, 1953), pp. 157–330.

their freedom for the preservation of the other, just as a wounded man has his arm cut off to save the rest of his body." Only with the third change do some men exceed the bounds of law, limited authority, and popular authorization. Law itself seems at best superfluous: "And as . . . laws, in general less strong than passions, contain men without changing them, it would be easy to prove that any government that, without being corrupted or altered, always worked exactly according to the ends of its institution, would have been instituted unnecessarily, and that a country where no one eluded the laws and abused the magistracy would need neither magistracy nor laws." In every society divided between rich and poor, limited political authority under law leads to further enslavement: "The law . . . serves the powerful as an offensive weapon, and as a shield against the weak; and the pretext of the public good is always the most dangerous scourge of the people."[4]

In *Emile* Rousseau was equally explicit in his denunciations of contemporary legality. Everywhere the law has taken the side of the strong against the weak: "In the civil state, there is a vain and chimerical equality of right, because the very means intended for its preservation serve to destroy it; and the public strength, joined to the power of the strongest to oppress the weak, destroys the sort of equilibrium nature had established among men." He partly concurs when Emile hesitates to join any of the European states they have visited and examined: "I knew that when you examined our institutions you would be very far from placing a confidence in them which they do not deserve. In vain do we seek liberty under the protection of the laws. The laws! Where is there any law?" And, shortly after advising Polish citizens to suffer anything rather than weaken the force of law, Rousseau warned them of the danger of many laws and the oppression resulting

4. *Discourse on Inequality*, pp. 187, 177–178, 188; *Discourse on Political Economy*, p. 258. See also *ibid.*, p. 273; *Social Contract*, p. 367n.

from relying upon political authority limited by law: "If we have laws, it is solely for the purpose of teaching us to obey our masters well, to keep our hands out of people's pockets, and to give a great deal of money to public scoundrels."[5]

There is no contradiction because Rousseau praised law only in one circumstance: where it is instituted to prevent political authority from being instituted. Law for Rousseau must eliminate, not merely limit, political authority. To the constitutionalist law's purpose is the curbing of extralegal privileges, the punishing of abuses of political authority, and the judging and punishing of guilty subjects in a fair, impartial manner; but to Rousseau its only purpose is preventing men from confronting each other as ruler and ruled. Law is laudable only when it prevents this confrontation.

With no commands coming from men in authority, the artificial individual retains his absolute independence, that natural condition of masterlessness which is literal self-government. Law can "reestablish the natural equality of men."[6] Law can make each citizen "perfectly independent of all his fellow citizens."[7] Free men obey themselves alone: "A free people obeys, but it does not serve; it has chiefs but not masters; it obeys the laws, but it obeys only the laws, and it is in virtue of the strength of the laws that it does not obey men. . . . In a word, liberty always follows the fate of the laws; it reigns or perishes with them. I know nothing more certain."[8] Both the use of the law by some men to command others and a man's

5. *Emile* (P, IV, 524, 857); *Government of Poland*, p. 958. Here and in some subsequent citations of passages in *Emile* I have omitted Rousseau's quotation marks to avoid confusion.

6. *Discourse on Political Economy*, p. 248.

7. *Social Contract*, p. 394.

8. *Letters from the Mountain*, p. 842. See also *Discourse on Political Economy*, pp. 248–250; *Fragments on Laws* (P, III, 492–494); *Geneva Manuscript* (P, III, 310); *Government of Poland*, p. 955; letter to Mirabeau (July 26, 1769; CG, XVII, 157).

placing himself above the law raise the problem of political authority itself. The question is not the possible abuse of authority, but its existence: "In relations between one man and another, . . . the worst that can happen to one is to see himself at the discretion of the other." Enslavement goes beyond any constitutionalist demands for universality and impartiality in the application of law: "For whatever the constitution of a government may be, if a single man is found who is not subject to the law, all the others are necessarily at his discretion."[9]

In the *Discourse on Political Economy* Rousseau contrasted the "natural force" of the public interest and self-imposed laws with the force of magistrates who rule: "If you have only a single ruler, you are at the discretion of a master who has no reason to love you; if you have several rulers, you must suffer both their tyranny and their divisions." Laws, however, can secure the "common liberty." When magistrates follow the "public reason which is the law," then arrangements of command and obedience between men are impossible, man's natural liberty is redeemed, and the dignity of man is realized. For then all members obey only self-imposed laws: "How can all members obey, yet no one commands? How can all serve, yet have no master, and be the more free, as, in apparent subjection, no one loses his liberty except for what might harm the liberty of another? These marvels are the work of the law." A citizen who places himself above the law does more than forfeit its advantages; he enslaves men through obedience to his will. To be free is to remain independent of the will of other men: "With whatever sophistry one tries to blur all this, it is certain that if someone can compel my will, I am no longer free."[10] When you have your "precious freedom," Rousseau reminded Genevans, "you have no other masters except the

9. *Discourse on Inequality*, pp. 181, 112.

10. *Discourse on Political Economy*, pp. 243, 258, 248. See also *Social Contract*, pp. 378–379.

wise law you have made, administered by upright magistrates of your own choice."[11]

Rousseau was so little concerned with orthodox constitutionalism that he showed little interest in a codified body of positive law for magistrates to "administer." Four types of law cover every basic relation among artificial individuals. First, the "action of the whole body politic on itself, that is to say, the relation of all with all, or of the sovereign with the state" constitutes "political" or "fundamental" laws. Second, the relation of the "members of the body politic among themselves, or of each within the entire body" defines "civil laws." Third, the relation between "the person and the law" involving disobedience and its penalty establishes criminal laws. Finally, there "must be added a fourth, the most important of all, which is inscribed neither on marble nor brass, but in the hearts of the citizens, a law which forms the true constitution of the state." It is "a law which sustains a nation in the spirit of its institution and imperceptibly substitutes the force of habit for the force of authority. I refer to [*moeurs*], customs and, above all, belief: this feature, unknown to our political theorists, is the one on which the success of all the other laws depends."[12]

Rousseau's account of these four kinds of law reveals his anarchism. Given the fourth kind of law, the others are unnecessary. Without it, other laws are inadequate, and in fact, become the instruments of increased enslavement. Multiplying civil laws can only further silence voices of civic duty in the hearts of citizens; the more civil laws, the greater the enslavement through public disenchantment and the more magistrates to share the plunder. Selling justice, duty, and the state in

11. *Discourse on Inequality*, p. 116.
12. *Social Contract*, pp. 393–394. The term *sovereign* denotes citizens in their active, legislative capacity and *state* the same citizens who obey, as subjects, self-imposed laws.

turn, magistrates enslave a people, using the civil law as pretext. Then they "substitute the cry of terror, or the lure of an apparent interest." Even the upright magistrate whose faithful administration of civil law inspires a love of the laws—and this "alone is the talent of reigning"—presides over a situation in which civil law is largely irrelevant: "If he could get everyone to act rightly, he himself would no longer have anythng to do; and, as the masterpiece of his efforts, he would remain idle."[13]

The few, simple civil laws necessary in a society of self-governing citizens must also correspond to the fourth and most important kind of law, the *"moeurs,* customs and belief" of common life. Civil laws which ignore or contradict common opinion are both oppressive and powerless. Rousseau heartily approved of Genevan sumptuary laws because they conformed to the genius of Genevan society and were an expression of the Genevan general will. But he found sumptuary laws inappropriate for corrupt Poland. An effort to redistribute wealth and to restrict the passion for luxury among the Polish nobility through civil law would have been ineffective and despotic.[14]

In general, the vain passions of corrupt men can be disciplined by the force of civil law, the constraint of opinion, and the objects of pleasure which signify the shared tastes of a people. Of the three, civil law is always the weakest, and it depends upon the other two. Louis XIV's attempts to abolish dueling were bound to fail: "Opinion, queen of the world, is not subject to the power of kings; they are themselves her first slaves."[15] And while arguing in the *Discourse on Inequality*

13. *Discourse on Political Economy,* pp. 253, 250.

14. *Government of Poland,* pp. 964–966. See also *Discourse on Inequality,* p. 116; *Letter to d'Alembert,* pp. 124–125. Rousseau recommended sumptuary laws in Corsica, if not retroactive. *Constitutional Project for Corsica,* pp. 936–937. See also *Letter to Raynal* (June 1751; P, III, 33); *Fragments on Laws,* p. 497; and *Fragments on Luxury, Commerce, and the Arts* (P, III, 517–521).

15. *Letter to d'Alembert,* pp. 28–29, 98. See also preface to *Narcisse* (P, II, 971). Dueling is Rousseau's recurring symbol for contemporary

that civil laws can only punish corrupt men without making them virtuous, Rousseau offered Sparta as a worthy example of a society which relied upon few civil laws. The society of self-governing citizens Rousseau imagined in the *Social Contract* also needs few civil laws. Internal dissension, exaggerated by foreign pressure, caused a need for civil laws in Corsica, but civil laws must still be simple, precise, and limited in number. In Poland, rescued from more brutal enslavement by Rousseau's proposals, there would be three codes of law, constitutional, civil, and criminal. But these few laws would necessarily be so clear and brief that every Polish child could commit them to memory. Whenever there are more civil laws than a citizen can know and recall, common life is irredeemably corrupt; and one who does not know the civil laws of his state cannot be a virtuous citizen.[16]

Correspondingly, Rousseau's hymns to the honorable and gentle yoke of the laws, obedience to which guarantees liberty and avoids slavery, refer to the first and fourth types of law, fundamental or political law and the *moeurs* of common life: "Laws are really nothing other than the conditions on which civil society exists. A people, since it is subject to laws, ought to be the author of them. The right of laying down the rules of society belongs only to those who form the society." When self-governing citizens obey self-imposed laws, both the "rules which a people as a whole make for the people as a whole" and the customs and beliefs which inhere in their society, then they must obey only themselves.[17]

Rousseau's demand for absolute liberty can be phrased another way. A constitutionalist summarizes the idea of limited

corruption. See *Discourse on Inequality*, pp. 159, 190; *Social Contract*, pp. 357, 459; *Emile*, pp. 544n–545n; *La Nouvelle Héloise* (P, II, 152–160).

16. *Discourse on Inequality*, pp. 187–188; *Social Contract*, p. 437; *Constitutional Project for Corsica*, pp. 903, 916; *Government of Poland*, p. 1001; *Fragments on Laws*, p. 492.

17. *Social Contract*, pp. 380, 379.

and responsible political authority in the phrase "a government of laws but not of men." With changes in civil and constitutional laws, however, men cannot obey laws without also obeying men who change laws, even when changes are accomplished by authorized persons employing legal means. Rousseau's idea of a true rule of law presents no such difficulty: the voice of fundamental law and of the *moeurs* of common life is never the voice of particular men. Rousseau's government of laws is no government in the conventional sense because self-governing citizens are completely independent of the will of other men, including magistrates.

There is no middle ground between literal self-government and dependence upon the will of others. Liberty or slavery. Citizens either participate directly in legislative assemblies and serve in a defensive militia, or they authorize representatives who sell the liberty of citizens to others and hire soldiers who enslave their fellow citizens themselves. When citizens do not participate directly in the affairs of common life, they are preoccupied with "particular" concerns involving commerce, the arts, luxury, and personal wealth. Greedy, cowardly men, preferring comfort to liberty, do not resist the efforts of a magistracy which finds it convenient not to convene assemblies. In his discussion of the forms of "legitimate government" in the *Social Contract*, Rousseau rejected Aristotle's distinction between a tyrant and a king. If the distinction were valid, then there has never been a king. Monarchical government, Rousseau asserted, must not be confused with executive "administration" of the laws by a single, virtuous magistrate. Princes are always wicked or incompetent. If they are only incompetent when they begin, they are always wicked when they end. When he urged a monarchical form of government for Poland, he was merely commenting on what its size and complexity demanded. Such a government would be either elective and free or established through forceful usurpation and enslavement: "Heredity in the crown and freedom in the nation will always be incompatible." The only tranquility a hereditary monarch assures is that of slavery. Again, in the *Social Contract,* Rousseau asserted that if state funds are not used for the public good, as in a "free state," they will become the personal resources of particular men, the magistrates. In the ensuing despotism people become so miserable that they are easily enslaved—as under a monarchy. For the institution of those fundamental laws which first define a political society of fellow citizens, there are two possible moments: peace and prosperity, or war, famine, and seditious chaos. A true lawgiver chooses the first; a charlatan and tyrannical usurper the second. During the subsequent establishment of magistracy by a sovereign people, citizens will either act to preserve their liberty, happiness, and virtue or, depriving neighbors of their liberty, they will seek to conquer others in search of wealth.[18]

The Scope of Politics

Rousseau judged every conceivable instance of social dependence in terms of the difference between liberty and slavery. Self-legislation is imperative in nongovernmental relations, for artificial individuals can be each other's victims as well as government's. Matters of common life involving the sciences and arts, religion, economic classes, and familial society all raise the issue of liberty or slavery.

The first of Rousseau's published works to attract wide attention, the *Discourse on the Sciences and Arts* (1750), makes this understanding of the scope of politics clear. Rousseau began by contrasting the civic virtue of free men in early, simple societies with the preoccupation of contemporary men with superfluous arts and sciences, commerce, and luxury: "While

18. *Ibid.,* pp. 427–431, 423n, 409–415, 390–391; *Government of Poland,* pp. 989–992, 1029. Lanson recognizes the "all or nothing" character of Rousseau's thought, although, he does not relate instances to a demand for absolute liberty. See Lanson, "L'Unité de la pensée de Rousseau," p. 8.

government and laws provide for the safety and well-being of assembled men, the sciences, letters, and arts, less despotic and perhaps more powerful, spread garlands of flowers over the iron chains with which men are burdened, stifle in them the sense of that original liberty for which they seem to have been born, make them love their slavery, and turn them into what is called civilized peoples. Need raised thrones; the sciences and arts have strengthened them. Earthly powers love talents and protect those who cultivate them." Rousseau pointed to a moment in Roman history when liberty and civic virtue were debased. In spite of the efforts of Cato the Elder, the Romans were corrupted by Athenian arts and sciences and were made "slaves of the frivolous men" they had conquered: "The sacred names of liberty, disinterestedness, obedience to laws were replaced by the names of Epicurus, Zeno, Arcesilas. . . . Behold how luxury, licentiousness, and slavery have in all periods been punishment for the arrogant attempts we have made to emerge from the happy ignorance in which eternal wisdom had placed us."[19] And the "first source" of these enslaving arts and sciences is "inequality" itself: political or moral inequality leads to wealth, which leads in turn to luxury and idleness, which permit respectively the fine arts and sciences.[20]

In 1762 Rousseau defended this judgment in his *Letters to Malesherbes*. Men either courageously serve the fatherland or engage in the hypocritical flattery of men of letters. The latter yields constant dissension between arrogant masters and happy

19. *Discourse on the Sciences and Arts* (P, III, 6–7, 13–15). I have used the translation in *Jean-Jacques Rousseau: The First and Second Discourses*, ed. Roger D. Masters, trans. Roger D. and Judith R. Masters (New York, 1964), pp. 31–64. See also *Jean-Jacques entre Socrate et Caton: Textes inédits de Jean-Jacques Rousseau (1750–1753)*, ed. Claude Pichois and René Pintard (Paris, 1972), pp. 10, 35–37, 40–44, 75–78, 96; Michel Launay, *Jean-Jacques Rousseau: Ecrivain politique (1712–1762)* (Grenoble, 1971), pp. 139–145, 148–152.
20. *Observations* (P, III, 49–50).

slaves. In the dedication to Geneva of the *Discourse on Inequality*, Rousseau contrasted the "august freedom" of contemporary Genevan women ("the chaste guardians of [*moeurs*] and the gentle bonds of peace") with the "pretended grandeurs [and] frivolous compensations for servitude" of women in other societies. Within the second historical period of the *Discourse on Inequality* appear glimpses of the arts and sciences which will later lead to property and, later still, to enslaving officials. Fathers in rustic families use the leisure of their solitary life to obtain superfluous objects, and then consider them true needs. Luxury in one class assures poverty in another: luxury, "in order to feed the crowds of lackeys and miserable people it has created, . . . crushes and ruins the farmer and the citizen." A savage man, after he had eaten, was at peace with his fellow men. The new "man of society" has delicate appetites which destroy the simple unity of the family: "It is first of all a question of providing for the necessary, and then for the superfluous; next come delights, then immense wealth, and then subjects, and then slaves." The words *mine* and *thine* divide a society against itself, yielding "cruel and brutal human beings known as masters and a group of rascals and liars known as slaves."[21]

Thus Rousseau objected to establishing a modern theater in Geneva. "I will be asked," he noted, "who forces the poor to go to the theater. I answer: first, those who establish it and give them the temptation. In the second place, their very poverty which condemns them to constant labor without hope of seeing it end, makes some relaxation necessary." Rousseau imagined the effect of a theater on mountain villagers in the vicinity of Neufchâtel whom he had visited during his youth. These happy, economically self-sufficient farmers and craftsmen enjoy the "sweetness of society," and "each is everything

21. *Letters to Malesherbes* (Jan. 1762; P, I, 1131–1137); *Discourse on Inequality*, pp. 119–120, 168, 206, 203; *Last Response* (P, III, 80).

for himself [and] no one is anything for another"; they are "free of poll-taxes, duties, commissioners, and forced labor"; they use their leisure harmlessly for fashioning countless useful and decorative objects often found on foreign markets; a stranger would mistake a farmer's living room for a mechanic's workshop or a simple laboratory in experimental physics. Villagers paint, sketch, and play the flutes they make. Families sing psalms in four parts which "are not taught them by masters but are passed down, as it were, by tradition." Even a little theater company—indeed, the very existence of the building—would destroy the liberty and simplicity of their common life. Effort slackens as work ceases to amuse. To the modest cost of tickets is added the expense of Sunday clothes and frequent changes of linen. Villagers powder and shave more often. Their goods become more expensive compared to those of industrious neighbors without a theater, and trade declines. In winter seasons, when the roads are not passable, new roads are made in the snow and perhaps paved. These public expenses—"and God grant that they do not put up lanterns" alongside these roads—lead to new taxes. Wives want to be dressed fashionably: "The wife of the chief magistrate will not want to present herself at the theater attired like the schoolmaster's. The schoolmaster's wife strives to be attired like the chief magistrate's." Husbands are ruined and perhaps won over by this vain competition. Riches and luxury are pursued. Sumptuary laws are disregarded. People become inactive and soft. Easy sociability and equality give way to rivalry. The self-governing citizen becomes a slave.[22]

22. *Letter to d'Alembert*, pp. 154, 80–85. This use of Neufchâtel suggests a negative judgment of contemporary Geneva. See also letter to Moultou (Jan. 29, 1760; *CC*, VII, 24), written after the publication of the *Letter to d'Alembert* but before *Emile* and the *Social Contract* were published and condemned by Genevan authorities. Rousseau's volatile judgments, fears and hopes for Geneva, in which his political status and writings were often at stake, constitute a separate, tangled story. For an appraisal of Rousseau's celebration of the small republics

Religious practices are also a political matter, in part because religion arises at a particular moment in man's evolution as a social being.[23] In the last chapter of the *Social Contract* Rousseau defended a "civil religion" in a free society. Although the chapter was added shortly before publication and although Rousseau later softened some aspects of it, he had described a civil religion as early as 1756 in his response to Voltaire's poem on the Lisbon earthquake.[24] This civil religion, which we examine in Chapter 9, is a consistent device for avoiding enslaving sectarianism in the ideal society he imagined in the *Social Contract*. Rousseau's politics of religion goes further than noting that heroic lawgivers must attribute the foundation of a free society to divine inspiration or that monarchs at the dawn of common life are often thought gods or that early societies are theocracies or even that civic and religious intolerance are inseparable because one cannot live in peace among citizens one considers damned. Even without governmental office, a body of clergy exercises political authority, inescapably. Priests who can refuse to marry citizens because of their nonconformity usurp direct, legislative responsibility of self-governing citizens and divide popular sovereignty. Even if the clergy forms nothing more than an unofficial particular society within a body

---

of the High Valais and the Genevan background to the theater controversy, see François Jost, *Jean-Jacques Rousseau, Swisse*, 2 vols. (Fribourg, 1961), I, 210–218, 243–259. Jost also argues (I, 155–189) that Rousseau's major writings reflect a Genevan heritage and an essentially favorable attitude toward Geneva. See, in contrast, Launay, *Rousseau*, pp. 341–352. Although a theater's effects upon *moeurs* were repeatedly debated in the eighteenth century (see Mornet, *Rousseau*, pp. 51–54), Rousseau again used Neufchâtel as an example of a free state in *Letters from the Mountain*, pp. 827, 866. This work also contains Rousseau's most detailed and uncompromising criticism of contemporary Geneva.

23. *Letter to Beaumont*, pp. 950–953. See also the fragments pertaining to this letter, pp. 1017–1018.

24. Letter to Rey (Dec. 23, 1761; *CC*, IX, 346); *Letters from the Mountain*, pp. 703–706; *Letter to Voltaire* (Aug. 18, 1756; P, IV, 1073–1074).

politic and possesses only a power of excommunication, it is the real "master" of an enslaved citizenry.[25]

This position was not uncommon among advanced thinkers in eighteenth-century France. But its basis, which would *require* a civil religion in a free society, is peculiarly Rousseau's. To accept the testimony of others in matters of divine revelation is to consent to human authority. Either a Christian follows unaided the message of the Gospels and is devoted to moral duty and liberty, or he is subject to the commands of priests. Furthermore, a pious man does not obey even God, should God appear tyrannic. Rousseau rejected the idea of original sin in part because it implies an awesome, distant God. Rousseau claimed that Adam's sin was not in breaking God's command, because God does not command men from afar in this fashion. God gave a paternal warning, not an absolute prohibition. God becomes a presence with whom to communicate directly, without the mediation of his supposed representatives on this earth. The proper worship of God is joyous assent to his creative presence rather than prayer for special benefits. One does not request miraculous changes; one does not ask God for the will to do good because that would be to ask Him to do one's own work while one garners the rewards. Rousseau's was not a God of grace.[26]

The very relationship between rich and poor is another instance of enslaving politics. The wealthy man commands re-

25. *Social Contract*, pp. 383-384, 460-463, 469. The treatment of the French clergy is less inhibited in the first version. See *Geneva Manuscript*, pp. 343-344.

26. *Letter to Beaumont*, pp. 938-941, 960-964, 986-996; *Social Contract*, p. 464; letters to Vernes (Feb. 18, 1758; May 25, 1758; *CC*, V, 33, 82-83); *Emile*, pp. 591-594, 604-606; *Letters from the Mountain*, pp. 751-752. See also *La Nouvelle Héloise*, pp. 684-685, 696-701, 715-716. For a discussion of Rousseau's religious ideas, which stresses the absence of "Christian doctrine" concerning sin, remorse, and redemption, see Robert Derathé, "Jean-Jacques Rousseau et le christianisme," *Revue de métaphysique et de morale*, LIII (Oct. 1948), 379-387, 410-414.

spect from the fearful and envious poor. Even without spending money, this "useless scoundrel" is obeyed. He uses his reputation to obtain submission to his will: "Does he travel through a dangerous place? There are escorts. Does the axle of his carriage break? Everybody rushes to his assistance. Is there a noise at his door? He speaks but a word, and all is silent. Does the crowd inconvenience him? He gestures and everybody disperses. . . . All these attentions cost him not a penny; they are the rich man's right, not the price of wealth." The case of the poor man, whose poverty testifies to his enslavement by the rich, is different: "The more humanity owes him, the more society refuses him." He is deprived of his rightful, legal opportunities, and if he obtains justice under law it is with great difficulty. He is summoned first when roads are repaired and militias are formed. People avoid him when he suffers the smallest accident: "If his wretched cart overturns, far from receiving anyone's assistance, I think him lucky if he avoids insults from the impudent servants of a young duke. In a word, all gratuitous assistance is denied the poor when they need it, precisely because they cannot pay for it."[27]

In *La Nouvelle Héloise* Julie comments on the political character of any wedded union: "It is not only in the interest of the wedded couple, but the common cause of mankind, that the purity of marriage shall not be tampered with. Every time two persons are joined by a solemn tie, there intervenes a tacit engagement with the whole human race to respect this sacred bond and to honor in them the conjugal union. . . . The public is in some fashion the guarantor of an agreement made in its presence." Moreover, the family, within itself, is also a political society. In "domestic government" the themes of the larger body politic occur: the character of the ruler, the rights of property, the common object or general will of the corporate whole, the division of sovereign authority, the character

27. *Discourse on Political Economy*, p. 272.

of obedience. In corrupt families, the talents of children, "victims of the misery of their parents or the barbarous shame of their mothers," are buried and their inclinations are "forced by the imprudent constraints of fathers." Enslaved by their parents' avarice, children "groan in indissoluble chains which the heart rejects and which gold alone has formed."[28]

Within the imaginary and unusual society of *Emile*, the relationship between Rousseau as tutor and his pupil Emile can only be one of liberty or one of slavery. This evolving politics of their common life lends integrity to the work. Interpreters have often limited the political significance of *Emile* to book five, in which Emile reaches maturity and Rousseau summarizes his principles of political right. But Rousseau conceived the scope of politics as much broader than a summary of principles. He expressed this scope in the whole story of Emile's education. As a description of the "natural education" of a single, self-governing citizen, *Emile* stops short of the decline of men into contemporary slavery. Emile is educated to virtuous citizenship within a miniature body politic whose members are beyond the enslaving authorities of contemporary Europe. Emile's education is not a "private" matter.

The politics of common life begins with birth in *Emile*, when Rousseau denounces the contemporary family. Neglectful parents and hired nurses who restrict an infant's movements are responsible for moral and physical deformities. Such "chains" make an infant "more miserable than a criminal in irons" and lead him to attempt to impose his will on others in retaliation. His voice alone still free, the infant cries. From this moment the problem of command and obedience is upon us: "Either we do what he wants or we demand that he do what we want. Either we submit to his whims or we subject him to our whims. There is no middle course; he must give or receive commands. Thus his earliest ideas are those of domin-

---

28. *La Nouvelle Héloïse*, pp. 359–360; *Discourse on Political Economy*, pp. 241–244; *Discourse on Inequality*, pp. 204, 205n.

ion and servitude. He commands before he can speak; he obeys before he can act; and sometimes he is punished for offenses before he is aware of them or even before they are committed." For his imaginary pupil, however, Rousseau finds a middle way by which to secure Emile's obedience without commanding it, without bending Emile's will to his own.

An infant is similarly enslaved through his own efforts to command his tutor. His plaintive cry asking assistance in obtaining an object beyond his reach must be carefully studied: "Infants' first tears are prayers; if one is not careful, they soon become commands; infants begin by asking for aid and they end by demanding service. Thus, from their own weakness, there first arises a feeling of dependence; then the idea of rule and tyranny is born." If Emile has simply misjudged the distance of the object, Rousseau may bring him the object . . . slowly. If his cries are a command that the object approach or that Rousseau bring it to him, Rousseau does not hear his cries: "He must learn in good time not to give commands, not to command men because he is not their master, or things because they cannot hear him." A response to valid cries should be generous, not submissive. When misjudged distance, rather than authoritative demand, entitles an infant to possession of an object, he should be carried to the object rather than having the object brought to him.

Emile never experiences the conflict of will we mistakenly think natural. He does not learn to dominate, or to suffer domination, or even to resist it. Because Emile must remain a stranger to the phenomenon of rule, he never hears or employs those empty but pernicious phrases of politeness used by the rich to command and subdue: "*If you please* means in their mouth *it pleases me*, and *I beg of you* means *I command you*." Later, in order to develop Emile's capacity for judgment and foresight, Rousseau faces the same choice. Is Emile to be like the free man of simple society or the civilized peasant of modern society who complaisantly accepts the routines imposed by others? Liberty or slavery. No one is as mentally sluggish as the modern peasant who is always doing what he has been commanded by others to do, what he sees his father doing, or what he himself has always done: "Habit and obedience have taken the place of reason." A pupil educated in this manner cannot move until directed by others: "He dare not eat when he is hungry, nor laugh when he is merry, nor cry when he is sad, nor offer one hand or the other, nor move a muscle unless commanded to do so. Soon he will not dare to breathe without orders." The education of a free man is very different. Tied neither to one place nor to tasks demanded by others, "obedient to no one, with no other law but his own will," he reasons with every event of his life and becomes self-reliant, alert, and inquisitive. Emile is educated in this manner. He never acquires "the habit of seeking help from others." For, "as he is always active, he is forced to notice many things, to understand many effects; he soon acquires a great deal of experience. He takes his lessons from nature, not man; . . . and he is always carrying out his own ideas, not those of other people." The difficult art of the tutor is one of "governing without precepts, and doing everything by doing nothing." This pattern of conscientiously eschewing all authoritative direction continues throughout *Emile*.[29]

It is never only those obedient to the commanding will of others who are enslaved. All rulers are themselves enslaved because they are dependent upon obedience by the ruled, as in the example of a tutor's reaction to an infant's cries. A "master" is the "slave" of the child's bargains. The child, in "the chains of his tyrant," is himself a "little tyrant" who in fact "controls" by clever extortion the ruling tutor. The child obtains what he wants by withholding or modulating the obedience his tutor demands. One hour of industry obtained

29. *Emile*, pp. 254, 261, 287–288, 312–313, 360–362. See also *La Nouvelle Héloïse*, pp. 572–573.

through authoritative insistence is paid for with a week of compliance to the tyrannic wishes of the pupil.[30]

Rousseau's condemnation, from both directions, of every authoritative arrangement is the essence of his anarchistic imperative of absolute liberty. Every arrangement of command and obedience, whatever its social circumference and its official status, is tyrannic: "Those who think themselves the masters of others are indeed greater slaves than they." He who commands always depends on the will of those he governs: "Domination itself is servitude when it is joined to opinion, because you depend upon the prejudices of others when you rule them by means of those prejudices. To direct them as you please, they must be led as they please. They have only to change their way of thinking, and you are forced to change your course of action."[31]

After the appearance of an economic division of labor and the usurpation of common property during the fourth historical period in the *Discourse on Inequality*, the rich are compelled by the resistance of the poor to establish civil laws and representative government. This struggle is one of reciprocal enslavement: "Having formerly been free and independent, behold man, due to a multitude of new needs, subjected so to speak to all of nature and especially to his fellowmen, whose slave he becomes in a sense even in becoming their master; rich, he needs their services; poor, he needs their help; and mediocrity cannot enable him to do without them."[32] Every authoritative relation remains a state of war, sometimes peace-

30. *Emile*, pp. 362, 366.
31. *Social Contract*, p. 351; *Emile*, p. 308. See also letter to Abbé de l'Etang [?] (Mar. 10, 1752 [?]; *CC*, II, 180). Rousseau justified his own need for solitude on the basis of his "dominant passion" for liberty, an "indomitable spirit of liberty which nothing can conquer, and before which honors, fortune, and even reputation are nothing to me." *Letters to Malesherbes*, pp. 1132–1133. See also letter to Voltaire (Jan. 30, 1750; *CC*, II, 124); *Letter to Beaumont* (fragment), p. 1019.
32. *Discourse on Inequality*, pp. 174–175.

ful in appearance and limited by law.[33] And this mutual enslavement cannot remain peaceful, as subsequent stages of
common life in the *Discourse on Inequality* suggest. Once
authoritative direction appears, there begins an accelerating
struggle of competing but mutually dependent wills. The only
alternative to mutual enslavement is a condition of common
life wherein each member respects the identical independence
to which fellow citizens are entitled: "Liberty consists less in
doing one's own will than in not being subject to the will of
others; it consists further in not subjecting the will of others
to our own. Whoever is master cannot be free; and to rule is
to obey."[34]

33. See *Fragments on the State of War*, pp. 608–612.
34. *Letters from the Mountain*, pp. 841–842. The context here contrasts "independence" and "liberty." The former—"doing one's own
will"—is that lawless impetuousness of presocial man which, in society,
enslaves all men. Or, as Rousseau wrote in the manuscript margin:
"Whenever there are slaves there are masters." *Ibid.*, p. 1693.

CHAPTER 6

Political Equality
and Absolute Liberty

The *Discourse on Inequality* not only rejects liberal individualism and introduces nonindividualism; it also contains Rousseau's first sustained statement of the anarchistic imperative. The *Discourse* depends on a continuous contrast between the equality in the presocial state of nature and the inequality that can occur in society. More specifically, the now familiar alternative of liberty or slavery appears within the panorama of the six historical periods of social dependence. As in the *Discourse on the Sciences and Arts* (where the simplicity of early society is contrasted with the enslaving degradation of contemporary society) and in *Emile* (where the self-governing man of simple society is contrasted with the enslaved peasant of contemporary society), Rousseau distinguished the first from the later three stages of social dependence. In the first, men are still self-governing. In the later three, men are progressively enslaved to one another because they have transferred their liberty through their acceptance of domination and obedience.

Natural Equality

The apparent flippancy with which Rousseau refers to his "true state of nature" can now be understood. He acknowledges that man's "primitive condition" is but a "supposition." He refers to "the hypothetical history" presented in the *Dis-*

course on Inequality.[1] He was uncertain about the precise physical specifications of original man. As we indicated in Chapter 3, the historical origins of herd societies, national communities, and an economic division of labor are speculative and awkward. "Let us begin therefore by setting all the facts aside," he asserted, "for they do not affect the question. The researches which can be undertaken concerning this subject must not be taken for historical truths, but only for hypothetical and conditional reasonings better suited to clarify the nature of things than to show their true origin."[2]

Nonetheless, and far beyond the required delicacy concerning Biblical "facts," Rousseau was very much concerned with the probable facts of the origin and evolution of social dependence. At great length he invited skillful observers of foreign *moeurs* to voyage to simple communities. He cautiously suggested experimental crossbreeding of men and orangutans to establish man's relation to the animal kingdom. He repeatedly apologized for describing the history of man in general while ignoring varieties of time and place. The presocial state of nature was obviously of extreme importance to him. And the reason is clear. He wanted to formulate precise judgments about the essential matter of liberty or equality. He wanted a critical point of view on the actual. To locate and evaluate the "source of inequality" among contemporary social men, we must view man "as nature formed him," in his "original constitution" and "primitive state." Thus, "I ventured some conjectures, less in the hope of resolving the question than with the intention of clarifying [the origin of inequality] and reducing it to its true state. . . . It is no light undertaking . . . to know correctly a state which no longer exists, which perhaps never existed, which probably never will exist, and about which it is nevertheless necessary to have precise notions

1. *Discourse on Inequality* (P, III, 160, 127).
2. *Ibid.*, pp. 134, 196–198, 132–133.

in order to judge our present state correctly."[3] As Rousseau reminds the mature Emile, proper concepts of natural man and the state of nature are indispensable. They are especially indispensable for one like Emile who is about to become a member of a body politic where he can live "free and independent, without having need to harm anyone and without fear of being harmed." Before choosing, Emile undertakes his own voyages of comparison to obtain that knowledge of "governmental matters, of public *moeurs*," which can combat the influence of contemporary prejudices and can permit one to determine "if men are born in slavery or freedom, associated together or independent, if they join together voluntarily or through force."[4]

Rousseau considered Montesquieu the only man in modern times capable of undertaking this complete study. But Montesquieu, according to Rousseau, ignored "the principles of political right" and was content to deal with the positive laws of established governments: "Nothing in the world is more different than these two studies." "Yet," Rousseau continued, "he who would judge wisely actual governments is obliged to combine the two: he must know what ought to be in order to appraise what is." Could we infer man's natural sentiments from his observable actions, we would conclude that he is a predator.[5]

In the *Discourse on Inequality* Rousseau argued that "among the differences that distinguish men, some pass for natural that are uniquely the work of habit and the various types of life

3. *Ibid.*, pp. 211, 122–123.
4. *Emile* (P, IV, 835–837).
5. *Ibid.*, pp. 836–837; preface to *Narcisse* (P, II, 962). See also *Rousseau juge de Jean-Jacques* (P, I, 728, 936); *Confessions* (P, I, 408–409); *Letter to Beaumont* (Mar. 1763; P, IV, 951–952); *Fragments on the State of War* (P, III, 609–611); *Moral Letters* (P, IV, 1092). Montesquieu perhaps thought the question of the "origin" of society a bit ridiculous. See *Persian Letters*, no. 94, in *Montesquieu: Oeuvres complètes*, ed. Roger Caillois, 2 vols. (Paris, 1949–1951), I, 269–270.

men adopt in society." By going backwards far enough he was able to distinguish "the equality nature established among men" from "the inequality they have instituted": "By common avowal, [men] are naturally as equal among themselves as were the animals of each species before various physical causes had introduced into certain species the varieties we notice."[6]

Two distinctly different, unrelated kinds of inequality exist among contemporary social men: "physical" inequality and "moral or political" inequality. Physical inequality, established by nature, "consists in the difference in age, health, bodily strengths and qualities of mind and soul." These are "barely perceptible" to natural men, and their influence is therefore "almost null." Moral or political inequality is different; it includes "different privileges that some men enjoy to the prejudice of others, such as to be richer, more honored, more powerful than they, or even to make themselves obeyed by them." Logically, moral or political inequality could not have arisen among presocial men: political authority "depends upon a sort of convention and is established, or at least authorized, by the consent of men." Rousseau denied the sanction of natural right to all arrangements distinguishing ruler from ruled: "[Physical] inequality . . . draws its force and growth from the development of our faculties and the progress of the human mind, and finally becomes stable and legitimate by the establishment of property and laws. . . . Moral inequality, authorized by positive right alone, is contrary to natural right whenever it is not combined in the same proportion with physical inequality." This distinction "sufficiently determines what one ought to think in this regard of the sort of inequality that reigns among all civilized people; since it is manifestly against the law of nature, in whatever manner it is defined, that a child command an old man, an imbecile lead a wise man, and a handful of men be glutted with superfluities while the starv-

6. *Discourse on Inequality*, pp. 160, 111, 123.

ing multitude lacks necessities." Merely to ask if there is "some essential link" between physical inequality and political inequality "would be asking, in other terms, whether those who command are necessarily worth more than those who obey, and whether strength of body or mind, wisdom or virtue, are always found in the same individuals in proportion to power or wealth: a question perhaps good for slaves to discuss in the hearing of their masters, but not suitable for reasonable and free men who seek the truth."[7]

What Rousseau said of moral or political equality in the *Discourse*, he also said of liberty. Liberty is "the most noble of man's faculties." Man is by nature "a free being." Unlike other beasts, he is not a prisoner of mere sensations, ideas, and instincts. He is a "free agent," and "it is above all in the consciousness of this freedom that the spirituality of his soul is shown." Man can will; he can choose and reject courses of action "by an act of freedom."[8] He alone is capable of purposeful adaptation to changes in his physical environment that threaten survival. The misuse of natural liberty, not "nature," is responsible for the moral degradation and physical calamities of civilized life: "As an untamed steed bristles his mane, paws the earth with his hoof, and breaks away impetuously at the very approach of the bit, whereas a trained horse patiently endures whip and spur, barbarous man does not bend his head for the yoke that civilized man wears without a murmur, and he prefers the most turbulent freedom to tranquil subjection."[9]

7. *Ibid.*, pp. 131–132, 193–194. Indeed, Rousseau attributed most observable differences of temperament and "strength of mind" to cumulative social effects. *Ibid.*, pp. 160–161. The notion of a ruling child is not innocuous, for a regency ruled in France from 1715, when Louis XV was five years of age, until 1723; and Louis did not rule alone until 1761.
8. *Ibid.*, pp. 183, 152, 141–142.
9. *Ibid.*, p. 181. See also letter to Franquières (Jan. 15, 1769; P, IV, 1141–1142); *Letter to Voltaire* (Aug. 18, 1756; P, IV, 1061–1066). In rejecting the significance Voltaire had attributed to the Lisbon earthquake, Rousseau argued that "moral evil," including civilized man's fear

Because man is ignorant of vice, his liberty in the presocial state of nature is unthreatened. Natural *amour de soi* does not require domination for satisfaction. Natural man's "inner impulse of commiseration" restrains him from harming other sensitive animals: "Let someone explain to me what is meant by this word oppression. Some will dominate by violence, the others will groan, enslaved to all their whims. That is precisely what I observe among us; but I do not see how that could be said of savage men, to whom one would even have much trouble explaining what servitude and domination are. A man might well seize the fruits another has gathered, the game he has killed, the cave that served as his shelter; but how will he ever succeed in making himself obeyed? And what can be the chains of dependence among men who possess nothing?" If one man, whose strength is "sufficiently superior" and who is "depraved enough," were to force another to provide for his subsistence, he must keep his captive constantly in sight and tie him up every night. If his vigilance relaxes for a moment or a sudden noise makes him turn his head, his captive takes twenty steps into the forest and is never seen again.

Social dependence is a necessary condition for mutual enslavement: neither is conceivable in the state of nature. The savage "breathes only repose and freedom"; the words *power* and *reputation* are without meaning to him; he wants only to live and remain idle. The artificial individual of society, however, lives outside himself, as he must. He also "pays court to the great whom he hates, and to the rich whom he scorns. He spares nothing in order to obtain the honor of serving them; he proudly boasts of his baseness and their protection; and proud of his slavery, he speaks with disdain of those who do

---

of death, and most of his physical ills, are his "own work." It is man himself, "man free, perfected, and completely corrupted" by restless vanity, who has chosen to live in crowded cities and to huddle in buildings: Rousseau, like Voltaire, knew the earthquake found thousands in churches for All Saints Day.

not have the honor of sharing it." For this reason Rousseau asserted that "in becoming sociable and a slave, [man] becomes weak, fearful, and servile." Men of society are "forced to flatter and destroy one another, and . . . are born enemies by duty and swindlers by interest." Civilized men, in the sixth stage of common life, "let themselves be oppressed [by magistrates] only insofar as they are carried away by blind ambition; and looking more below than above them, domination becomes dearer to them than independence, and they consent to wear chains in order to give them to others in turn. It is very difficult to reduce to obedience one who does not seek command; and the most adroit politician would never succeed in subjecting men who want only to be free."[10]

Yet this distinction between nature and society is not the important matter; the two can be compatible. The fundamental alternative remains liberty or slavery, not natural isolation or society, not private man or public society, not man or citizen, not the individual or the group, not spontaneity or opinion. Man cannot choose between liberty and society because both are essential to him once the state of nature has ended. Similarly, both nonindividualism and anarchism are fundamental to Rousseau's thought. They are the warp and woof of his political philosophy. To ignore or slight either, or to interpret society and liberty as competitive principles, is to miss the integrity and meaning of Rousseau's philosophy.

The contrast between the earliest and the last three historical periods of common life in the *Discourse on Inequality* makes it clear that Rousseau's primary concern was always with the choice between liberty and slavery. The third period, with its small nation of families "united by [*moeurs*] and character, not by regulations and laws," was the stage "least subject to revolutions, the best for man." This epoch, "maintaining a

10. *Discourse on Inequality*, pp. 161, 192–193, 139, 203, 188. See also *Letters from the Mountain* (P, III, 842n).

golden mean between the indolence of the primitive state and the petulant activity of our vanity, must have been the happiest and most durable epoch." That simple peoples still in this earlier period of common life reject European *moeurs* "seems to confirm that the human race was made to remain in it always; that this state is the veritable prime of the world, and that all subsequent progress has been in appearance so many steps toward the perfection of the individual and in fact toward the decrepitude of the species."[11] This society, unlike its successors, reconciles the requirements of absolute liberty with those of social dependence.

In the *Discourse*, a number of circumstances accompany the enslavement of later social men: men use the leisure of simple life in national communities to seek superfluous commodities now considered necessities; a quickened vanity, no longer satisfied with competitions during public festivals, leads to contempt, shame, or envy; and "contrived inequality," arising from a division of labor. The division between wealthy, idle owners of property and poor laborers represents a conclusive "destruction of equality," so that common life now exhibits the "usurpations of the rich, the brigandage of the poor, [and] the unbridled passions of all."[12]

The relentless momentum of this descent of man through later historical periods owes nothing to such fortuitous events as those Rousseau imagined initiating earlier stages. Political authority itself is responsible. Once moral inequality is instituted, once the desire to dominate others appears, there is sufficient cause for permanent and accelerating war between enslaved men; and inevitable revolutions underscore the precarious and servile position of those who seek to command others and the inevitability of resistance from those enslaved to the will of others. Once men rule other men, whether as

11. *Discourse on Inequality*, pp. 169, 171. See also *ibid.*, pp. 220–222.
12. *Ibid.*, pp. 168, 170–176.

masters or slaves, the appetite for further domination is insatiable. Without enslaving political authority, historical evolution might have lingered, motionless, at the time of small, simple nations.[13]

Before the establishment of representative government and civil law, "a man did not . . . have any other means of subjecting his equals than by attacking their goods or by giving them some of his." When government is established to secure the ill-gotten possessions of the rich, constant war between political societies occurs. "The rich, for their part, had scarcely known the pleasure of domination when they soon disdained all others, and using their old slaves to subdue new ones, they thought only of subjugating and enslaving their neighbors: like those famished wolves which, having once tasted human flesh, refuse all other food and henceforth want only to devour men." Rulers successful in war seek to make their magistracy hereditary; they "call their fellow citizens their slaves, count them like cattle in the number of things that belonged to them, and call themselves equals of the gods and kings of kings."[14]

In this incessant struggle among predatory men, natural goodness disappears and civic virtue is impossible. Violent despotism tolerates no sort of loyalty; and "as soon as it speaks, there is neither probity nor duty to consult, and the blindest obedience is the sole virtue which remains for slaves." A limited, representative rule of men has led inevitably to the rule of force. "Here is the ultimate stage of inequality, and the extreme point which closes the circle and touches the point from which we started. Here all individuals become equals again because they are nothing. . . . Here everything is brought

13. *Ibid.*, pp. 171, 176, 189–190; *Observations* (P, III, 49–50); preface to *Narcisse*, pp. 968–969. See Jouvenel, "Essai," pp. 25–28, 149–150. For a discussion of this fatalism, see Jean Starobinski, *Jean-Jacques Rousseau: La Transparence et l'obstacle* (Paris, 1958), pp. 9–10, 13, 17–18, 22, 25–28, 241–243. Starobinski also sees a necessary opposition between nature and society in Rousseau's thought.

14. *Discourse on Inequality*, pp. 179, 175–176, 187.

back to the sole law of the stronger, and consequently to a new state of nature different from the one with which we began, in that the one was the state of nature in its purity, and this last is the fruit of an excess of corruption." Whatever the outcome, the constant revolutions of civilized life are of no significance to natural right; thus, "no one can complain of another's injustice, but only of his own imprudence or his misfortune." The slavery of political authority among civilized men irrevocably replaces the equality men enjoyed in small national societies. We have come to ourselves. Contemporary life in common is an unmitigated tyranny of violent forces: whatever its momentary disguises, the Hobbesian state of war, correctly understood and located, is now and forever.[15]

Contracts, Consent, and Representation

Before Rousseau reached this characterization of contemporary life in the *Discourse*, he discussed the establishment of a political society and the designation of magistrates. This discussion appears to imply concern for nothing more than a lag in time between the formation of a political society with civil laws and the subsequent appointment of magistrates, and again between the appointment of magistrates with legal and limited authority to govern and their subsequent assumption of arbitrary and unlimited powers. The discussion has a very different intent. It permitted Rousseau to identify all surrenders of liberty to particular men as enslaving inequality. Natural right prohibits every division between rulers and ruled.

Rousseau first noted that "inconveniences and disorders had to multiply continually in order that men finally thought of confiding to private persons [*des particuliers*] the dangerous trust of public authority, and committed to magistrates the

15. *Ibid.*, p. 191. See also *Fragments on Luxury, Commerce, and the Arts* (P, III, 523); *Fragments on the State of War* (P, III, 602–603, 608–616). Berman, *Politics of Authenticity*, pp. 131–141, also notes Rousseau's Hobbesian characterization of contemporary politics.

care of enforcing obedience to the deliberations of the people."
Moreover, "to say that the chiefs were chosen before the confederation was created and that the minister of laws existed before the laws themselves is a supposition that does not permit
of serious debate." Thus, Rousseau rejected an immediate
"voluntary establishment of tyranny" through a contract between a people and a magistrate, the one transferring its liberty
to the other. This would indicate the sudden, irreparable degradation of man's nature. It would be an offense to "the author of one's being to renounce without reservation the most
precious of all his gifts and subject ourselves to committing all
the crimes he forbids us in order to please a ferocious or in-
sane master." Invoking Locke as an authority, Rousseau asserted that "no one can sell his freedom to the point of subjecting himself to an arbitrary power which treats him
according to its fancy" because this would mean selling one's
own life—of which one is not the master. Yet Rousseau's fas-
tidious concern with the exact sequence by which men establish government is at odds with his simple assertion, moments
earlier, that the institution of this political society with civil
laws is itself slavery. It "destroyed natural freedom for all
time, established forever the law of property and inequality,
. . . and subjected the whole human race to work, servitude,
and misery."[16] The subsequent tyranny of arbitrary magistracy merely strengthens the tyranny of the wealthy through
the additional sanction of enforceable law.

As with constitutionalism, the contradiction disappears once
the requirement of absolute liberty receives its proper emphasis. Any government authority established through a contractual transfer of liberty is slavery because the authorized magistrates divide common life between rulers and ruled. However
convenient Rousseau's invocation of Locke, it is misleading.
Locke defended natural rights. Rousseau defended as a matter

16. *Discourse on Inequality*, pp. 180, 182–183, 178.

of natural right absolute liberty itself. Locke was a constitutionalist who traced representative government to a contract in which men, surrendering one natural power to magistrates authorized to govern them, retained other private liberties. Rousseau was interested in the original character and extent of governmental authority only insofar as it was necessary to account for the origin and devolution of tyranny. Any magistracy which commands, any government which governs, represents an enslaving surrender of liberty.

This is why Rousseau next denied in the *Discourse on Inequality* the legitimacy of any contract between a people and its magistrates. Whether the authorization is voluntary or forced, temporary or permanent, limited or unlimited, is of no importance, for every surrender of liberty to others places men at the discretion of others. Consent does not justify enslavement: "Pufendorf says that just as one transfers his goods to another by conventions and contracts, one can also divest himself of his freedom in favor of someone else. That, it seems to me, is very bad reasoning: for, first, the goods I alienate become something altogether foreign to me, the abuse of which is indifferent to me; but it matters to me that my freedom is not abused, and I cannot, without making myself guilty of the evil I shall be forced to do, risk becoming the instrument of crime." Moreover, because the right of property is "only conventional and of human institution," every man can do whatever he pleases with his property. In contrast "life and freedom" are "essential gifts of nature." "By giving up the one, one degrades his being, by giving up the other one destroys it insofar as he can; and as no temporal goods can compensate for the one or the other, it would offend both nature and reason to renounce them whatever the price [in return]." Even "if one could alienate his freedom like his goods," parents' contractual authorization of magistracy could not be binding for their children; and so, "just as to establish slavery violence had to be done to nature, nature had to be changed to per-

petuate this right; and the jurists, who have gravely pro-
nounced that the child of a slave would be born a slave, have
decided in other terms that a man would not be born a man."[17]
Slavery, then, does not begin when appointed magistrates
violate civil law. And when later magistrates do resort to the
force of the stronger which the establishment of magistracy
was intended by the contracting parties to remedy, this "is
only their corruption and extreme limit." Men already were
enslaved as soon as they agreed to divide their labor, as soon as
the rich seized property, and as soon as rich and poor agreed
to establish a political society. If there are "inevitable abuses"
in every political contract between a people and magistrates, it
is because citizens are obeying particular men. It was only to
describe enslaved men of corrupt society that Rousseau, following what he called "common opinion," used the concept of
a political contract between a people and its magistrates.[18]

When Rousseau referred in the *Social Contract* to contractual exchanges among men, he defended the idea of absolute
liberty with equal vehemence. He again argued that a political
society must have been founded first, before magistrates were
designated. But his reason for making this point is to reject
that "so-called right of slavery" implicit in every theory of
natural and contractual inequality: "The words 'slavery' and
'right' are contradictory, they cancel each other out."[19]

Rousseau first attacked Grotius' view that liberty is and
should be alienable. Grotius went so far as to justify conventional slavery on the basis that, if the vanquished can legitimately become the slave of a conqueror, an entire people can
submit to the political authority of a prince. Rousseau asserted

17. *Ibid.*, pp. 183–184.
18. *Ibid.*, pp. 184–185. Similarly, that this political society was earlier
instituted through conquest or a union among the weak, instead of the
contractual swindle by a man of wealth, is a matter of "indifference" for
"what I want to establish." *Ibid.*, p. 179.
19. *Social Contract* (P, III, 356, 358).

that Grotius was merely offering a fact as a proof of right: "It is possible to imagine a more logical method, but not one more favourable to tyrants." Grotius' assertion, Rousseau continued without dallying over distinctions, was identical to the views of Hobbes and of the Emperor Caligula as reported by Philo: "These authors show us the human race divided into herds of cattle, each with a master who preserves it only in order to devour its members." The surrender of liberty to this extent must be rejected: "To speak of a man giving himself in return for nothing is to speak of what is absurd, unthinkable; such an action would be illegitimate, void, if only because no one who did it could be in his right mind. To say the same of a whole people is to conjure up a nation of lunatics; and [political] right cannot rest on madness." Moreover, a contract establishing absolute authority for one party and unlimited obedience for the other is self-contradictory. Where there is no mutual obligation among equal participants, contractual exchange is inconceivable: "There is peace in dungeons, but is that enough to make dungeons desirable? The Greeks lived in peace in the cave of Cyclops awaiting their turn to be devoured."[20]

But the basis of Rousseau's objections to Grotius is that every contract between ruled people and ruling magistrate involves an alienation of liberty itself: "To renounce freedom is to renounce one's humanity, one's rights as a man and equally one's duties." There is no possible indemnity "for one who renounces everything. Indeed such a renunciation is contrary to man's very nature; for if you take away all freedom of the will, you strip a man's action of all moral significance." The timing, extent, or expected benefit in every surrender of liberty to others is not the issue. Every transfer of liberty to others, however voluntary or revocable, is incompatible with natural right and contrary to the common end of fellowship—man's

20. *Ibid*, pp. 352–353, 355–356.

absolute liberty. Contractual alienation yields not equal citizens with binding ties but slaves with competing particular interests: "There will always be a great difference between subduing a multitude and ruling a society. If one man successively enslaves many separate individuals, no matter how numerous, he and they would never bear the aspect of anything but a master and his slaves, not at all that of a people and their ruler [*chef*]; an aggregation, perhaps, but certainly not an association, for they would neither have a common good nor be a body politic. Even if such a man were to enslave half the world, he would remain a private individual, and his interest, always at variance with that of the others, would never be more than a personal [*privé*] interest." Indeed, justifying any contractual surrender of liberty to others, of whatever extent and at whatever time and price, is simply another way of defending the idea of natural slavery. Before Grotius, Hobbes, and Caligula, Aristotle had said that "men were not at all equal by nature, since some were born for slavery and others born to be masters." Aristotle was correct, Rousseau continued, but he mistook the effect for the cause: "Anyone born in slavery is born for slavery—nothing is more certain. Slaves, in their bondage, lose everything, even the desire to be free. They love their servitude even as the companions of Ulysses loved their life as brutes. But if there are slaves by nature, it is only because there has been slavery against nature. Force made the first slaves; and their cowardice perpetuates their slavery."[21]

21. *Ibid.*, pp. 356, 359, 353. Rousseau's rejection of contractual authorization is grounded in extensive arguments against what he calls four "false notions of the social bond" among citizens: the extension of parental authority, the claims of men of wealth, the right of the strongest, and "prescription" or "tacit acquiescence." See *Geneva Manuscript* (P, III, 297–305); *Social Contract*, pp. 352–359, 365–367. See also *Letters from the Mountain*, pp. 806–807; *Émile*, pp. 836–839. For a view which recognizes that Rousseau's own contract cannot be a "pact of submission" but argues that Rousseau misunderstood and was unfair to modern natural law theorists like Grotius and Pufendorf, see Derathé, *Rousseau et la science politique*, pp. 48–52, 71–84, 181–182, 192–207, 269–272.

There is, of course, a "contract" which, because he found it appropriate to self-governing citizens, Rousseau respected. It is a curious contract. A people, contracting with itself, agrees only to obey itself. It has "alienated" its liberty to itself alone. It has established its own "supreme authority," the sovereignty of a corporate legislative will, which preserves rather than destroys the moral or political equality of presocial nature. The contract involves no "real renunciation" of liberty because the corporate whole always legislates for itself directly and because the people have not authorized any men to govern or command in any manner: Rousseau's contract assures literal self-government. Each participant in this social contract, "while uniting himself with the others, obeys no one but himself, and remains as free as before." This "act" of political self-definition precludes all other contracts and all other kinds of alienation. It precludes everything which establishes a ruled and ruling arrangement between men. The sovereignty of the corporate whole must remain absolute and indivisible because the liberty of artificial individuals must be absolute and indivisible. In contrast to the contractual transfer of liberty to magistrates in the *Discourse on Inequality*, the *Social Contract* conceives a subsequent, noncontractual establishment of "legitimate government" by self-governing citizens. Because this does not involve the delegation of authority to govern, it cannot involve the alienation of liberty: magistrates are never entitled to legislate for or to command subjects who are obligated to obey. Because free men never "undertake to obey a master," legitimate government does not govern, in the usual sense: "the supreme authority can no more be modified than it can be alienated; to limit it is to destroy it. It is absurd and self-contradictory that the sovereign should give itself a superior."[22]

Popular sovereignty, the only "authority" Rousseau per-

22. *Social Contract*, pp. 375, 360, 432–433.

mitted, means direct legislative action by all citizens. Those who exercise it are truly independent of the will of others. Their natural equality is redeemed. The sovereignty of a people, "being nothing other than the exercise of the general will, can never be alienated; and . . . the sovereign, which is simply a collective being, cannot be represented by anyone but itself." The essential condition for the creation and maintenance of a common life of self-governing citizens, men "as free as before," is the corporate society's inalienable "authority" to legislate directly for itself. Obedience to fundamental laws and to the *moeurs* of a society assures that obedience to the very conditions of common life which avoids the enslaving authority of men. So also must all members of a political society make additional civil laws directly. One day's society of self-governing citizens cannot even be bound in principle by the civil laws it willed yesterday: "it is not only through [civil] law that the state keeps alive; it is through legislative power. Yesterday's law is not binding today, but for the fact that silence gives a presumption of tacit consent and the sovereign is taken to confirm perpetually the laws which is does not abrogate. . . . Everything which it has once declared to be its will, it wills always," unless it revokes it.[23] Once again, limited authority in a constitutionalist sense, or even popular sovereignty limited by law, is not an issue. Life in common for free men originates in and remains in principle a daily plebiscite. It avoids every form of slavery. Liberty is permanent and unmediated participation in legislation. Liberty is literal self-government. Each day among self-governing citizens is a celebration of the social bond of their fellowship, a renewal of their common life which establishes and preserves their equality.

Rousseau's hostility to the very idea of representative government is a final, direct instance of his anarchistic imperative, for his concern was not the scope, responsibility, or account-

23. *Ibid.*, pp. 368, 424.

ability of representative political authority, but the division between those who command and those who obey.[24] He insisted that the English people were mistaken to think themselves free. They authorized enslavement when they selected legislative representatives. The English people were free only at that instant they assembled to elect representatives and before an actual choice of representatives was made: "In the brief moments of its freedom, the English people makes such a use of that freedom that it deserves to lose it." That the size of modern, complex states often dictates a representation of the general will by governing magistrates means that few contemporary societies have true laws. The idea of legislative representation is itself a modern one, coming from the "iniquitous and absurd" feudal scheme of government "under which the human race is degraded and which dishonors the name of man."

In ancient republics representatives and the very word *representative* were unknown: "Among the Greeks, all that the people had to do, it did itself; it was continuously assembled in the market place. The Greek people . . . was not at all avaricious; slaves did the work, its chief concern was its free-

24. For contrasting views, which argue that Rousseau's hostility to representation is based upon the likely independence of representatives from their constituents, the influence wielded by hereditary monarchs, the corruption of electoral systems, or the limited suffrage of his day, see T. H. Green, *Lectures on the Principles of Political Obligation* (London, 1960), pp. 83–86; Cobban, *Rousseau and the Modern State*, pp. 39–45, 49; Masters, *Political Philosophy of Rousseau*, pp. 410–413; Derathé, *Rousseau et la science politique*, pp. 266–280; Olivier Krafft, *La Politique de Jean-Jacques Rousseau: Aspects méconnus* (Paris, 1958), pp. 72–84; Plamenatz, *Man and Society*, I, 399–403, 409–411. These considerations do account for the reservations of philosophes who admired English institutions. See Voltaire, *Philosophical Letters*, letters 8–9; Baron d'Holbach, *Système social; ou, principes naturels de la morale et de la politique du l'influence du gouvernement sur les moeurs*, 2 vols. (Paris, 1795), II, 338–342. For the view that Rousseau was not opposed to representative government as such because he rejected only a representation of popular sovereignty, see Hall, *Rousseau*, pp. 149–150.

dom." Rousseau unfalteringly continued: "What? Is freedom to be maintained only with the support of slavery? Perhaps. The two extremes meet. Everything outside nature has its disadvantages, civil society more than all the rest. There are some situations so unfortunate that one can preserve one's freedom only at the expense of someone else; and the citizen can be perfectly free only if the slave is absolutely a slave. Such was the situation of Sparta. You peoples of the modern world, you have no slaves, but you are slaves yourselves; you pay for their liberty with your own." Perhaps Rousseau implied a distinction between slaves attached to the household and slaves of the state. But this too would be inconsistent with his demand for radical equality. How could the members of a common life be free if citizenship were exclusive and if citizens depended upon the obedience of their slaves? Rousseau immediately recognized this: "I do not mean by all this to suggest that slaves are necessary or that the right of slavery is legitimate, for I have proved the contrary. I simply state the reasons why peoples of the modern world, believing themselves to be free, have representatives, and why peoples of the ancient world did not. However that may be, the moment a people adopts representatives it is no longer free; it no longer exists."[25]

Rousseau's unqualified rejection of legislative representation illustrates his objection to every surrender of liberty of whatever extent, sequence, and apparent benefit. It also suggests the difficulties Rousseau had in locating a society of self-governing citizens in historical time and space—except of course at the midpoint of the "hypothetical history" in the *Discourse on*

---

25. *Social Contract*, pp. 430–431. See also *Government of Poland*, pp. 975, 979. However, Rousseau applauded what he called the "liberties" of redress some English nobles could claim against their monarch, in comparison to what the Genevan constitution permitted. *Letters from the Mountain*, pp. 874–879. Similarly, Bomston contrasts an idle and tyrannical aristocracy with that true nobility in England who are the "friends," not the "slaves," of the English monarch. *La Nouvelle Héloise*, (P, II, 168–171).

Inequality and among mountain villagers near Neufchâtel before the introduction of a modern theater. In any case, the political disaster of any representation of the general will is never a mere matter of the failure of designated officials to be responsible to their constituents. It is a matter of the illegitimacy of representation itself. Liberty, consequently, is possible only in small communities where all citizens know one another and are able to gather together in the public square for legislative assemblies.[26] This limit upon size is dictated not by the consideration that the voice of a ruler must be audible to citizens but by the anarchistic imperative: there must be no division of common life between rulers and ruled.

Montesquieu's conception of republican government required a partial delegation of popular sovereignty to representatives in order to avoid the "extreme equality" of disorder.[27] Rousseau's refusal to permit any representation of the general will, or any contractual authorization of governing magistrates by citizens, was designed to guarantee extreme equality. Whenever the general will is represented, men are necessarily obedient to the particular will of magistrates who form an exclusive group less than the corporate whole; thus, no members of the whole are self-governing. The instrument for their freedom, the sovereign "authority" of all members, becomes an instrument enslaving them to particular persons. If by chance the particular will of governing magistrates corresponds to the demands of the general will, if magistrates conscientiously attempt to interpret the general will of civic virtue, then representation is simply unnecessary. When the general will is opposed to the particular will of magistrates, then a rule of pure force exists; and an entire people is enslaved to the will of a master dependent in turn upon the will of those who formally obey. Opposition between the general will and the particular

26. *Social Contract*, pp. 390, 397, 405, 425–427, 429, 431.
27. Montesquieu, *Spirit of the Laws*, bk. 8, chaps. 1–4, in *Oeuvres complètes*, II, 349–353.

will of governing magistrates is unavoidable, Rousseau added, because the particular will "inclines by its very nature towards partiality, and the general will towards equality." A society of free men can be "governed" in such a way as to achieve their common good of equality, but not by magistrates: "The general will alone can direct the forces of the state in accordance with that end which the state has been established to achieve—the common good." This common good, the shared moral purpose of all indivisible members of the body politic, must be the absolute liberty of each citizen in all of his inescapable engagements with his fellow citizens. Man's perfection in society remains the social equivalent of his natural origin, namely his political independence: "If a people promises simply and solely to obey [other men], it dissolves itself by that very pledge; it ceases to be a people; for once there is a master, there is no longer a sovereign, and the body politic is therefore annihilated."[28]

This inalienable sovereignty of the corporate whole over itself, this recourse to the general in preference to the particular, is one instance of the manner in which nonindividualism and anarchism converge within Rousseau's political thought: a united and disciplined common life alone assures literal self-government for all artificial individuals.

28. *Social Contract*, pp. 368–369. See also *ibid.*, p. 391; *Geneva Manuscript*, pp. 294–297, 305–308.

PART THREE

A UNITY AND DISCIPLINE OF COMMON LIFE

CHAPTER 7

The Virtuous Citizen: Sincerity

The first two parts of this study have located the basis for Rousseau's political philosophy in his nonindividualism and anarchism. Both are essential. If one ignores Rousseau's understanding of the organic character of social engagement which takes individuals to be fellow creatures of a common life, then realizing absolute liberty would involve social disengagement and dispersal. Simple exile or respected solitude would be the necessary conditions for achieving liberty. If one ignores Rousseau's radically egalitarian imperative, his ideas appear haphazard and contradictory, and Rousseau becomes a curiously recalcitrant companion to Montesquieu, Hume, and Burke.

The two principles cannot be separated. Nonindividualism and anarchism converge in Rousseau's understanding of the scope and character of politics and of the circumstances of common life essential for the realization of absolute liberty. Artificial individuals are themselves public men. All areas of shared experience, from the limited circumference of the family to the larger circumference of the state, are also public; a threat of enslavement haunts every form of social engagement. Because social men are neither entitled to command nor obligated to obey one another, absolute liberty must be a shared condition of their common life. The "perfect independence" of every artificial individual must be the political equality of their common life. Rousseau often called this liberty "civil" or "moral," in contrast to the lawless independence of bestial men in a presocial state of nature.

More specifically, Rousseau's nonindividualism and anarchism converge in the conception of a unity and discipline of common life. This conception encompasses various contingent and instrumental arrangements assuring absolute liberty for public men: social division of every form is slavery. Citizens can remain independent of the will of one another only when their common life has a solidarity, a simple, vigorous, and unmediated concreteness. Rousseau thus promulgated the most general society and the general will in preference to the particular societies and particular wills which enslave all men. As we have seen, the unrepresentable and indivisible sovereignty of a people avoids a division of the body politic between magistrates who govern and subjects who are governed; similarly, every member of society remains masterless only when their common life is a united and disciplined whole. A failure to conform to one's general will signifies the beginning of enslaving struggles for mastery: the members of a corporate whole no longer command and obey themselves simultaneously when common life is divided.

At the center of this conception of a united and disciplined common life is Rousseau's idea of civic virtue. The self-governing individual is a special type of social man, a virtuous citizen. His actions express his conscientious adherence to his indestructible general will. The virtue of this citizen is his passionate affection for his fellow citizens and for the reciprocal conditions of their common life. Rejecting particular desires, the virtuous citizen remains absolutely free, continuously confirming and celebrating his indebtedness to the common life he shares with other self-governing citizens. When public men together are citizens of the whole, each "will of all" closely approximates their general will: truly virtuous citizens make and obey rules, but they never rule or are ruled by one another.

Rousseau's demand for a unity and discipline of common life does not alter his sensitivity to variety and national genius. In some societies, because of pernicious customs and beliefs, unity and discipline are difficult to achieve. Most modern men are doomed to servitude and degradation. Hence Rousseau's characteristic attitude toward disunity. He condemned all the various obstacles or distractions that interfere with the performance of civic duties in the societies we know. But when it is impossible to obtain self-government, this is not because of some necessary incompatibility between the abstract and the concrete, or between ideal demand and factual circumstance: common life is as essential in the realization of liberty as in its denial. Moreover, on other appropriate occasions, Rousseau intended his recommendations and exhortations to cauterize historical change, to postpone an accelerating fragmentation of the body politic. Historical circumstances, then, do vary the form, scope, possibility, and expected benefits of Rousseau's demand for a united and disciplined common life. But Rousseau's general criticisms and intentions were everywhere identical, for the question of social man's liberty or slavery is always at stake. The only possibility for most contemporary men, because they are possessed by ambitious mimicry, is some sort of palliative that postpones conclusive fratricide.[1]

1. Rousseau's pervasive pessimism is argued in Jouvenel, "Essai," pp. 18–20, 35–37, 138–141. See also Jouvenel, "Rousseau the Pessimistic Evolutionist," pp. 83–96, which, however, takes the *Social Contract* and *Emile* to be "recipes" for avoiding further deterioration for the Corsican "patriot" and the "private" Frenchman; and Jouvenel, "Théorie des formes de gouvernement chez Rousseau," *Le Contrat social*, VI (Nov.-Dec. 1962), 345–351, which employs *government* and *authority* synonymously. See also Iring Fetscher, "Rousseau, auteur d'intention conservatrice et d'action révolutionnaire," in *Rousseau et la philosophie politique*, pp. 51–75, which discusses the pessimism underlying Rousseau's Corsican and Polish proposals but sees the ideas of *Emile* providing salvation for some contemporary individuals. For the view that Rousseau was both optimist and pessimist, see Starobinski, *Rousseau*, pp. 16–24. For the view that Rousseau was a quasi-Marxist who believed in

Rousseau's apostrophes to the forgotten citizen and to civic virtue and his hostility to vain particular wills are a recognition that public men can avoid slavery only by a united and disciplined common life. Though common life is itself unnatural and accidental, it is consecrated because it alone assures the dignity of man, his liberty. Civic virtue is only a means, albeit the essential means, to realizing absolute liberty. Man is naturally good, but not naturally virtuous; only liberty, as perfect independence of the will of others, carries the sanction of natural right. Further, the demands of this instrumental civic virtue often conflict with natural goodness. Criminals are punished and enemies are killed in war; both actions go against man's natural pity for his species. The civic duty to perform useful work completely repudiates natural indolence. Risking one's life while defending the fatherland contradicts man's natural love of self.

The reasoning behind Rousseau's demand for social unity also led him to repudiate as both enslaving and illusory the various "free markets" defended by traditional liberals. Their

---

sudden, perhaps revolutionary redemption through contemporary man's capacity to "reassert himself over history," see Einaudi, *Early Rousseau*, pp. 11, 23–25, 40–41, 142, 153–161, 233–237, 242–278.

Rousseau asserted that there can be no "remedy" for contemporary slavery; it is impossible to "restore men to their original equality, that preserver of innocence and the source of all virtue." *Observations* (P, III, 56). See also *Moral Letters* (P, IV, 1088). As the "Frenchman" in *Rousseau juge de Jean-Jacques* observes: "[In all his writings Rousseau] has shown us the human species better, wiser, and happier in its primitive constitution and blind, unhappy, and wicked as it draws farther away from it. His aim is to redress the errors of our judgment in order to slow down the progress of our vices, and to show us that where we seek glory and brilliance we find in fact only error and misery. But human nature never retrogresses, and we can never go back to the times of innocence and equality once we have left them." *Rousseau juge de Jean-Jacques* (P, I, 934–935). Similarly, Rousseau feared and thought inevitable revolutions which could only worsen contemporary *moeurs*. See *Discourse on Inequality* (P, III, 189–191); *Emile* (P, IV, 468). See also Jouvenel, "Essai," pp. 79–84, and Benda, "Rousseau's Early Discourses," *passim*.

reliance, within some limits, upon competitive exchange, their applause for social fragmentation and for eccentricity and originality, and their fears of suffocating uniformity and monopolistic concentration—these could not be Rousseau's views. To Rousseau competitive disunity, however anonymous or unofficial, is slavery because competitors must depend upon the will of one another. In some circumstances, Rousseau defended a harsh and even vindictive discipline for men whom particular passions consume or who only nominally attend to civic duties. Greater enslavement is always possible. Hence Rousseau is thought to condone, or even require, an authoritarian suppression of individuals, the surrender of personal identity and eccentric passion before the oppressive monopoly of the state. These interpretations ignore fundamental aspects of Rousseau's thought: he demanded literal self-government; he insisted that the realization of absolute liberty be a shared condition of common life; he found insignificant the existence of magistrates and civil laws to the achievement—but not the failure—of a united and disciplined common life; and he attended to varieties of historical time and space.

Accusations of repressive "collectivism" also result from imposing individualism upon Rousseau's thought, especially the idea that society is a naturally fluid aggregation of discrete individuals and groups. Those who approach Rousseau's thought using distinctions between individual and society or private liberty and public order, dismiss him for failing to locate individual liberty in processes of action and reaction among the separate parts, each of which is a "private citizen" exercising opportunities for unaided association, bargaining, persuasion, and competition with other private men.[2]

2. Vaughan, pursuing the contradiction he sees between Rousseau's early individualism and later collectivism, finds that the latter works "subordinate the individual ruthlessly to the community at large." Rousseau's thought contains "two strands" which are "necessarily inconsistent." He is a "champion of individual liberty [and] . . . of the

In a society, self-interest is particular, and, because it derives from membership in society, cannot be private. The motives of public men, whether vicious or virtuous, are not per

sovereignty of the State": the moment a social contract is concluded "the individual ceases to be his own master" because "his life, his will, his very individuality are merged in those of the community." Unlike Locke's contract which "is expressly designed to preserve and confirm the rights of the individual," Vaughan continues, "that of Rousseau's ends, and is intended to end, in their destruction." Vaughan, ed., *Political Writings*, I, 4, 21, 47–48, 70. Similar views dominate nineteenth-century interpretations of Rousseau by Constant, Proudhon, Tocqueville, Guizot, Lamartine, Lemaître, Lasserre, Faguet, Duguit, and Vecchio. See Derathé, introduction to the *Social Contract* (P, III, cxiii–cxiv); J. L. Talmon, *Political Messianism: The Romantic Phase* (New York, 1963), pp. 317–334; and Roger Bonnard, "Les Idées politiques de Jean-Jacques Rousseau," *Revue du droit public et de la science politique en France et à l'étranger*, XXVII (Oct.–Dec. 1907), 784–794.

More recently, Watkins has contrasted "liberal" and "individualist" aspects of Rousseau's thought involving Kantian "rationalist" ideas of individual moral responsibility and perfectibility with an "authoritarian" or "totalitarian" principle which distrusts "the creative potentialities of ordinary individuals" to maintain social order. Hence Rousseau's recourse to the lawgiver (or a "scientifically competent elite"). The lawgiver is not a despot. His "institutions . . . [are], however, strictly totalitarian in character," because of the "minimization of private interests and activities [in] the complete absorption of the individual in the collective life of the state" and because all "forms of private association," "private property," "private religion," and "private amusements" are abolished or discouraged. Watkins, introduction, *Rousseau: Political Writings*, pp. xix–xxxv. Talmon identifies Rousseau's position with the sensationalism of the philosophes, whose ideas are driven by that "vague Messianic expectation," "secular religion," or "rationalist politics" which offers mankind "one universally valid pattern." Rousseau's "original individualism" of private rights to life, liberty, and property is lost in the "positive pattern" of a harmonious social order. Rousseau's "fundamental problem" of "the individual versus the social order" yields a "bundle of contradictions" in which Rousseau is "yearning to return to nature, given to reverie, in revolt against all social conventions" on the one hand and "the preacher of discipline and the submergence of the individual in the collective entity" on the other. Because the general will provides an "objective" or "external" criterion "incompatible with obeying one's own will," Rousseau was Robespierre's teacher: "Rousseau's sovereign is the externalized general will and . . . stands for essentially the same [order] as the natural harmonious order. In marrying this

sonal, exclusive, and private. The lonely egotist, prudently
calculating his long-range interests without overt influence
from fellow citizens and disregarding the general will, deceives

concept with the principle of popular sovereignty, and popular self-
expression, Rousseau gave rise to totalitarian democracy. . . . If the
people does not will [the general will], it must be made to will it, for
the general will is latent in the people's will." J. L. Talmon, *The Origins
of Totalitarian Democracy* (New York, 1960), pp. 19, 26, 36–40, 23, 43.
Two additional, somewhat milder accusations are James I. McAdam,
"Rousseau and the Friends of Despotism," *Ethics*, LXXIV (Oct. 1963),
34–43, and Sergio Cotta, "La Position du problème de la politique chez
Rousseau," in *Etudes sur le* Contrat social, pp. 177–190. McAdam argues
that Rousseau's state, like Locke's, was intended to be a legal fiction
whose members, as the subject of rights and duties, exist as a quasi-
entity in the eyes of the law. But Rousseau, failing to " 'place law above
men,' " became a champion of the very despotism he rejected, that
representation of popular sovereignty defended by Hobbes, Grotius, and
Pufendorf. Because the decisions of a majority "must be taken as the
decision of the general will and regarded as law," a "sovereign majority"
overrules "conscientious objectors." Rousseau was preoccupied with a
"legislative" liberty of direct participation, rather than Lockeian
personal liberties. All rights are irrevocably "surrendered" to the state.
See also Eméry, *Rousseau l'annonciateur*, pp. 131–134, 167–168; John
Charvet, *The Social Problem in the Philosophy of Rousseau* (London,
1974), pp. 33–34, 71, 85–86, 95, 98, 107, 124–128, 139, 146.
    Finally, the most dogged accusation. Crocker argues that Rousseau
"opened the door to collectivism and totalitarianism—if he indeed did
not walk through it": the suppression of individuals and the total transfer
of their rights to a "collectivity," the failure to allow for minority
rights, the absence of political parties, and an educational program of
thought control and conditioning reveal a genuine, if partially unintended, "sacrifice of the individual to the collective whole." Crocker,
"The Relation of Rousseau's Second *Discours* and the *Contrat social*,"
pp. 38–44. Elsewhere, Rousseau's state becomes the "absolute of totalitarianism." In contrast to Diderot, who trusted the competence of
natural reason and preserved individual rights independent of coercive
law, Rousseau believed that whatever is willed is right, that the expressed will of society is "*always* and *necessarily* in conformity to the
general good and so to justice." Lester G. Crocker, "The Priority of
Justice or Law," *Yale French Studies*, XXVIII (Fall–Winter, 1961–62),
34–42. Crocker also argues that Rousseau's totalitarianism is not a question of historical influence, for his influence among democratic movements has been very great. Rather totalitarianism is the "internal sense"
or "profound direction of his thought," which Crocker contrasts with
that "pluralism" of a "liberal society" which places an "accent" on

himself if he thinks he labors alone and unaided. He fails to recognize debts to common tastes, standards of pleasure, and notions of worth. Similarly, the general will does not issue from an unfamiliar, external source. In the inescapable common life of a historical corporate whole, the general will can be active or mute, but others can never create or impose it.

"individualism": Crocker appraises Rousseau's denial of privacy, reliance upon thought control and dictatorial guidance, and preference for an absolutist general will in the context of the "rights of the state or collectivity" on the one hand and the "rights of individuals or minorities" on the other. Crocker, "Rousseau et la voie du totalitarisme," in *Rousseau et la philosophie politique*, pp. 99–136. Crocker has brought together these views in *Rousseau's Social Contract: An Interpretive Essay* (Cleveland, 1968). Rousseau's thought is defined by the "conflict between man's nature as an ego and as a social being, or between the individual and society" (p. 179). Crocker contrasts an "open or pluralistic society" with Rousseau's recourse to that "duplicity, manipulation, and reflexive conditioning" (p. 35) which leave "in the personality no sanctuary that is inviolable" (pp. 48–49). Rousseau's state capitalism "outlines the idea of what Chinese communists call communes" (p. 27). His social contract involves a "surrender of the individual as complete and absolute as in Hobbes," for "freedom is swallowed up by this collective monolith" (pp. 60, 61). A general will "comes out of the vote" (p. 112n); and, as a "metaphysical entity existing independently of any actual wills" (p. 88), the general will requires deception and thought control by a permanent lawgiver (pp. 50–61, 73–87, 101, 164–166, 180). Rousseau himself "incarnates the authoritarian's attitude toward men and the world" (p. 163); he had a "deep-seated *need* for order, that is for a rigid value system" (p. 5). Rousseau was "a perfect model of what we now refer to as the 'authoritarian personality'" (p. 36), and he exhibited "virtually" all the sixteen characteristics of the authoritarian personality Crocker lists (p. 186). One paragraph of this study (pp. 94–95) discusses Rousseau's notion of legitimate government in the *Social Contract;* no mention is made of Rousseau's distinction between sovereignty and government and of that principled opposition to monarchical government which preclude a permanent lawgiver.

For a study addressed to the charge of totalitarianism, see Chapman, *Rousseau—Totalitarian or Liberal?*. Chapman sees competing liberal and totalitarian aspects, with the former predominant. He contrasts ideas of moral freedom and a deliberative process (which makes a general will) with an idea of political liberty that leads to totalitarian social integration. See also R. A. Leigh, "Liberté et autorité dans le *Contrat social*," in *Jean-Jacques Rousseau et son oeuvre*, pp. 249–262, which argues for a "balance" between individual liberty and political order in Rousseau's

The composite personality of each socially dependent creature must always include the "unchanging" and "indestructible" general will of common life, "the moral self common to the whole."

Even when common life is disintegrating, actions spring from particular wills deriving from social dependence. Competition and war are never collisions among self-defined parts in a free market. Both internecine rivalry and war follow historically (as in the *Discourse on Inequality*) the loss of a disciplined common life: *amour-propre* is not a natural attribute of man. Whether in liberty and civic virtue or in slavery and degradation, artificial individuals retain their public character. Enslaved, debased men suffer the imperfection of their social bond, not the absence of one.

Self-mastery, then, is self-government for a social man who wants to remain independent of the will of others. Because natural right demands absolute liberty for every composite self, there is a hierarchy of particular and general wills, with the most general society and the general will at the apex. Self-government requires sincere obedience to one's general will: only in a unified and disciplined fellowship can public man continue "to obey himself alone" and remain as free as he was in the state of nature. Conversely, a particular will is self-inflicted violence, an abuse of natural liberty. A member of a society of dismembered parts cannot be at peace with himself because loyalty to a particular identity, divisive as a result of its partial nature, necessarily enslaves a man to the will of others. The particular will expresses a desire for political in-

---

thought. Because the object as well as the source of the general will must be general and because "total alienation" in the *Social Contract* is merely a definition of political right, a "natural right" of religious conscience survives in civil society; an unconfiscated "private sector" of "particular wills" constitutes the persisting "invulnerability of a citizen's private life" outside the scope of popular sovereignty. In short, liberal individualist tenets are also used to refute accusations of totalitarianism.

equality, or it would not be a particular will; and the individual who expresses it is the first victim of the situation to which he aspires. The general will is the will to be and remain free.

Reciprocated feelings and proud memories, the renewal of social affections, and the rehearsal of patriotic sentiments mark the common life of virtuous citizenship. True citizenship is not simply the expression of an enlightened state of mind. Reason, which is not natural to man and develops late in the evolution of social men, is itself passionate. When unaccompanied by virtuous sentiments, it cannot be right reason, for then it is the instrument of particular passions which estrange a man from himself and his fellow citizens. Rousseau argued against the forms and disguises in which the pernicious *amour-propre* of enslaved men appears, but not because the general will is either less passionate or more rational than any particular will. True, Rousseau often characterized the virtue of a self-governing citizen by distinguishing "reason," "natural law," and "conscience" from appetite and desire. But the superiority of the general will lies in the serviceability of the passion it embodies. The general will has as its end the welfare of the corporate whole and all its parts in their capacities as self-governing citizens.

When the temptation to profit at the expense of fellow citizens is rejected, then the interest of a citizen, his true and most general interest as a creature of the inclusive body politic, is identical with civic duty and civic fervor. The virtuous citizen is a whole man undivided by conflicting public identities. He has no need or desire to harm others and no reason to fear harm from his fellow citizens. With all true needs satisfied, he is immune to envy, vanity, contempt, and shame. He knows nothing of domination. Beyond that division of rulers and ruled which is slavery in every form within every society of whatever sort, the fulfillment of one citizen is the simultaneous perfection of his fellow citizens. The true profits, the absolute liberty and integrity of one citizen, do not spell a fellow citizen's loss or disgrace. Allegiance to one's fellow citizens is that loyalty to oneself, to one's new self, which transcends all problems of egoism and self-denial or selfishness and asceticism.

In short, for Rousseau society and nature need not clash. Nonindividualism and anarchism converge and are sustained in the demand for a united and disciplined common life, and in the relentless criticism of its absence. Self-governing social men are virtuous citizens, obedient to their highest and most noble passion alone, their general will of civic virtue.

Natural Goodness and Civic Virtue

Rousseau employed the idea of civic virtue initially in his *Discourse on the Sciences and Arts* to indict the slavery and degradation of his "enlightened age." But it is once again the *Discourse on Inequality* that systematically exhibits his basic principles. Natural men, "not having among themselves any kind of moral relationship or known duties, could be neither good nor evil, and had neither vices nor virtues"; but, as we have seen, there is an important sense in which Rousseau insisted that this presocial man is naturally good. Natural *amour de soi* cannot prejudice the liberty and preservation of other men in a state of nature. Moreover, man is a naturally compassionate beast, capable of an "inner impulse of commiseration." This "natural virtue" is his instinctive repugnance at the sight of the suffering or perishing of any sensitive being, especially a member of his species. Only during accidents of occasional and forgotten conflict, when one man is temporarily threatened and compelled to prefer himself over others, do natural men harm one another.[3]

The inconsistency of Rousseau's terms here is a bit awkward.

3. *Discourse on Inequality*, pp. 152, 126. See also *Letters to Malesherbes* (Jan. 1762; P, I, 1135–1136); *Rousseau juge de Jean-Jacques*, pp. 934–935.

Clearly, however, Rousseau both contrasted and connected the natural goodness of presocial man with the civic virtue of some artificial men. He contrasted the innocent and disinterested passivity of man who, in the state of nature, does not harm others and is ignorant of vice, with the positive duties and conscientious compassion of virtuous citizens. He connected the citizen's compassionate regard for the well-being of his fellow citizens—his conscience—to the passions comprising man's natural goodness. Virtuous passions "flow" from the natural passions of pity and love of self. The virtue of generosity among fellow citizens is pity applied to the weak; clemency and humanity are pity applied to the guilty and to mankind. "Benevolence and even friendship are, rightly understood, the products of a constant pity fixed on a particular object: for is desiring that someone not suffer anything but desiring that he be happy?" Love of self is "a natural sentiment which inclines every animal to watch over its own preservation, and which, directed in man by reason and modified by pity, produces humanity and virtue."[4]

In *Emile* Rousseau developed the contrast between natural goodness and civic virtue. Social man requires sincere willfulness or a conscientious self-discipline even to refrain from harming others: "The good man is good only so long as he finds it pleasant; goodness falls to pieces and perishes at the shock of human passions; the good man is good only to himself." Although the virtuous citizen remains passionate, his obedience to his highest will requires studious mastery of particular passions: "The word *virtue* is derived from the word *strength* [*force*]; strength is the foundation of all virtue. Virtue belongs to a creature weak by nature and strong by will; that is the merit of the honorable man; and though we

4. *Discourse on Inequality*, pp. 126, 155, 219. See also *Letter to Beaumont* (Mar. 1763; P, IV, 935–937); *Fragments on the State of Nature* (P, III, 476–478); *Fragments on Honor and Virtue* (P, III, 504–505); preface to *Narcisse* (P, II, 971n).

call God good, we do not call him virtuous because He does good without effort." The virtuous man, then, "follows his reason, his conscience; he does his duty; he is his own master and nothing can distract him from his duty." Rousseau added that you cannot distinguish between those passions which are lawful and those which must be resisted because they are unlawful: "All are good when we remain their masters; all are bad if we are dominated by them. . . . We cannot resist feeling or not feeling passions, but we can rule ourselves. Every sentiment under our control is lawful; those which control us are criminal."[5]

To obtain self-mastery in this fashion is to obey the general will of civic virtue alone. Social man's most comprehensive and therefore noblest passion in that for civic virtue, an expanded love of self and an expanded compassion that have become a fervent love of one's fellow citizens and one's civic duty: "Only with passions can we control our passions; their rule must control their tyranny, and nature herself must always provide us with the means to control them." When the intentions and actions of artificial individuals are grounded in their general will alone, common life has unity and discipline. When natural equality is confirmed by a peaceful and compassionate fellowship that does not admit a distinction between ruler and ruled, each virtuous citizen secretly applies the word "everyone" to himself when he votes in a public assembly of a sovereign people. For the life of both the body politic and a member of the body politic is "the self common to the whole, the reciprocal sensibility and internal correspondence of all its parts. Where . . . the contiguous parts belong to one another only by juxtaposition, the man is dead or the state is dissolved."[6]

5. *Emile*, pp. 817–819. See also letter to Franquières (Jan. 15, 1769; P, IV, 1143–1144); *Rousseau juge de Jean-Jacques*, pp. 670–671; *Rêveries* (P, I, 1052–1054); *La Nouvelle Héloïse* (P, II, 682).

6. *Emile*, p. 654; *Discourse on Political Economy* (P, III, 245). See

The discipline of virtue among self-governing citizens, then, is more a matter of reciprocated feelings than of reason. Justice and goodness are "no mere abstract words, no mere moral conceptions formed by the understanding, but true affections of the heart clarified by reason, the orderly outcome of our primitive affections." Reason, unsupported by natural passions of pity or "conscience," cannot establish any "natural law" of civic duty among social men, and every notion of "natural right" among social men is chimerical if it does not rest upon some instinctive need of the human heart. Reason alone can neither prescribe virtuous action to a citizen nor assure virtuous action by his fellow citizens: "The wicked man takes advantage of the uprightness of the just and of his own injustice; he is happy to have everybody just except himself. . . . But when the enthusiasm of an expansive heart identifies me with my fellow creature, so that I share, so to speak, his feelings, so that I will not let him suffer lest I should suffer too, then I care for him because of my love of self; and the reason of the precept is found in nature herself, which inspires me with the desire for my own welfare wherever I may be." A political society of self-governing citizens is based not upon rational calculation or contractual exchange among unchanged, aggregated partners, but upon the shared feelings of benevolence awakened by common life.[7]

Reason develops when pernicious passions emerge, and remains the instrument of particular passions which, in dismembering common life, enslave all men: "Astronomy was born

---

also *Social Contract* (P, III, 363, 373, 429, 438–439); *Discourse on Political Economy*, p. 255.

7. *Emile*, pp. 522–523. See also *Geneva Manuscript* (P, III, 284–287); *Social Contract*, p. 363. The window breaking episode in *Emile* (pp. 333–338) dramatizes the inadequacy of unaided reason. In the larger European society, ordinary treaties and alliances only ratify states' relative power and conflicting interests: aggressive states take advantage of honest nations which rely upon mere reason. *Perpetual Peace* (P, III, 568–577), and *Critique of Perpetual Peace* (P, III, 592–595).

from superstition; eloquence from ambition, hate, flattery, and falsehood; geometry from avarice; physics from vain curiosity; all, even moral philosophy, from human pride." The "defect of origin" of these coveted sciences and arts is confirmed by applications of reason: "What would we do with arts without the luxury that nourishes them? Without the injustices of men, what purpose would jurisprudence serve? What would history become, if there were neither tyrants nor wars nor conspirators? In a word, who would want to spend his life in sterile speculations if each of us, consulting only the duties of man and the needs of nature, had time for nothing except his fatherland, the unfortunate and his friends?" The "prudent man" of contemporary society is also permanently estranged—from himself: "Reason engenders vanity and reflection fortifies it; reason turns man back upon himself, it separates him from all that bothers and afflicts him."[8]

The arts and sciences originate in the idleness of corrupt men and distract from civic duty. An "irreparable loss of time is the first injury they necessarily cause society. In politics as in ethics, it is a great evil to fail to do good, and every useless citizen may be considered a pernicious person." Illustrious scientists and philosophes, driven by an invidious "passion to

8. *Discourse on the Sciences and Arts* (P, III, 17–18); *Discourse on Inequality*, p. 156. See also *La Nouvelle Héloïse*, p. 359. Rousseau often equated a sincere dedication to civic duty with "the secret voice of conscience" and the cause of true "reason." *Discourse on Inequality*, pp. 116–117; *Geneva Manuscript*, p. 286. This usage underscores the viciousness of mere prudence: "The art of reasoning is never reason; often it is the abuse of it. Reason is the faculty of ordering all the faculties of our soul in conformity to the nature of things and their relationship with us." *Moral Letters*, p. 1090. See also *ibid.*, pp. 1095–1100; *Rousseau juge de Jean-Jacques*, pp. 861–862. For the argument that these considerations do not make Rousseau an "anti-rationalist," see Wright, *Meaning of Rousseau*, pp. 13–16, 25, 159; and Weil, "Rousseau et sa politique," pp. 5–6, 9–11, 13–15. For a discussion of Rousseau's notion of virtue as "primarily" a political or civic consideration, in contrast to the classic rationalist conception of virtue, see Strauss, *Natural Right and History*, pp. 255–264, 269–277.

gain distinction," undermine the habits of common life and consume the economic substance of society. They are "enemies of public opinion" who shatter solemn bonds. These "vain and futile declaimers go everywhere armed with their deadly paradoxes, undermining the foundations of faith, and annihilating virtue. They smile disdainfully at the old-fashioned words of fatherland and religion, and devote their talents and philosophy to destroying and debasing all that is sacred among men."[9] Among his many exhortations addressed to Genevan citizens, Rousseau cautioned against listening to "sinister interpretations and venomous discourses, the secret motives of which are often more dangerous than the acts that are their object."[10] And in the free society depicted in the *Social Contract*, deliberation is more important for what it might signify than for what it usually accomplishes. Long debates, dissension, and tumult in legislative assemblies often show the ascendency of vain, particular passions. Agreement might signify instead that a "will of all" corresponds to the general will. Nevertheless, citizens must never be fearful of speaking in assemblies; unanimity can also announce the lapse into servitude of free men who worship or curse a master in silent fear or flattery.[11]

9. *Discourse on the Sciences and Arts*, pp. 18–19. See also preface to *Narcisse*, pp. 968–969; *Observations*, pp. 40–41; *Last Response* (P, III, 72–75); *Moral Letters*, pp. 1088–1090; and letter to Voltaire (Sept. 10, 1755; CC, III, 164–166).

10. *Discourse on Inequality*, p. 117.

11. *Social Contract*, pp. 439–441. See also *Rêveries*, pp. 1026–1029, 1033. Rousseau exempted "geniuses" or a "few men" of great talent and unusual virtue, provided their studies are not allowed to corrupt through popularization the simple tastes of ordinary men. Such men are "exceptions which prove the rule." *Discourse on the Sciences and Arts*, pp. 28–30; preface to *Narcisse*, pp. 970–971. See also *Observations*, pp. 37–39; *Last Response*, p. 78. For an interpretation which partially identifies this exception with the classical distinction between knowledge and opinion and the notion of natural inequality, see Strauss, "On the Intention of Rousseau," pp. 461–469, 475n. Strauss detects two voices for two audiences in Rousseau's writings. For the view that Rousseau rejected only "wrong" philosophy and that his lawgiver is a kind of

It follows that Rousseau would view modern printing as the means to the immortalization of dangerous errors. Even good books are obviously worthless since in France, a home to academies and literary societies, the people are less virtuous and less happy than elsewhere in Europe.[12] Vain passions deceive. Ignorance is the only certain means of avoiding pernicious error.[13] Mere reason cannot persuade to virtue, as the arguments of priests involving interpretations of scripture and authentication of miracles testify. Ignoring their civic duties, clerics assume arrogant powers that only promote discord. Simple faith is replaced by obstinacy and vanity; battles and even massacres follow the publication of books on subjects of theological subtlety as each party to a dispute seeks to impose its views.[14] But the philosophe remains the prime example of lapsed citizenship, of civic indifference and sectarian squabbling. Philosophy is born at the courts of kings together with the desire to command.[15] A "taste for philosophy weakens all those ties of esteem and mutual benevolence which attach men to society." The pleasure of study "soon renders every other attachment insipid." The philosophe comes to despise the men he studies, so that *family* and *fatherland* become "words without meaning: he is neither parent, nor citizen, nor man; he is philosophe."[16]

Platonic philosopher, see Benda, "Rousseau's Early Discourses," pp. 16–20, 23–24.

12. Letter to Tscharner (Apr. 29, 1762; CC, X, 225–226).

13. *Discourse on the Sciences and Arts*, pp. 11–12, 26–28; preface to *Narcisse*, pp. 965–966; *Fragments on Luxury, Commerce, and the Arts* (P, III, 516).

14. *Observations*, pp. 45–49; *Letters from the Mountain* (P, III, 694–700, 724–726); *Letter to Beaumont*, pp. 969–975.

15. *Fragments on Honor and Virtue*, p. 505.

16. Preface to *Narcisse*, p. 967. See also *Observations*, pp. 55–56. Rousseau's most savage attack against the philosophe is *Rousseau juge de Jean-Jacques*, pp. 844–845, 862–865, 889–891, 964–969. The philosophes' intolerant ambition and "taste for domination" imitate that of their greatest enemies, the Jesuits; together, the two constitute a dual power

In educating his imaginary pupil to virtuous citizenship, Rousseau does not arrange for Emile to teach himself to read until the age of twelve. Emile ultimately acquires a basic scientific knowledge, but from simple and practical experiments of his own fabrication, seldom from books. Knowledge obtained from books is always superficial and impermanent. "I hate books," Rousseau added; "they only teach us to talk about things we know nothing about. It is said that Hermes engraved the elements of science on pillars, to shelter his discoveries from a deluge. If he had implanted them in men's heads, they would have been preserved by tradition. Well-trained minds are the monuments on which human knowledge is best engraved." The Savoyard vicar in *Emile* similarly expresses his disdain for "the European mania for books" and contentious learning. Either a man will learn his civic duty without depending upon the authority of writers and eloquent spokesmen or he is not capable of ever knowing it. Man must "reason" for himself in the depths of his conscience and read "the book of nature" himself; and true "reasoning" will always remain faithful to man's natural goodness. The Savoyard relates that he is often torn between particular and general demands, between his "reason which judges everything by selfish interest" and his "conscience," those "natural sentiments which speak for the common interest." And he concludes: "I serve God in the simplicity of my heart. I seek to know only what is important for my conduct. As for those dogmas which affect neither actions nor morality, and over which so many people torment themselves, I do not worry about them in the least."[17] In contrast, modern students, their minds adorned by useless knowl-

---

like that of Rome and Carthage. For discussions of Rousseau's self-promotion as "Citizen of Geneva" in exile, as an exemplary and exceptional free man, see Starobinski, *Rousseau*, pp. 43–44, 47–56; Burgelin, *La Philosophie de l'existence de Rousseau*, pp. 41–86, 91–103; and Groethuysen, *Rousseau*, pp. 52–66.

17. *Emile*, pp. 454, 620, 602, 627.

edge and their judgments corrupted by pernicious maxims of self-interest, can never become virtuous citizens. Because they are taught everything "except their duties," they will continue to write meaningless verse and learn to fashion specious arguments: "They will not know what the words magnanimity, equity, temperance, humanity, courage are; that sweet name fatherland will never strike their ear; and if they hear of God, it will be less to be awed than to be afraid of him." Today "we have physicists, geometers, chemists, astronomers, poets, musicians, painters; we no longer have citizens; or if a few of them are left, dispersed in our abandoned countryside, they perish there indigent and despised."[18] Yet contemporary life in common could be even worse. Modern societies would do well to retain present academies, colleges, libraries, and dramatic theaters rather than to suffer other, more pernicious effects of *amour-propre*. It is "better to live among knaves than brigands."[19]

Rousseau repeatedly proclaimed his admiration for Cato the Elder, especially compared with Socrates. Socrates was the better philosopher, but Cato was a true citizen: "Athens was already ruined, and Socrates no longer had a fatherland except the whole world. Cato always carried his fatherland in the depth of his heart; he lived for it alone, and could not bear to outlive it." Socrates "instructed a few individuals, opposed the Sophists, and died for truth; but Cato defended his state, its liberty, and its laws, against the conquerors of the world, and finally departed from the earth when he no longer had a fatherland to serve."[20] Similarly, Rousseau preferred the discipline of civic virtue at Sparta to the discordant indulgence of Athe-

18. *Discourse on the Sciences and Arts*, pp. 24, 26.
19. Preface to *Narcisse*, p. 972. See also *Letter to Beaumont*, pp. 965–968; *Rousseau juge de Jean-Jacques*, p. 935.
20. *Discourse on Political Economy*, p. 255. See Henri Gouhier, *Les Méditations metaphysiques de Jean Jacques Rousseau* (Paris, 1970), pp. 185–202.

nians. The Spartans wisely chased poets and scientists from their walls and "eternally put to shame a vain doctrine." Sparta was a "republic of demi-gods rather than men, so superior did their virtues seem to human nature." At Athens, in contrast, the tyrant Pisistratus gathered the writings of Homer; and subsequent preoccupations with frivolous arts and sciences assured the permanent ruin of the city and its citizens.[21] Athens was never in fact a democracy but was "a very tyrannical aristocracy, governed by learned men and orators."[22]

Enlightened Europeans are dissolute Athenians in modern dress. The very meaning of *city* is lost to modern men when *town* and *city* are thought identical and a citizen is mistakenly regarded as a resident burgher: "People forget that houses may make a town, while only citizens can make a city." Citizenship conveys the equal legal right and mutual obligation of every member to participate in the common affairs of the sovereign whole. The passions of civic virtue must be prominent in the life of all free peoples because the sovereign "authority" of a people over itself is everywhere the same. A society where citizens are subject only to the laws which inhere in common life and self-imposed civil laws is a republic, whatever its form of government, "for then, and then alone, does the public interest govern and then alone is the 'public thing'—the *res publica*—a reality."[23]

Here, as always, in Rousseau, politics involves a judgment of qualities, not the calculation of quantities. A society is never the sum of its parts. A free society is a kind of life, a fellowship of mutual compassion; for "geometrical precision has no

21. *Discourse on the Sciences and Arts*, p. 12.
22. *Discourse on Political Economy*, p. 246. See also *Discourse on the Sciences and Arts*, p. 30; *Last Response*, pp. 81–89, 94–95; *Fragments on Sparta and Rome* (P, III, 538–543). Rousseau's Sparta and Roman Republic were never the Sparta and Rome familiar to historians. See Rousseau's indirect admissions of this discrepancy in *Social Contract*, pp. 381n, 444.
23. *Social Contract*, pp. 361n–362n, 405, 379–380.

place in moral calculations." And "moral dimensions have no precise standard of measurement" in judgments of common life.[24] "Where is the fatherland?" Rousseau asked: "Neither men nor walls make up the fatherland; it is the laws, the *moeurs*, the customs, the government, the constitution, the manner of being which results from all these things. The fatherland is in the relationships of the state to its members; when these relationships change or are destroyed, the fatherland vanishes."[25] Citizens are free, or avoid slavery, only when they are truly virtuous: "The fatherland cannot exist without liberty, just as liberty cannot exist without virtue, nor virtue without citizens; . . . without citizens, there are only vicious slaves, beginning with the magistrates themselves."[26]

The Danger of Hypocrisy

The distintegration of common life begins when, to satisfy particular passions for invidious esteem, citizens seize property and establish a division of labor. When corrupt men fence off common land and claim exclusive possession of what they usurp, they create barriers between themselves and others, barriers which finally eradicate all traces of the compassion that once made possible the common life of families united in small nations. Hypocrisy is one inevitable vice. The political society subsequently established is in reality a clever swindle to protect property. Among vain competitors driven by the ambition to dominate, distrust and duplicity become accepted habits and destroy all prospects of equality. Everyone attempts to conceal his aggressive intentions and actions behind the pretense to benevolence and the common good.[27]

24. *Ibid.*, pp. 398, 419.
25. Letter to Pictet (Mar. 1, 1764; CC, XIX, 190). Here Rousseau concedes that his Genevan "fatherland" no longer exists and that the "country" which remains dishonors its memory. See also *Fragments on the Fatherland* (P, III, 534–536); *Observations*, p. 43.
26. *Discourse on Political Economy*, p. 259.
27. *Discourse on Inequality*, pp. 174–175.

In contrast, the sincerity of self-governing citizens, the genuine compassion of virtuous men for one another, permits no discrepancy between appearance and reality, neither a mask of philanthropy, nor the studied dishonesty of men of property, nor the pretense to humility in the man of letters. A self-governing citizen truly loves his civic duty, and his motives and deeds are completely visible. Citizens of a united whole seek their wellbeing in the unobstructed intimacy of common life, in that "ease of seeing through each other" which spares them many vices. True citizens are conscientious men who cannot be "deceived by the appearance of right" in the fashion of the "happy slaves" of our enlightened age who have "the semblance of all the virtues without the possession of any." Our ritual of agreeable politeness and professions of good will only conceal the *amour-propre* that motivates them: "Richness of attire may announce a wealthy man; . . . the healthy, robust man is known by other signs. It is in the rustic clothes of a farmer . . . that strength and vigor of the body will be found. Ornamentation is no less foreign to virtue, which is the strength and vigor of the soul. The good man is an athlete who likes to compete in the nude. He disdains all those vile ornaments which would hamper the use of his strength, most of which were invented only to hide some deformity."[28] Rousseau warned Genevans that the slightest disrespect for fellow citizens, the "least germ of bitterness or distrust," is a "deadly leaven" which will destroy their common liberty.[29] Furthermore, the best civil laws become the most dangerous when they bind insincere men who harbor jealousy of one another. Having no civil laws at all is better than furtive disobedience or nominal compliance based on fear of detection and punishment: "The worst of all abuses is to appear to obey the laws,

---

28. *Discourse on the Sciences and Arts*, pp. 7–8. Or, as Wolmar observes: "Propriety is only the mask of vice. Where virtue prevails, it is useless." *La Nouvelle Héloise*, p. 424.
29. *Discourse on Inequality*, p. 116.

only in order actually to break them with security." Among self-governing citizens, among truly virtuous citizens, "the first law must be to respect the other laws."[30]

Rousseau insisted repeatedly that the magistracy, civil laws, and especially the threat of criminal sanctions are tyrannic and inadequate means for achieving sincerity. The "harshness of punishments is only a vain device contrived by small minds in order to substitute terror for the respect which [magistrates] have no other means of obtaining." As men cannot be persuaded to virtue by books, they cannot be dissuaded from vice by criminal sanctions. Virtuous citizens unhesitatingly obey their laws because they do sincerely love their society as themselves; those who do not love society will always find a way of eluding the law.[31] In a free society few punishments are needed, not because pardons are frequent but because criminals are rare. Frequent punishments signify a government's oppression and moral impotence. Criminal sanctions temporarily restrain vicious men and punish violators but always without reforming corrupt hearts.[32]

At the same time, Rousseau sometimes proposed severe penalties for disobedience. Such penalties do not disregard his assertions as to the ineffectiveness of punishment or even his general statement in the *Social Contract* that no criminal should ever be executed, even as an example for others, if he can be left to live without endangering common life.[33] For there are occasions when disobedience threatens that solemn integrity of common life upon which liberty depends. On such occa-

---

30. *Discourse on Political Economy*, pp. 253, 249. For a comprehensive analysis of Rousseau's demand for sincerity, and his rejection of remoteness, concealment, and dissonance, see Starobinski, *Rousseau*, *passim*.

31. *Discourse on Political Economy*, pp. 249, 252–253.

32. *Government of Poland* (P, III, 965–966); *Constitutional Project for Corsica* (fragments) (P, III, 940); *Social Contract*, p. 377; *Letter to d'Alembert*, pp. 87–90.

33. *Social Contract*, p. 377.

sions the criminal is viewed as an impostor, a renegade guilty of insincerity. He is a mortal danger to common life which depends upon the principle of sincerity. He has betrayed the trust without which common life is slavery. He has attacked himself as well as the body politic, because he is himself the maker of the law to which he now gives the lie. When justifying punishment Rousseau did not distinguish crime from treason. An accused is tried and, if convicted, punished as a traitor to the common life: public disgrace, death, and banishment—the penalties Rousseau scattered throughout his writings—are fair punishments for one who is already a fugitive from common life, an orphan in the society of his fellow citizens.

For this reason Rousseau warned that negligence must not be confused with moderation or leniency with weakness. Legitimate governments must not hesitate to employ their administrative powers: "One must be severe in order to be just; to tolerate vice when one has the right and the power to repress it, is to be oneself vicious." When an assembly of the sovereign people has collected and assigned the funds of the entire state, for example, "the very nature of these revenues, in a sense, is changed; the revenues become so sacred that it is not only the most infamous theft but treason to divert the smallest amount from the purpose for which it was intended."[34] Death or banishment, Rousseau explained, is appropriate punishment for a foreign enemy: "Since every wrongdoer attacks the society's law, he becomes by his deed a rebel and a traitor to the [fatherland]; by violating its law, he ceases to be a member of it; indeed, he makes war against it. And in this case, the preservation of the state is incompatible with *his* preservation; one or the other must perish; and when the guilty man is put to death, it is less as a citizen than as an enemy. . . . Such an

34. *Discourse on Political Economy*, pp. 254, 265. See also *Perpetual Peace*, pp. 575–576.

enemy is not a [moral] person, but a man, and therefore the right of war makes it legitimate to kill him."[35]

Rousseau never claimed that severe punishment or even its threatened use could render men virtuous or successfully protect virtuous citizens from the effects of insincerity. That is never the point. But precisely because virtue cannot be legislated, it must be protected; and citizens must take seriously, as a case of war, everything which threatens the quality of their common life. Therefore Rousseau never mellowed on the question of severity of punishments, even when advising Corsicans to follow the Roman practice of permitting an accused to depart in peace without confiscation of property or the threat of sentence of death.[36] Public disgrace, death, and banishment are not really so different for social man. Perhaps public disgrace and banishment are slower, even more effective forms of execution. These punishments emphasize an earlier loss of life: expulsion from the common life of fellow citizens.

Insincerity cannot be punished in contemporary society, for the same reason that liberty cannot be found. Modern men have irreparably lost the capacity for honest speech and true, disinterested compassion. A modern man no longer dares to appear to others as he is nor to follow his benevolent inclinations. Ultimately the "perpetual constraint" of a deceitful propriety destroys all trust. Men are left with a precarious, hollow dignity.[37] They have frequent recourse to duels. The contemporary belief that "bravery can take the place of all the duties of society" is "the wildest and most barbarous opinion which

35. *Social Contract*, pp. 376–377. I discuss in Chapter 9 Rousseau's second, different justification of punishment in the *Social Contract* (a criminal remains a citizen and punishes himself). Both justifications suggest the difficulty of sustaining the anarchistic imperative in cases of disobedience.

36. *Constitutional Project for Corsica* (fragments), p. 940.

37. *Discourse on the Sciences and Arts*, pp. 7–9, 15–16, 21–22. See also *Confessions*, pp. 408–409; preface to *Narcisse*, pp. 965–969.

ever entered the human mind." Yet modern men believe that "a man is no longer a cheat, rascal, or slanderer, that he is civil, humane, and polite when he knows how to fight; that falsehood is changed into truth, robbery becomes legitimate, perfidy honesty, infidelity praiseworthy, as soon as all this is maintained sword in hand; that an affront is always made good by a sword thrust; that a man is never wrong in relation to another provided that he kill him."[38] And among European states there is constant war because the relations that actually obtain are hidden. Hereditary governments are elective in appearance. Each European prince acts as if he were self-sufficient; in fact, each is dependent on the others, as the incessant struggles among them testify.[39]

The Liberty of Sincere Obedience

The specific cause of disguise is *amour-propre,* a will to dominate. Desires for distinction are the "secret pretensions of the heart of every civilized man." *Amour-propre* "inclines each individual to have a greater esteem for himself than for anyone else [and] inspires in men all the harm they do to one another." The result is an inversion of morals: "Continence becomes a criminal precaution and the refusal to give life to one's fellow-man an act of humanity."[40] Our laws only increase the tumult of enslaving particular wills.[41] And modern theorists defend a "rational system" of self-interest which does not even admit the reality of civic virtue and casts scorn on the "duties of man and citizen." Mandeville "suggests that there are neither virtues nor vices and that moral good and evil are chimeras."

38. *Letter to d'Alembert,* p. 98.
39. *Perpetual Peace,* p. 569.
40. *Discourse on Inequality,* pp. 203, 219, 205.
41. *Discourse on Political Economy,* pp. 252–253; *Fragments on the Social Pact* (P, III, 483–484); *Discourse on Inequality,* pp. 188–189; *Fragments on Luxury, Commerce, and the Arts,* pp. 516–524; *Letters from the Mountain,* pp. 896–897; *Letter to Beaumont,* p. 937.

Hobbes claims "that men are wolves and can devour one another with clear conscience."[42]

Absolute liberty demands that the "social bond" be respected, that citizens accede to their general will of civic virtue: the "social order" is a "sacred right," the basis of all reciprocal liberties enjoyed by members of the corporate whole. When the "social tie begins to slacken," when the general will is rendered powerless, politics is emptied of meaning: "In the end, when the state, on the brink of ruin, can maintain itself only in an empty and illusory form, when the social bond is broken in every heart, when the meanest interest impudently flaunts the sacred name of the public good, then the general will is silenced; everyone, animated by secret motives, ceases to speak as a citizen any more than as if the state had never existed; and the people enacts in the guise of laws iniquitous decrees which have private [particulier] interest as their only end." On the other hand, if social feelings deepen, politics becomes a reality. For the "less the object of our care is directly joined to ourselves, the less there is to fear from the illusion of particular interest; the more general this interest becomes, the more just it is; and the love of the human race is nothing but the love of justice within us."[43]

Citizens must be "secured against seduction" by particular wills if they are to avoid slavery: "When the citizens love their duty, and the trustees of the public authority [the magistrates] sincerely apply themselves to the nourishing of that love by their example and their attentions, every difficulty vanishes; and administration becomes so easy that it avoids the art of darkness, whose blackness is only mystery." When the public has been properly educated "to recognize what it desires" and

42. Preface to *Narcisse*, pp. 965–966; *Discourse on the Sciences and Arts*, p. 27. See also *Rousseau juge de Jean-Jacques*, pp. 970–972; *Rêveries*, p. 1022; *Government of Poland*, pp. 956, 969.
43. *Social Contract*, pp. 352, 438, 368; *Emile*, p. 547. See also *Geneva Manuscript*, pp. 329–330; *Discourse on Political Economy*, pp. 250–251.

when individuals "subordinate their will to their reason," there is a "union of understanding and will in the social body." The dependent parts of the corporate whole are brought into "perfect harmony" and "lift the whole to its fullest strength." Such conformity of a "will of all" to the general will is a veritable "reign of virtue" in which the "voice of the people is the voice of God."[44] For "as we say that beauty is only an assemblage of the most common traits, we can say that virtue is only a gathering of the most general wills." Civic virtue assures that each citizen, never commanding or obeying other men, remains free: truly virtuous citizens obey only law. Because this law is largely defined by the very conditions of common life, absolute liberty also requires that additional, self-imposed civil laws should be as limited as possible. Then "each citizen shall be . . . perfectly independent of all his fellow citizens and excessively dependent on the republic" of which he is a creature.[45]

More specifically, there are "two kinds of dependence: dependence on things, which comes from nature; and dependence on men, which comes from society." The former, "having nothing to do with morality, can do no injury to liberty and can engender no vices." But "dependence on men, being prohibited, engenders all vices, and through this dependence master and slave become mutually depraved." The only way to avoid dependence on men is "to substitute law for man and to furnish the general wills with a real strength superior to the action of all particular wills. If the laws of societies, like the laws of nature, were able to have an inflexibility which no human power could ever break, then dependence on men would become dependence upon things." And this rule of law would "combine in the republic all the advantages of a state of nature with those of civil society; one would join to the

44. *Social Contract*, p. 380; *Discourse on Political Economy*, pp. 253–254, 252, 246. See also *Letters from the Mountain*, pp. 862–863.
45. *Fragments on the Social Pact*, p. 483; *Social Contract*, p. 394.

liberty which preserves a man from vice the morality which raises him to virtue." In such a society isolation becomes an evil: "The most vicious of men is he who isolates himself the most, who most concentrates his heart in himself; the best is he who shares his affections equally with his kind." Indeed, compared to virtuous citizenship, man's "perfect independence" and "liberty without rule" in the presocial state of nature exhibit an "essential vice harmful to the development of the most excellent faculties": natural man's isolation lacks "that bond among parts which constitutes the whole" so that he can never know "the most delightful sentiment of the soul, which is the love of virtue."[46]

Because sincerity is essential, and because even virtuous citizens are unlikely at all times to sustain the voice of civic duty in their hearts, Rousseau recommended several means for postponing violent discord. One means, on some occasions, is public watchfulness, a kind of unofficial although intolerant public "conscience" or censorship. A penetrating public gaze expresses approval and disapproval, overseeing the inner disposition of social men. Rousseau was pleased to find that Genevans did not attempt to hide their conduct "from the eyes of the public"; they were "born censors of one another." To preserve some semblance of unity and discipline in Poland, he relied in part upon public watchfulness. Certain effects of Polish history —foreign threats, aristocracy, an appetite for luxury, and formal arrangements involving representative government and a hereditary monarch—made sincerity difficult. Therefore Rousseau suggested public watchfulness: "Arrange things so that every citizen will feel himself to be constantly under the public eye; that no one will advance or succeed save by the favour of the public; that no office or position shall be filled save by the will of the nation." If all Poles become "so dependent on

46. *Emile*, p. 311; *Letter to d'Alembert*, p. 158; *Geneva Manuscript*, p. 283.

public esteem that nothing can be done, nothing acquired, no success obtained without it," then "out of the effervescence excited by this mutual emulation will arise that patriotic intoxication which alone can raise men above themselves, and without which liberty is but an empty word, and laws but a chimera." The virtue of Polish magistrates was to be proclaimed by merit badges. These would inspire worthy emulation; each magistrate would be wearing his virtue on his sleeve (or over his heart). Unlike the medals of enslaved men, the monetary value of Polish badges would be in inverse proportion to a magistrate's merit and responsibility. After a three-year probationary period, a worthy magistrate would display first gold, then silver, and finally blue steel plaques.[47]

This tense atmosphere of watchful judgment within Geneva and Poland recalls Rousseau's defense of severe punishment. Characteristically, Rousseau recommended death as punishment for disobedience which threatened the political integrity of the Polish whole. If a representative to the plenary diet were found guilty of ignoring the precise instructions of his constituents, he could be put to death. If a deputy in the federal diet misused the discredited *liberum veto* of the old constitution, that deputy would be immediately placed on public trial. The only possible verdicts by a court of the wisest and most respected citizens were to be death and acquittal. The latter would bring public honors and ample compensation. Even a dead monarch was to be judged. An immediate posthumous trial reviewing the entire career of the monarch would be held, and every citizen would somehow contribute to the verdict. Here too only two verdicts were possible. If found honorable, the deceased king would be inscribed on the honor

47. *Letter to d'Alembert*, p. 79; *Government of Poland*, pp. 1019, 1020–1021. Contemporary *moeurs* are too corrupt to bear governmental censors. *Discourse on Inequality*, pp. 222–223. See Hendel, *Rousseau*, I, 76–90; Jean Starobinski, "La Pensée politique de Jean-Jacques Rousseau," in *Jean-Jacques Rousseau*, pp. 98–99.

list of former kings similarly acquitted and granted the official epithet *"of glorious memory."* His widow would be given a pension, and his children honored by a grateful citizenry. If he should fail this posthumous inspection, his name would be stricken from the record of kings, his memory condemned, and a simple burial arranged. Thus, even after death a Polish king might be judged a traitor to common life, becoming, as we might say, a nonperson retroactively deprived of his social and historical existence. For obvious reasons, the verdict was to be announced in the presence of the king's successor.[48]

Public watchfulness is a way of indicating how much sincerity matters in a society of self-governing citizens. Where sincerity can be counted on, however, public watchfulness is unnecessary. Where it cannot be counted on, public watchfulness may help only to postpone greater hypocrisy. Thus Rousseau built public watchfulness into the constitution of Poland, whose citizens suffered the effects of centuries of deceit and self-deceit. But in his constitutional proposal for Corsica, a society whose *moeurs* were simple, public watchfulness is not even mentioned.

A man who evades his general will by succumbing to particular interests commits a crime against the self and remains a divided self of conflicting public identities. His conduct is riddled with contradictions because his very being is a torment of antagonistic desires and obligations caused by insatiable *amour-propre*. He mirrors a society divided against itself: "The body of society is actually divided into other bodies, whose members adopt a general will which is good and just with regard to these new bodies, but unjust and vicious with regard to the whole from which each has been dismembered." His behavior is also similar to that of a performer on the contemporary stage who "annihilates" himself before audiences of equally corrupt men. Both are impostors, degrading themselves

48. *Government of Poland*, pp. 979–901, 996–990, 1031 1036.

as well as the persons they portray: "What is the talent of the actor? It is the art of counterfeiting himself, of putting on another character than his own, of appearing different than he is, of becoming passionate in cold blood, of saying what he does not think as naturally as if he really did think it, and, finally, of forgetting his own place by dint of taking another's." Rousseau added that the actor may not precisely deceive his audience because he does not seriously intend to be taken for the person he imitates. The actor simply cultivates "by profession the talent of deceiving men and of becoming adept in habits which can be innocent only in the theater and can serve everywhere else only for doing harm." The actors of modern societies are performers outside theaters, the enslaved and ignoble marionettes of corrupt *moeurs* who "play the roles of decent men in society."[49]

"What makes for human misery," Rousseau observed, "is the contradiction to be found between our condition and our desires, between our duties and our inclinations, between nature and social institutions, between man and the citizen. Restore man's unity, and you make him as happy as he can be." A vigilant civic virtue would be its own reward. For only the sincerely virtuous citizen is a whole and happy man. He is at peace with himself and his fellow citizens. He triumphs over the particular passions that make him miserable. He enjoys his sentiments—his feelings of compassion and the confidence that they will be reciprocated. Contradiction is impossible because the source of it—the struggle for domination between fellow citizens—is absent: "The good man orders his life for the sake of the whole; the wicked orders the whole for his own sake. The latter places himself at the center of all things; the former measures his radius and holds fast to the circumference."[50]

49. *Discourse on Political Economy*, p. 247; *Letter to d'Alembert*, pp. 106–108. See Starobinski, *Rousseau*, pp. 47–57.
50. *Fragments on Public Happiness* (P, III, 510); *Emile*, p. 602. That

True law can prevent every sort of division. It avoids all divisions between ruler and ruled. Enshrining sincerity, it eliminates division between the voice of vain interest and the voice of civic duty. True law is a "celestial voice which dictates to each citizen the precepts of the public reason and teaches him to act according to the rules of his own judgment, and not to be in contradiction with himself." Justice and utility are not opposed in a united and disciplined society of truly virtuous citizens because "what right permits" is combined with "what interest prescribes." The civic duty and the interest of every public man, his "true self-interest," are indeed identical in the personality of the sincerely virtuous citizen. Truly virtuous citizens willingly celebrate together their shared origin and their natural destiny of absolute liberty, as a matter of civic obligation: "The commitments which bind us to the social body are obligatory only because they are mutual; and their nature is such that in fulfilling them a man cannot work for others without at the same time working for himself." The general will, which such "commitments" describe, "derives its generality less from the number of voices than from the common interest which unites them—for the general will is an institution in which each necessarily submits himself to the same conditions which he imposes on others; this admirable harmony of interest and justice gives to social deliberations a quality of equity." And the end of every self-imposed civil law in a society of truly virtuous citizens remains the common good of these citizens—their freedom and equality. Freedom and equality always imply a shared condition of common life, that very "social order" or "sacred bond" of common life to which every creature of social dependence is indebted, "free-

---

true happiness requires a proper hierarchy of social identities is discussed by Bretonneau, *Valeurs humaines de Rousseau,* pp. 42–56, 201–215, 238–241, 278–279. For contemporary man's prospects, Bretonneau's interpretation is an optimistic one.

dom because any individual dependence means that much strength withdrawn from the body of the state, and equality because freedom cannot survive without it."[51]

51. *Discourse on Political Economy*, p. 248; *Social Contract*, pp. 351, 373, 374, 391, 438–439; *Discourse on Inequality*, pp. 116–117. See also *Geneva Manuscript*, pp. 288–289, 310; *Fragments on the State of Nature*, p. 475; *Letters from the Mountain*, pp. 806–808.

CHAPTER 8

The Virtuous Citizen: Simplicity

Contemporary slavery, according to Rousseau, expresses mankind's decline into civilized old age from the simplicity of its youth. During what Rousseau occasionally called the golden age, the compassionate fellowship of self-governing citizens appears spontaneous. A nearly perfect convergence exists between absolute liberty and social dependence, between "nature and social institutions"; each "will of all" seldom strays from the given general will because citizens are seldom in situations which oppose civic duty to interest. A rule of law is a kind of eternal present. It is sustained as a matter of revered custom, for men are most likely to be virtuous citizens when common life itself is simple.[1]

1. Rousseau distinguished simple *moeurs* from the discipline of civic virtue, just as he contrasted (and connected) natural goodness and civic virtue. See, for example, *Emile* (P, IV, 467–468); *Constitutional Project for Corsica* (P, II, 901–902). But the distinction between simplicity and virtue describes neither different periods of common life nor separate and incompatible ideals. Civic virtue would have preserved equality within the third period of simple *moeurs* described in the *Discourse on Inequality;* and evolution beyond this common life of families united in small nations constitutes a new historical period of slavery and vice.

For a contrasting view, see Jouvenel, "Essai," pp. 56–67, and "Rousseau, évolutionniste et pessimiste," in *Rousseau et la philosophie politique*, pp. 1–19. Jouvenel argues that a "social" ideal of simplicity, or of virtuous conduct without the discipline of virtue, animates Rousseau's thought. See also Groethuysen, *Rousseau*, pp. 52–140, which argues for a "duality" of incompatible "ideals": the "private" or "natural" man who is good

As a kind of patriot adviser to Corsicans, Poles, and Genevans, Rousseau offered as palliatives adaptations of recoverable
aspects of earlier societies. Modern men cannot return to a

---

and the "civil" man or "man as part of a common whole" who is
virtuous. See also Judith N. Shklar, *Men and Citizens: A Study of
Rousseau's Social Theory* (Cambridge, 1969), pp. 3–32, 60–74, 85, 94,
127–150, 208–214. Shklar's elaboration of the "polar opposition" between
two utopias draws the sharpest distinction between simplicity and civic
virtue. The first utopia, illustrated by Wolmar's estate and *Emile*, is the
"tranquil household" of the golden age of simplicity and, occasionally, a
Swiss village whose members concentrate their activities in their respective families. A second utopia, described in the *Discourse on the Sciences
and Arts* and the *Discourse on Political Economy*, is the Spartan city,
with Rousseau's evocations taken for the Sparta familiar to historians.
Although Shklar discusses some similarities between natural man's "self-
expression" within familial society and a citizen's "self-repression" within
a state, the unity of Rousseau's thought involves two utopias: agricultural
simplicity, domestic education, and moral virtue are opposed, respectively, to a stern military-civic ethos, political education, and civic
virtue. Indeed, "the Spartan city is built on the destruction of the
family and of all its emotional and social gratifications": a citizen "loses
his personal identity" as a member of a "collectivity"; in "the citizen-
army, the *moi humain* is really crushed by the *moi commun*"; the
citizen "utterly lacks . . . any opportunity for self-expression"; and the
Spartan city "excludes all private affections and associations, not only
the family." This interpretation recalls individualist views of "collectivist"
repression cited earlier. See also a discussion of Rousseau's theory of
personal friendship in Ronald Grimsley, *Jean-Jacques Rousseau: A Study
in Self-Awareness* (Cardiff, 1961), pp. 86–94.

In another distinction between simplicity and virtue, simplicity is
taken to describe presocial indolence and ignorance, so that Rousseau
advocated or yearned for a return to the state of nature—the ideal of
a noble savage. See, for example, Irving Babbitt, *Rousseau and Roman-
ticism* (Cleveland, 1955). For a refutation of this view, see Arthur O.
Lovejoy, "The Supposed Primitivism of Rousseau's *Discourse on
Inequality*," *Modern Philology*, XXI (1923), 165–186. The noble savage
accusation is not without lineage. Voltaire acknowledged receipt of
Rousseau's *Discourse on Inequality* by thanking him for his "new book
against the human species" and by expressing regret that sixty years
in an upright position makes crawling on all fours impossible. Letter
to Rousseau (Aug. 30, 1755; *CC*, III, 156–157). Palissot's play, *Les
Philosophes* (1760), portrays a disciple of Rousseau entering on all fours

golden age of simple *moeurs*. Nevertheless, if some men restore part of its unmediated concreteness, they may postpone
the conclusive slavery of civilized barbarism. Rousseau's invocation of simplicity also underlies his indictments of contentious debates, well-written books, pernicious reasoning by enlightened men, and representative government: liberty is found
only in the honest speech and unadorned habits of farmers
lingering in the European countryside, in the happy ignorance
of "Spartans," and in short, uncomplicated, memorizable codes
of civil law.

The third historical period described in the *Discourse on Inequality* is the "best society for men." Simple men are organized in small, stable nations. Each family is economically self-
sufficient, and together citizens use their considerable leisure
for festivals of singing and dancing.[2] Elsewhere, Rousseau
described a lost past of simple *moeurs* as a time when the personal interest of every citizen remained a reciprocated love of
his society, a time before passions for political domination and
personal property.[3] And the Corsican age of simplicity was
that time before the separation of "two inseparable things, the
body which governs and the body which is governed. In the
original constitution of government, these two bodies are but
one; they become separate only through the abuse of that constitution." Rousseau also advised Corsicans, whose opportunity
he claimed unique compared to that of other European societies, to restore conditions that favored the sentiments of
equity, humanity, and good faith of their "national character."
Corsicans, he asserted, should follow the example of Swiss republics before their decline: "Since needs and interests did not

munching vegetables. Rousseau tirelessly denied this charge. See, for
example, *Discourse on Inequality* (P, III, 207–208); letter to Voltaire
(Sept. 7, 1755; CC, III, 164–166). And the inseparability of civic virtue
and simplicity confirms his denial.

2. *Discourse on Inequality*, p. 171.
3. Preface to *Narcisse* (P, II, 967–970).

conflict, and no one depended [economically] on anyone else, their only relations with one another were those of benevolence and friendship; peace and concord reigned in their numerous families." Marriages, "almost the only subjects of negotiation between them," were never "contracted for reasons of ambition, or prevented on grounds of interest and inequality. This people, poor but not needy, and enjoying the most perfect independence, thus multiplied in unshakable unity; . . . This hard-working and independent life attached the Swiss to their fatherland with a strength which gave them two great means of defending it, namely, harmony in council and courage in battle." Corsicans were also admonished that only generous pride could be an "instrument of so great an enterprise as the creation of a national body." Deriving self-esteem from truly estimable objects and common purposes is historically closer to the state of nature than is vanity, the emblem of corrupt *moeurs*.[4]

We can grasp Rousseau's understanding of the nature of simplicity from these and similar examples. In early societies the needs and hopes of citizens were few. As versatile amateurs, citizens knew only useful trades. Neither economic competition, complicated civil laws, nor talented magistrates threatened their fellowship: self-government was nearly a matter of unreflective habit. The crystalline immediacy of trustful companionship did not permit hazard, mystery, hypocrisy, or conflict. It allowed kindness and gaiety. Rousseau's "nostalgia" for man's lost simplicity expresses his preference for the calm attentiveness and firm loyalty of youth over the cacophonous disruption and distraction of old age. He preferred sincerity over brittle, unfeeling remoteness, the confident liberty of self-sufficient farmers and the open air over crowded towns, commercial exchange, and class conflict.[5]

4. *Constitutional Project for Corsica*, pp. 901, 913–915, 937–938. See also *Social Contract* (P, III, 392).

5. See also Saint-Preux's description of the High Valais region and

Rousseau's proposals for modern men reflect his grudging acceptance of inherent limitations, for no patriot can repeal or avoid the cumulative givens of his time and place: "The reason Diogenes did not find a man was that he sought among his contemporaries the man of a time that no longer existed. Cato . . . perished with Rome and freedom because he was out of place in his century."[6] Contemporary men will persist in accepting the advice of scientists and philosophes who advocate precepts of vicious self-interest.[7] Moreover, as old age and death destroy the body of man, so fratricidal division is inevitable: "If Sparta and Rome perished, what state can hope to last for ever?" Thus, "free peoples must remember this maxim: liberty can be gained but never *regained*." Though a people might make itself free in its youth, it cannot do so when its "civil energies" are exhausted: "Once customs are established and prejudices rooted, reform is a dangerous and fruitless enterprise; a people cannot bear to see its evils touched, even if only to be eradicated; it is like a stupid, pusillanimous invalid who trembles at the sight of a physician."[8]

Rousseau preferred to live in "a happy and tranquil republic," one whose past was lost "in the darkness of time." A common life of virtual stasis is preferable to "a newly instituted

---

some aspects of Wolmar's estate [*La Nouvelle Héloise* (P, II, 79–82, 527–557)]; *Rousseau juge de Jean-Jacques* (P, I, 668–673, 676–677, 828–829); and *Letter to Beaumont* (P, IV, 936–937). For a similar understanding of Rousseau's golden age, see Burgelin, *La Philosophie de l'existence de Rousseau*, pp. 273–287, 317–328. For Rousseau's reliance upon ancient theorists and modern travelers' reports, see Michel Collinet, "L'Homme de la nature et la nature de l'homme," *Le Contrat social*, VI (May–June 1962), 151–153.

6. *Discourse on Inequality*, p. 192.

7. *Last Response* (P, III, 231); *Social Contract*, p. 420n; *Government of Poland* (P, III, 969).

8. *Social Contract*, pp. 424, 385. Lanson, "L'Unité de la pensée de Rousseau," pp. 26–28, 30, and Pickles, "The Notion of Time in Rousseau's Political Thought," pp. 367–388, stress the conservative, restorative aspects of Rousseau's proposals.

republic," however good its laws. Contemporary patriots must therefore beware of "selfish and ill-conceived projects and the dangerous innovations" of the sort that destroyed equality in Athens: "It is above all the great antiquity of laws which makes them holy and venerable." Great evils are often introduced to correct lesser ones on the pretext of making improvements: "For freedom is like those solid and rich foods or those hearty wines, which are proper to nourish and fortify robust constitutions habituated to them, but which overpower, ruin, and intoxicate the weak and delicate who are unsuited to them. Once peoples are accustomed to masters, they are no longer able to do without them." All popular revolutions "necessarily" entail "frightful dissensions [and] infinite disorders." Once dismemberment of common life commences, greater slavery is inevitable; men are further deprived of liberty when the tattered bonds of a common life are fragmented by the particular will of rebels. In fact, a tyrant may abdicate or be overthrown, but subjects do not have the "fatal right" to depose him.[9]

Rousseau's pessimism was responsible for the conservative and meliorative character of his Polish proposals, for he intended only to restore, in imperceptible fashion, some semblance of a lost simplicity. He offered his Polish plan on the assumption that the Poles were a "people which, without being wholly free from vices, still had a certain amount of resilience and virtue." If Poles had already become "radically venal and corrupt," it would be futile to attempt even partial restoration.[10]

One of the givens of modern Poland was constitutional slavery. The active portion of the Polish state was confined to a small, hereditary nobility, for burghers and peasant serfs participated in neither legislation nor government: the Polish nation was a "body made up of a large number of dead members, and of a small number of disunited members," the nobles'

9. *Discourse on Inequality*, pp. 112–114, 185–186.
10. *Government of Poland*, p. 1022.

passion for wealth preventing their pursuit of common goals. Rousseau left no doubt that the "law of nature, that holy and inprescriptible law, which speaks to the heart and reason of man," repudiated this usurpation of a corporate whole's sovereignty over itself. Civil laws were not "binding on anyone who has not voted for them in person" or through their legislative representatives (representation being a reluctant allowance for the size of Poland). Polish nobles deceived themselves if they thought themselves free "as long as [they] hold [their] brothers in chains."[11]

Yet if restoring peasants and burghers to active membership was "a great and worthy enterprise," it was also "bold, perilous, and not to be attempted lightly." For "liberty is a food easy to eat, but hard to digest; it takes very strong stomachs to stand it. I laugh at those debased peoples who, allowing themselves to be stirred up by rebels, dare to speak of liberty without having the slightest idea of its meaning, and who, with their hearts full of all the servile vices, imagine that, in order to be free, it is enough to be insubordinate." Thus, Rousseau proposed that serfs and burghers be reabsorbed into the body politic "without any perceptible revolution." Public lists would register degrees of promotion while censorial committees judged aspirants. A scrupulously impartial administration of civil law would encourage burghers and serfs to "attach [their] affections to the fatherland and even the government" in the meantime: "You will enkindle in all the lower orders an ardent zeal to contribute to the public welfare; you would finally succeed in animating all parts of Poland, and in binding them together in such a way that they would no longer be anything more than a single corporate group; . . . and this with the inestimable advantage of having avoided all abrupt and rapid changes, and the danger of revolution."[12]

11. *Ibid.*, pp. 953–954, 973, 974.
12. *Ibid.*, pp. 974, 1024–1028.

Early, simple societies were also small; and Rousseau said that he preferred a state where "neither the obscure maneuvers of vice nor the modesty of virtue could be hidden from the notice and judgment of the public, and where that sweet habit of seeing and knowing one another turned love of the fatherland into love of the citizens rather than love of the soil."[13] The social bond is loosened through excessive numbers and extent of territory, for citizens cannot love one another when they are strangers from distant provinces exhibiting confusing customs and obeying different laws.[14] The "radical defect" of the Polish nation was its sheer size: the extensiveness of states is "the first and principal source of the misfortunes of the human race, and above all of the innumerable calamities that sap and destroy civilized peoples."[15]

Rousseau proposed to deal with the problem of size in part by restoring traditional Polish federalism. He sketched a plan involving thirty-three provinces, composed of still smaller territorial units.[16] This arrangement of federal units must not, of course, threaten "the bond of common legislation which unites them" or their "common subordination to the body of the republic."[17] But a more likely palliative than federalism was "simplicity itself," as Rousseau noted when explaining his educational reforms. Poland must be given the "vigour and stability of that of a small republic." It must undergo a "second birth," so that it could "recover in this new age all the vigour of a nation in the process of birth." National education could give all members that "national formation" appreciated only by the ancients. Polish education, conducted by Polish citizens of superior virtue, would be unlike "studies of the usual sort, directed by foreigners and priests." National education, appro-

13. *Discourse on Inequality*, p. 112.
14. *Social Contract*, p. 387.
15. *Government of Poland*, p. 970.
16. *Ibid.*, pp. 980–989, 998–999.
17. *Ibid.*, p. 971.

priate only to "free men," is a deliberate and historically condensed duplication of man's transformation from discrete private self to new public creature, and its proper end is civic virtue. "When first he opens his eyes, an infant ought to see the fatherland, and up to the day of his death he ought never to see anything else. Every true republican has drunk in love of [fatherland], that is to say love of law and liberty, along with his mother's milk. This love is his whole existence; he sees nothing but the fatherland, he lives for it alone; when he is solitary, he is nothing; when he has ceased to have a fatherland, he no longer exists; and if he is not dead, he is worse than dead." Polish children should play together, out of doors, so that all will aspire to a "common goal." Even children whose parents prefer domestic education must play together so that all children will become accustomed at the earliest age "to equality, to fraternity, to competition, to living under the eyes of their fellow-citizens and to desiring public approbation." The future citizen, Rousseau asserted, should know at ten years of age all his fatherland's products; at twelve he should know its roads, provinces and towns, at fifteen the entire history of Poland, and the next year all of its civil laws. A "mock state" of the sort utilized in Bern, a replica of Polish institutions, was to be a nursery for future citizens.[18]

Earlier, in the *Discourse on Political Economy*, without specific reference to a single European nation, Rousseau expressed an unwillingness to permit domestic education. A father may be prejudiced. Although a single family is frequently impermanent, the "great family" of the state endures in one form or another forever. Moreover, a single member of the corporate whole obtains in common under the name of citizen the same authority over his children that he would otherwise exercise separately as father. And only national education can "trans-

18. *Ibid.*, pp. 966–970.

mit from age to age, to future generations . . . the courage
and virtues of citizens."[19]

National education cannot repress the passions of corrupt
men. Rather, it gives children's passions a new direction, a
worthy object of affection and loyalty that prevents vices
from arising. If Europeans could reform their respective systems of education, then self-governing citizens would rejoice
together in that comprehensive society which gives them life
and excludes no member. "If, for example, they were accustomed from an early age to consider their individuality only
in its relations to the body of the state, and to perceive, so to
speak, their own existence only as a part of the state, they
could at length come to identify themselves in some manner
with this greater whole, to feel themselves members of their
fatherland, and to love it with that exquisite sentiment which
every isolated man has only for himself." Children "educated
in common in the bosom of equality, . . . imbued with the
laws of the state and the maxims of the general will, . . . sur-
rounded by examples and objects which constantly remind
them of the tender mother who nourishes them, of the love she
has for them, of the inestimable benefits they receive from her,
and of the return they owe her," such children have learned
"to cherish one another as brothers, never to will anything contrary to the will of society, to substitute the actions of men
and citizens for the futile and vain babble of sophists, and to
become in time the defenders and fathers of that fatherland of
which they have been so long the children." When generous
sentiments of pity and humanity are not enfeebled by attempting to embrace mankind, "we voluntarily will what is willed
by the people whom we love."[20] Patriotism is a love of one's
new, noble self.

19. *Discourse on Political Economy* (P, III, 259–261).
20. *Ibid.*, pp. 259, 261, 254. See also letter to Usteri (Apr. 30, 1763;
CC, XVI, 127–128); *Letters from the Mountain* (P, III, 706n); *Fragments
on the Fatherland* (P, III, 536).

The same reasoning underlies Rousseau's rejection of d'Alembert's proposed dramatic theater for Geneva. A theater would be a dangerous innovation or "revolution" in the relatively modest and austere life Genevans enjoy. It would be a "monument of luxury and softness . . . elevated on the ruins of our antique simplicity and threatening from afar the public liberty." It would deter Genevans from "the simple and modest virtues which make the good citizen."[21] Citizens forget themselves at the theater: "People think they come together in the theater, and it is there that they are isolated. It is there that they go to forget their friends, neighbors, and relations in order to concern themselves with fables, in order to cry for the misfortunes of the dead, or to laugh at the expense of the living."[22] An audience at the performance of contemporary tragedies is "instructed" in the triumph of villains. The educational effect of comedies is no less pernicious. Molière's "greatest care is to ridicule goodness and simplicity and to present treachery and falsehood so that they arouse our interest and sympathy." Though his characters sometimes make fun of vices, virtue is never loved. All the "most sacred relations" essential to common life are scandalously overturned. The most criminal acts of infidelity, forgery, theft, lying, and cruelty are subjects of playful amusement.[23]

Indeed, the effect of contemporary plays would be so disastrous that "only two years of theater [in Geneva] and everything will be overturned." It would supplant traditional Genevan *cercles*, the small groups of citizens gathered for innocent amusement, who "still preserve some image of ancient [*moeurs*]" and still speak forthrightly of fatherland and virtue

21. *Letter to d'Alembert*, pp. 165, 131, 129, 156.
22. *Ibid.*, pp. 20–21. See also *ibid.*, p. 33.
23. *Ibid.*, pp. 75, 45–46. See also *Discourse on Inequality*, p. 155; *Memoire à M. de Mably* (P, IV, 16, 24); *La Nouvelle Héloise*, pp. 251–254; *Emile*, p. 677.

without fear of ridicule. Genevans should instead institute "decent and innocent" festivals which would continue to make "friends, citizens and soldiers out of the same men." Rousseau proposed entertainments like those Greek citizens enjoyed: joyous festivals, reviews, public prizes, and competitions in sailing and cannon would be unpoisoned by the "odor of constraint and selfishness" and could be held in the open air without concealment. The performers at the best festivals are themselves citizens: "Plant a stake crowned with flowers in the middle of a square; gather the people together there, and you will have a festival. Do better yet; let the spectators become an entertainment to themselves; make them actors themselves; do it so that each sees and loves himself in the others so that all will be better united."[24]

Entertainments of this sort are celebrations of common life that can strengthen the bonds of equality: "All the societies constitute but one, all become common to all. It is almost a matter of indifference at which table one seats himself." And the Calvinist prohibition on innocent gaiety and dancing is a tyrannic affront to nature and reason. Rousseau proposed that during winter months Genevans hold indoor dances open to all young marriageable persons. A "comfortable and honorable section" of the hall would be reserved for elderly people who, "having already given citizens to the [fatherland], would now see their grandchildren prepare themselves to become citizens." Upon entering and leaving the hall Genevans would salute the elderly with a deep bow. Such dances would provide "a frequent means for reconciling divided families." Dances "would

24. *Letter to d'Alembert*, pp. 149, 140–142, 168–169. Rousseau did not mention that membership in the *cercles* often included burghers opposed to the ruling oligarchy. He later defended *cercles* as a mean between that "public education" of Greek republics which is no longer possible and the "domestic education" of contemporary monarchies in which "all subjects must remain isolated and have nothing in common but obedience." Letter to Tronchin (Nov. 26, 1758; *CC*, V, 242).

maintain the body of the people better in the spirit of its constitution; . . . [they] would bring the people together not so much for a public entertainment as for the gathering of a big family."[25]

Rousseau asserted that his plan for reconsecrating Genevan simplicity followed insofar as possible the Spartan example of public instruction: "It is not only because of their object but also their simplicity that I find [Spartan practices] worthy of recommendation; without pomp, without luxury, without display, everything in them breathes, along with a secret patriotic charm which makes them attractive, a certain martial spirit befitting free men." But just as Rousseau, preferring to live among knaves rather than brigands, recommended the retention of European academies, he found a modern theater appropriate entertainment in corrupt societies. Here it is useful "for occupying those who are too rich or aspire to be so; . . . for distracting the people from its miseries; . . . in a word, for preventing corrupt [*moeurs*] from degenerating into brigandage."[26]

As a kind of continuation of national education Rousseau recommended Polish festivals to Polish patriots. These could reform the hearts of men who clung "to personal privileges rather than to greater and more general advantages." Restoring the "ancient usages" of Poland would encourage Polish society to become an "indissoluble body," approaching in its fervor the height of Spartan and Roman citizens who had "the fatherland constantly before their eyes" in their laws, their games, their rewards, affections, and festivals. In this way Polish patriots would "elevate souls to the level of the souls of the ancients" and bring "patriotism and its attendant virtues to the

---

25. *Letter to d'Alembert*, pp. 170, 173, 175–176. See also letter to Lenieps (Nov. 8, 1758; *CC*, V, 212–213).

26. *Letter to d'Alembert*, pp. 181, 86.

highest possible degree of intensity." This is the only effective rampart against foreign conquerors: "If you see to it that no Pole can ever become a Russian, I guarantee that Russia will not subjugate Poland."[27]

Especially in view of Rousseau's sweeping condemnation of the large, modern "country" composed of "private citizens," we must distinguish his invocations of patriotic fervor from those associated with modern nationalism.[28] Whatever subsequent uses others have made of isolated aspects or of the tone of Rousseau's proposals, the only significance of civic virtue, in the full context of his political thought, is negative expedience: patriotic loyalty may postpone greater enslavement. Civic fervor could develop that leaven of good will which exists in the hearts of all men, "the very existence of which has not yet been so much as suspected by our corrupt maxims, our outworn institutions, our egotistical philosophy which preaches and kills."[29]

That patriotism was of only instrumental significance to Rousseau is seen at the beginning of his Polish plan. He noted the favorable consequences of the recent loss of some Polish people to foreign partition, and he warned of the foreign entanglements, disastrous to "national" unity, of Polish efforts to regain lost areas. Even with Rousseau's other proposals, Poles could never enjoy "the stability and vigor" of small republics. The "first reform" of the Polish nation must therefore be a further, voluntary contraction of territorial boundaries: "Perhaps your neighbors are thinking of doing you this service. It would no doubt be a great misfortune for the dismembered parts; but it would be a great boon to the body of the na-

27. *Government of Poland*, pp. 995, 957, 960–961.
28. For a contrasting view, see Cobban, *Rousseau and the Modern State*, pp. 99–125; Léon, "Rousseau et les fondements de l'état moderne," pp. 222–238.
29. *Government of Poland*, p. 969. See also *ibid.*, p. 956.

tion."[30] Because a demand for absolute liberty, or the avoidance of greater slavery, animates Rousseau's philosophy, he insisted upon the gradual reabsorption of serfs and burghers into Polish society and he welcomed earlier and future exclusions, on a territorial basis, of excess numbers from the body of the same Polish "nation."

The negative expedience of patriotic fervor is also seen when Rousseau condemned one especially pernicious form of contemporary vanity, the studied, disingenuous cosmopolitanism of enlightened men. They boast that they love humanity, Rousseau asserted, merely as a pretext for hating their neighbors.[31] Modern cosmopolitanism only conceals a European tendency to imitate the corrupt *moeurs* of the French: "Today, no matter what people may say, there are no longer any Frenchmen, Germans, Spaniards, or even Englishmen; there are only Europeans. All have the same tastes, the same passions, the same [*moeurs*], for no one has been shaped along national lines by peculiar institutions. . . . What do they care what master they obey, under the laws of what state they live?"[32] Yet Rousseau adopted a flexible, circumstantial attitude toward the cosmopolite, just as he did toward the geographical scope of membership in the modern country. Most modern men, their natural sentiment of pity silenced, think it their duty to murder foreigners. During "national wars, battles, murders, and reprisals which make nature tremble and shock reason," however, there are still "a few great cosmopolitan souls" who include the whole human race in their sentiments of benevolence.[33] Again, it is preferable to live among knaves than brigands.

Thus, if Poles were to postpone greater slavery, their "na-

---

30. *Ibid.*, pp. 970–971.
31. *Geneva Manuscript* (P, III, 287); *Emile*, pp. 248–249.
32. *Government of Poland*, p. 960.
33. *Discourse on Inequality*, pp. 178–179.

tional" society had to be self-sufficient: "The spirit of imitation seldom produces anything good, and never anything great." By restoring her own "natural and national disposition" or "genius," Poland would be "always herself, not someone else." Rousseau even suggested that Poles develop their own distinctive military organization and tactics, rather than imitating "slavishly the tactics of other nations." Even if some Polish customs were unworthy, they could be useful "provided that the vice be not radical." Polish citizens should always be ill at ease when they find themselves in the company of foreigners.[34]

In the *Social Contract* Rousseau saluted Corsica as the only state in contemporary Europe enjoying the social youthfulness that permits a people to receive its fundamental laws from a true lawgiver. Corsicans, he wrote, combine the "cohesion" of an ancient people with the "malleability" of a new nation.[35] Three years later, in *Constitutional Project for Corsica*, Rousseau asserted that Corsicans "can begin at the beginning, and take steps to prevent degeneration." The unusual opportunities consisted of Corsica's fortunate size and the extraordinary vigor and simplicity of common life remaining after thirty-five or forty years of uninterrupted war with pirates and the Genoese. The Genoese tyranny had nearly destroyed the Corsican nobility: "You are fortunate that they have taken upon

34. *Government of Poland*, pp. 1017–1019, 1013, 962. For a discussion of that perfect "intimacy" or "insularity" which, in a variety of social contexts, can dissolve one's sense of space and time, see Henri-Frederic Amiel, *Jean-Jacques Rousseau*, trans. Van Wyck Brooks (New York, 1922), pp. 34–36; Starobinski, *Rousseau*, pp. 114–126, 135–138; Collinet, "L'Homme de la nature et la nature de l'homme," pp. 148–150; Ronald Grimsley, *Rousseau and the Religious Quest* (London, 1968), pp. 21–22, 33–34, 42–43, 65–68, 88–107, 117–123.

35. *Social Contract*, p. 391. See also *Constitutional Project for Corsica* (fragment), p. 950; letter to George Keith (Dec. 8, 1764; *CG*, XII, 123); *Confessions* (P, I, 648–651). In the last two citations Rousseau explained his reluctance to undertake the project and his pessimism about the implementation of his "reveries."

themselves the odium of this enterprise, which you might not have been able to do if they had not done it before you." Ignoring foreign powers and *moeurs* as if they did not exist, the Corsican people can "give itself, by its own efforts, all the stability of which it is capable." For only some unfortunate legacies of the Genoese occupation must be combatted. An indomitable and ferocious temper, a propensity for dissension, and an inclination to theft and murder were stimulated by impunity under an oppressive foreign government.[36]

Accordingly, Rousseau did not recommend national education and public watchfulness, official or unofficial. The very habits of Corsicans' premodern common life could be their mutual instructions: a united Corsican nation would comprise self-sufficient farmers spread throughout the countryside, enjoying the "equality and simplicity of rural life." A geographical dispersal of farmers is designed to assure social unity, to discourage both the necessity and the possibility of contractual exchange in a free market. The exchange of agricultural products and manufactures in crowded cities is always a forced bargain for a farmer. He is turned into "a petty trader, a petty salesman, and a petty rascal" in the process. Modern commerce divides common life between the idle rich and starving peasants, with the small farmer's way of life becoming "either an article of commerce and a species of manufacture for the powerful farmer, or else the last resource of poverty for the mass of the peasantry."[37]

Rousseau proposed that instead of contractual exchange Corsicans depend upon barter, communal warehouses, county registers, and, if temporarily necessary, a purely imaginary unit of currency for comparative evaluation of the few objects to be exchanged. As a "final goal" every Corsican should strive to become economically self-sufficient. Money, employed for competitive advantage, is only a remote and relative token of

---

36. *Constitutional Project for Corsica*, pp. 902, 908, 903, 917.
37. *Ibid.*, pp. 905, 920. See also *ibid.*, pp. 926–928.

worth, a symbol of value that obstructs citizens' visions of each other. Soon money becomes a reality in the minds of men and they forget what it was meant to represent or provide. Corrupt men obtain money for one purpose and use it for another, far from public sight.[38]

Corsicans, like the early Romans, should rely upon small taxes paid in kind, and especially upon corvées. The word *corvée* should not frighten true republicans, Rousseau added, because "the fewer the intermediaries between need and service, the less onerous the service should be." And there are no intermediaries, whether of men or money, in a simple rural life that does not permit commerce: citizens join to use "their labor, their arms and their hearts, rather than their purses, in the service of the fatherland, both for its defense, in the militia, and for its utility, in corvées on public works." Elaborate financial arrangements are a recent invention; the word *finance* was no more known to the ancients than *tithe* and *capitation*. "I regard finance as the fat of the body politic," Rousseau continued, "fat which, when clogged up in certain muscular tissues, overburdens the body with useless obesity, and makes it heavy rather than strong." In barren areas of the Corsican countryside Rousseau permitted some manufacturing, favoring those artisans whose products are useful to agriculture and "advantageous to human life." Carpenters, blacksmiths, and weavers were to be welcome, but not practitioners of the "idle . . . arts of pleasure and luxury," such as woodcarvers, goldsmiths, and embroiderers.[39]

Economic simplicity would make Corsicans self-governing citizens. The "concurrence of all members of the state in the exercise of supreme authority" places citizens on a "plane of perfect equality," for apart from civic virtue, "democracy

---

38. *Ibid.*, pp. 924, 904–905, 916–917, 920–921. For a more extensive discussion of the enslaving character of economic exchange, see *La Nouvelle Héloise*, pp. 548–551.

39. *Constitutional Project for Corsica*, pp. 929–932, 926.

recognizes no other nobility except that of liberty."[40] Yet Rousseau also warned Corsicans of the decline that awaits every free state. Because there is in every body politic a "progression, a natural and necessary development, from birth to destruction," Corsican patriots would be wise to emphasize a restoration of the historical period that immediately preceded the attainment of maximum unity.[41] And to assure that attachment to the land would encourage love for fellow citizens and laws, Rousseau suggested that Corsicans, "gradually and automatically, through the simple operation of the passage of time," be classified into three categories: citizens, patriots, and aspirants. The first act establishing the restored constitution should be a solemn oath of allegiance sworn by all Corsicans twenty or older. Those who so swore would be immediately enrolled "without distinction" as citizens. Corsicans born on the island but not of age would be aspirants; and each aspirant would become a patriot when legally married and the possessor of land apart from his wife's dowry. A patriot, whether married or widowed, would become a citizen when he had two children, a house of his own, and enough land to support his family.[42] A free people grants "no distinctions save for merit, virtues, and patriotic service," which can be no more hereditary than actions on which such distinctions are based.[43]

---

40. *Ibid.*, pp. 907, 909.

41. *Ibid.*, pp. 1728–1729. See also *Social Contract*, pp. 421, 424.

42. *Constitutional Project for Corsica*, p. 919. Thus women of all ages are excluded from citizenship, a matter I discuss in Chapter 10. See also *ibid.*, pp. 943–944, for Rousseau's rough draft of an oath of allegiance to be taken by Corsicans "under the sky and with one's hand on the Bible." The terms of this oath correspond to the original contract in the *Social Contract*. But the Corsican oath is actually a ceremony of renewal or reunion, because mere reason or contractual commitment does not yield binding and reciprocal ties of common life.

43. *Ibid.*, p. 910. Like badges for Polish magistrates, the three Corsican ranks might suggest classical theories of virtue or distributive justice. But Rousseau's attention to individual merit differs from classic theories of proportionate equality. Magistrates' judgments of merit can take into

With his usual though often reluctant attention to variations of time and space, Rousseau noted that the economic simplicity appropriate to a republic could not even be attempted in a large, monarchical state.[44] Nevertheless, the attraction of self suffi cient farmers proved irresistible when Rousseau formulated his Polish proposal seven years later. Rousseau presented Polish patriots with a choice between two "incompatible" purposes which if mistakenly combined must yield a double failure. If Polish patriots chose the first, they were told to refrain from reading the rest of Rousseau's recommendations because "all my remaining proposals are directed exclusively to the second." As always, Rousseau saw no middle ground between slavery and liberty. If Poles' "only wish is to become noisy, brilliant and fearsome, and to influence other peoples of Europe, their example lies before you. . . . Cultivate the arts and sciences, commerce and industry; have professional soldiers, fortresses, and academies; above all have a good system of public finance which will make money circulate rapidly, and thereby multiply its effectiveness to your great profit; try to make money very necessary, in order to keep the people in a condition of great dependence." In this way "you will create a scheming, ardent, avid, ambitious, servile and knavish people, like all the rest; one given to the two extremes of opulence and misery, of license and slavery, with nothing in between." The alternative is "to create a free, wise and peaceful nation, one which has no fear or need of anyone, but is self-sufficient and happy." Here "you must preserve and revive among your

---

account only the "actions" or "services" of citizens, never "the judgment of persons." The latter can be judged only by "public esteem" or "the people." *Discourse on Inequality*, pp. 222–223. And "in a well-constituted state, all citizens are so equal that none is able to prefer the wisest or even the best dressed, but at most the best; even this last distinction is itself often dangerous because it makes knaves and hypocrites." Preface to *Narcisse*, p. 965.

44. *Constitutional Project for Corsica*, p. 933.

people simple customs and wholesome tastes, and a warlike spirit devoid of ambition; you must create courageous and unselfish souls; devote your people to agriculture and to the most necessary arts and crafts; you must make money contemptible and, if possible, useless, seeking and finding more powerful and reliable motives for the accomplishment of great deeds." Philosophes "will burn you no incense" but you will live "in true prosperity, justice and liberty."[45]

Poles too must employ to the greatest extent possible payment in kind, corvées, and nonmonetary rewards of official honors. Modern theorists who mistakenly think "pecuniary interest" a natural passion of men overlook the "reserve of grand passions" in every heart. Those who truly "know the human heart" affirm that a desire for personal profits is the "least and weakest" as well as "the worst, the basest and the most corrupting" of all passions. Indeed, the acquisitive man is not truly passionate: "The miser has no truly dominant passion; he aspires to money only as a matter of foresight, in order to be able to satisfy such passions as may thereafter come to him."[46]

These censures against economic acquisition and commerce are applications of the "principles of political right" Rousseau had developed in the *Social Contract*. Money permits corrupt men "to serve the state with their purse rather than their person." Mercenaries enslave a people and salaried representatives sell the state to the others: "Use money thus, and you will soon have chains. The word 'finance' is the word of a slave; it is unknown in the true republic. In a genuinely free state, the citizens do everything with their own hands and nothing by means of money; far from paying for exemption from their duties, they would pay to discharge them in person. I am very

45. *Government of Poland*, pp. 1003–1004. See also *Discourse on Inequality*, p. 120.
46. *Government of Poland*, pp. 1005–1008.

far from sharing received ideas: I believe that compulsory service is less contrary to liberty than is taxation."[47] Among truly virtuous citizens, of course, there would be nothing compulsory about corvées, for a sincerely virtuous citizen wills what is willed by the citizens whom he cherishes.[48]

Nevertheless, Rousseau's reliance in Poland and Corsica upon self-sufficient farmers represents a fragile compromise. Each citizen would own and cultivate enough land to permit all to postpone the slavery of an economic division of labor and contractual exchange; but such men have already traveled beyond the preproperty "best state" described in the *Discourse on Inequality*.

On the one hand the motivation for the original acquisition of land is unrelated to natural bodily needs, for possession is dictated by a desire for public esteem. From the perspective of natural equality, Rousseau left no doubt regarding the legitimacy of this claim to exclusive possession, this "new kind of right," this "precarious and abusive right." Industrious or strong men, who build the first wall around land and labor on it, are "destitute of valid reasons to justify" their "usurpations" of common land: "Who gave you its dimensions, . . . and by virtue of what do you presume to be paid at our expense for work we did not impose on you?"[49] On the other hand, there is no denying that many men of all contemporary societies do own and do expect to continue to own land. Efforts to deprive men of property would be the sheer force of a particular will, duplicating the force of original acquisition. Because contemporary men have authorized representative government to protect their "life, liberty and property," Rousseau asserted

47. *Social Contract*, pp. 428–429.
48. *Discourse on Political Economy*, p. 254. See also *Last Response*, p. 82; *Discourse on Inequality*, p. 190; *Fragments on the State of War* (P, III, 614); *La Nouvelle Héloise*, p. 108.
49. *Discourse on Inequality*, pp. 174, 176.

that the "civil right" of property has become, for them, "the most sacred of all the rights of citizens."[50]

Self-sufficient farmers are thus a compromise. Although Rousseau declared in his Corsican proposals that he preferred common ownership of all land, although he suggested arrangements for establishing some common land in Corsica, he accepted the impossibility of eliminating personal ownership. But Corsicans should confine personal ownership within the "narrowest possible limits." They should "give it a measure, a rule, a rein which will contain, direct, and subjugate it, and keep it ever subordinate to the public good." Sumptuary laws and an agrarian law prohibiting large acquisitions could not be retroactive, but they would help to prevent further inequalities.[51] In Poland, however, sumptuary laws would be a futile and tyrannic expedient, so opposed to Polish habits of action and belief that acquisitive desires would be further stimulated by efforts at legal restraint.[52] And because in every society there exists a natural tendency toward a division between rich and poor, civil laws must constantly combat personal acquisition that exceeds natural need.[53] Rousseau defended the principle of proportionate taxation which takes into account citizens' relative property, the relation between necessities and luxuries,

50. *Discourse on Political Economy*, pp. 248, 263. See also *ibid.*, pp. 269–270. Rousseau's misleading use of the Lockeian phrase is not accidental: later in the manuscript margin he has scribbled, "See Locke." *Ibid.*, p. 1406. Rousseau added that this new civil right of property is "more important in some respects than liberty itself" because it is more essential to the preservation of life, more vulnerable, and "the true foundation of civil society." This last point means only that personal possessions are "the true guaranty of the obligations of citizens, for if properties were not answerable for persons, nothing would be easier than to evade one's duties and laugh at the laws." *Ibid.*, p. 263. See also *Fragments on the Social Pact* (P, III, 483).

51. *Constitutional Project for Corsica*, p. 931.

52. *Government of Poland*, pp. 964–966.

53. *Discourse on Inequality*, pp. 187–188; *Letter to d'Alembert*, p. 155; *Government of Poland*, p. 1002.

and the relative advantages for rich and poor derived from membership in a state. A citizen with ten times the property of another ought to pay ten times the tax. A citizen possessing only the necessities for life should pay no tax. The tax on a wealthy man, who alone profits from the "social confederation," may be extended to everything he has in excess of necessities. He will "claim that, when his rank is taken into account, what may be superfluous to a man of inferior rank is necessary for him. But this is a delusion, because a duke has two legs, just like a herdsman, and but one stomach, too." Moreover, severe taxes on frivolous possessions cannot encourage fraudulent concealment, because the reason for their possession is to be visible.[54]

For the true republic described in the *Social Contract*, Rousseau observed that possessions need not be absolutely identical for every citizen but that "no citizen shall be rich enough to buy another and none so poor as to be forced to sell himself" to others. In fact, there is very little range for unequal possessions in this cautious formulation because men are bought and sold as soon as there is contractual exchange. And wealthy men and beggars are "equally fatal to the common good" because one buys and the other sells the "public freedom." Virtuous citizens avoid the "wretchedness" of the poor and "usurpation" by the rich, for the "social state is advantageous to men only when all possess something and none has too much." And personal property, in every society and of whatever amount, remains a "civil right," never a private or presocial natural right: "The right of any individual over his own estate is always subordinate to the right of the community over everything." Personal property is justified only when everyone's limited possessions are sanctioned by the express warrant of a sovereign people.[55]

Thus, in spite of man's natural indolence, useful work for

54. *Discourse on Political Economy*, pp. 271, 276–277. See also *Government of Poland*, pp. 1010–1012.
55. *Social Contract*, pp. 391–392, 367. For a similar view of Rousseau's

one's subsistence is a civic duty. The "severe working-conditions" of self-sufficient Corsicans will prevent the vice of idleness: "The stupid pride of the burghers serves only to debase and discourage the farm-worker. A prey to indolence and its attendant passions, they plunge themselves into debauchery and sell themselves for pleasure. Selfishness makes them servile, and idleness makes them restless; they are either slaves or mutineers, never free men."[56] Indeed, men who do not perform unofficial corvées of personal sustenance repudiate common life by leaving unpaid their "debt to society." An idle son who inherits the property of a wealthy father is a "thief" and "scarcely differs from a brigand who lives off those who pass his way." He "owes more to others than if he had been born with nothing," because he is wealthy. "It is not just that what one man has done for society should discharge another's debt, for since every man owes all that he is to society, he can only pay his own debt, and no father can transmit to his son the right to be useless to his fellow citizens; . . . Rich or poor, powerful or weak, every idle citizen is a knave."[57]

Finally, all the aspects of a united and disciplined common life are also arguments against professional mediation and recall the amateur virtuosity of early citizens. Such citizens neither exercise nor suffer the intimidating skills of specialists and professional interpreters. "Our distinction between the legal and military castes was unknown to the ancients," Rousseau reminded Polish patriots: "Citizens were neither lawyers nor

---

consistency about property and his rejection of Locke's private right to property, see Einaudi, *Early Rousseau*, pp. 197–201. For a contrasting understanding, specifically the view that Rousseau had a Lockeian view of property in the early writings and a collectivist view in the later ones, see Havens, "Diderot, Rousseau, and the *Discours sur l'inégalité*," pp. 255–256; Derathé, introduction to the *Discourse on Political Economy* (P, III, lxxv–lxxvi).

56. *Constitutional Project for Corsica*, pp. 904, 911. See also *Social Contract*, p. 427.

57. *Emile*, pp. 469–470.

soldiers nor priests by profession; they performed all these services as a matter of duty. That is the real secret of making everything proceed toward the common goal, and of preventing the spirit of faction from taking root at the expense of patriotism, so that the hydra of chicanery will not devour a nation."[58] As we have seen, Rousseau would punish as treason the theft of state funds. But "virtue is the only effective instrument" and "integrity . . . the only curb" against this assault upon the citadel of common life: "Books and auditors' accounts tend less to expose frauds than to conceal them; and prudence is never as quick to conceive new precautions as knavery is to elude them. Forget, then, about account books and papers, and place public revenues in honest hands; that is the only way they will be honestly handled."[59]

If Corsicans rely upon "great talents" in the magistracy, they no longer love their fatherland and respect their magistrates. The official responsibility for tax collection should become a "test of ability and integrity" for younger citizens, "the novitiate, so to speak, for public employment, and the first step toward the winning of magistracies." In contrast, "professional tax-farmers" are a "fatal example" to citizens, "an example which, all too promptly diffused throughout the nation, destroys all worthy feelings by making illicit wealth and its advantages respectable, and by casting unselfishness, simplicity, morality and all the virtues under a cloud of scorn and opprobrium." By tilling his field the Corsican citizen acquires everything necessary for true magistracy, namely virtuous passions and common sense. The only administrative office that will require "skill, calculation, and thought" is a state accountant who records efforts to maintain an optimum proportion of tax contributions in money and kind.[60]

58. *Government of Poland*, p. 1000.
59. *Discourse on Political Economy*, pp. 265–266.
60. *Constitutional Project for Corsica*, pp. 940–941, 933–935.

Poland's precarious international position permits experience and talent, but not social rank or economic fortune, to be considered in selecting military officers. The Polish monarch, to become an elective position, may also regain the military leadership which should accompany his office. The Polish army itself, however, must become a militia of citizens performing corvées. Because the experiences of "every free state" demonstrate that its members are its "true defenders," every citizen must remain "a soldier by duty, none by profession." A monarch can enslave his fellow citizens only by employing professional forces, "because it is inconceivable that the nation could be used to oppress itself, at least when all those who comprise it are given a share of freedom." Even in the cause of national education, Polish patriots must not make teachers a caste: "No public man in Poland should have any other permanent rank than that of citizen." When necessary, judges possess the discretionary power to supplement legal decisions "in the light of natural justice and common sense." But citizens' integrity and knowledge of civil law are usually sufficient to assure justice. A complicated mass of civil laws leads only to endless discussions and litigation in which men become the prey of eloquent professionals who poison an atmosphere of mutual trust: "To eliminate arbitrary judgments, [the English] have subjected themselves to a thousand judgments which are iniquitous and even absurd. Hordes of lawyers devour them, endless lawsuits consume them; and with the mad idea of trying to provide for every eventuality, they have turned their laws into an immense labyrinth where money and reason alike are lost." The legal calling, "intrinsically so respectable, grows vile and degrading as soon as it becomes a trade." Positions involving legal service and judgment should remain temporary and honorific: "I should like every public function to serve in this way as a stepping-stone to another, so that no one, in the expectation of staying in any one office, will turn it into a lucrative profession, and place himself above the judgment of men."[61] This versatility Rousseau demanded is also an adaptation of the general qualifications for magistrates of "legitimate government" in the *Social Contract*. Because qualities of "common sense, justice and integrity" suffice, magistrates are selected by lot from among all citizens.[62]

The slavery of professionalism, however, is never confined to official estates. Every particular will and partial society, nongovernmental as well as governmental, unorganized and organized, threatens the unity and discipline of common life. Perfect harmony is never possible for, even in the simplicity of the golden age, self-governing citizens are also fathers and husbands. Yet free men remain essentially members of the corporate whole, sincerely virtuous citizens.

For this reason doctors commanding submissive patients represent threats to the integrity of the whole identical at least in form to those posed by official talents. No doubt the art of medicine is useful to some men, Rousseau observed, but medicine does more harm to mankind than all the evils it professes to cure: "I myself do not know of what illness doctors cure us, but I do know that they infect us with very fatal diseases: cowardice, timidity, credulity, the terror of death. If they cure the body, they kill the courage." The virtuous citizen exhibits no alarm when summoning himself to the performance of his duties: "Doctors with their orders, philosophes with their precepts, priests with their exhortations are the ones who debase the heart, and make us forget how to die."[63]

Rousseau observed in the *Social Contract* that when common life is simple and sincere, citizens actually consider themselves a single body by joyfully acceding to their general will

---

61. *Government of Poland*, pp. 1013–1016, 967, 1000–1002. See also *Letter to Grimm* (Nov. 1, 1751; P, III, 69).

62. *Social Contract*, pp. 442–443. Military leadership, however, is determined by election.

63. *Emile*, pp. 269–270. See also *ibid.*, pp. 256–257, 1306; *Favre Manuscript* (P, IV, 85–86); *Discourse on Inequality*, pp. 138–139.

of civic virtue. Should occasion require new civil laws, the citizen who first proposes them merely voices "what everyone already feels." There is no need for "intrigues or eloquence" when citizens are not consumed by particular wills: "Then all the animating forces of the state are vigorous and simple; its principles are clear and luminous; it has no incompatible or conflicting interests; the common good makes itself so manifestly evident that only common sense is needed to discern it. Peace, unity, equality are enemies of political sophistication."[64] The citizens depicted in the *Social Contract* are free because they are virtuous: the temporal location of a true republic must be a historical period of simple *moeurs*. And all the institutional arrangements in the *Social Contract*, especially "legitimate government," are designed to prevent that dismemberment of common life which is slavery. Magistrates in the *Social Contract* do mediate. But their mediation does not divide the corporate whole between rulers and ruled. Legitimate government guarantees literal self-government, and only in part because this government must not become an opaque profession of the talented.

64. *Social Contract*, p. 437.

PART FOUR

A VISION OF
SELF-GOVERNMENT

CHAPTER 9

Citizens as Subjects

Rousseau was a lawgiver without a constituency, a lawgiver of the pen who could fix in words alone the contours of a true republic and the education of a self-governing citizen. Although the story of Emile's education does not constitute a legal treatise, both the *Social Contract* and *Emile* concern social men who remain free. The difference in social scale presents no problem since numbers have no intrinsic significance to a nonindividualist philosopher: the fussy, detailed *Emile* and the apparently lean and taut *Social Contract* are companion political writings. Nonindividualism and anarchism are perfectly, if fragilely, realized in Rousseau's imaginary societies.[1]

1. This view of the companion character of the *Social Contract* and *Emile* contrasts with interpretations cited earlier which distinguish within Rousseau's thought a collectivist civil liberty from an individualist moral liberty, and civic virtue from simplicity, and public from private education. See, in addition, Lanson, "L'Unité de la pensée de Rousseau," pp. 19–20, 24–25; Wright, *Meaning of Rousseau*, pp. 67, 70, 100; Hendel, *Rousseau*, I, 75–79; Martin Rang, "L'Education publique et la formation des citoyens chez Rousseau," in *Etudes sur le* Contrat social, pp. 253–262; Derathé, "L'Unité de la pensée de Rousseau," pp. 214–218; Derathé, introduction to *Social Contract* (P, III, xcvii–xcviii); Burgelin, *La Philosophie de l'existence de Rousseau*, pp. 474–565; Jouvenel, "Essai," pp. 85–88, 93–94; Jean Château, *Jean-Jacques Rousseau: Sa philosophie de l'éducation* (Paris, 1962), pp. 91–98, 129–156, 181–190, 235–241; Broome, *Rousseau*, pp. 85, 95–96, 100–102, 121–124; Paul H. Meyer, "The Individual and Society in Rousseau's *Emile*," *Modern Language Quarterly*, XIX (June 1958), 99–114; Masters, *Political Philosophy of Rousseau*, pp. 85–98, 348–353.

I do not examine the short, unfinished sequel to *Emile*. See *Emile et*

The self-government Rousseau envisioned in the *Social Contract* and *Emile* stands in stark contrast to the modern state. He never relinquished the perspective of the presocial condition of natural liberty and goodness, but contemporary slavery is only a side issue in the *Social Contract* and *Emile*. These writings are reveries on the "great and useless science" of political right.[2] In the societies Rousseau described, slavery is avoided, not accounted for or deflected. As parallel fictions, these societies embody his criterion of political legitimacy: literal self-government provides a conceivable and feasible standard for judging contemporary slavery.

Consequently, the "events" in the *Social Contract* must occur within the third period described in the *Discourse on Inequality*, that irretrievable "best society" of simple *moeurs:* they could never follow historically or remedy the later events described in that work. The lawgiver's foundation of a free society and a virtuous citizenry's subsequent establishment of legitimate government are both irreconcilable with the slavery men authorize in later periods of common life. Emile's education is also premodern. The *Discourse on Inequality* traces the cumulative transformation in the "life of the species" over a "multitude of centuries" by following a single, representative society to our own state of war. Emile's metamorphosis as a single, representative creature of his association with Rousseau repeats only the first half of this transformation: virtuous citizenship remains the political fulfillment of naturally free and good men. Rousseau's understanding of the sensibility and the

Sophie; ou, les solitaires (P, IV, 881–924). For a discussion of Emile's "betrayal" by Sophie's "treason," and of possible endings to *Emile et Sophie*, see Pierre Burgelin, introduction (P, IV, cliii–clxvii). For an interpretation consistent with my own view of *Emile*, see Jack W. Deaver, "La Liberté individuelle dans *Emile et Sophie*," in Michel Launay, *et al.*, *Jean-Jacques Rousseau et son temps* (Paris, 1969), pp. 151–158. See also Starobinski, *Rousseau*, pp. 157–169.

2. *Emile* (P, IV, 836).

gradually awakened faculties of a single infant in *Emile* parallels his understanding of the original "infant"[3] of the species in the *Discourse on Inequality*. In short, the *Social Contract* and *Emile*, together, are profoundly melancholic *histoires*. As forcefully as explicit indictments, they testify to the depth of Rousseau's rejection of contemporary society. They are a monument to Rousseau's self-exile, for compassionate fellowship is unavailable to modern slaves, and *Emile* is not a remedial instruction manual for modern parents.[4]

3. *Discourse on Inequality* (P, III, 160). Masters translates "child" for *enfant*.

4. For interpretations which argue that the *Social Contract* provides a basis for contemporary men's remedial or revolutionary action, see Wright, *Meaning of Rousseau*, pp. 71, 92; Broome, *Rousseau*, pp. 34–35, 48–49, 52–53, 63–77, 104–114; Crocker, "The Relation of Rousseau's Second *Discours* and the *Contrat social*," pp. 35–37; Zygmunt Jedryka, "Du gouvernement de la liberté selon Rousseau," *Le Contrat social*, VI (Nov.–Dec. 1962), 356–364; Jean Fabre, "Réalité et utopie dans la pensée politique de Rousseau," *Annales*, XXXV (1959–1962), 192–213; Hendel, *Rousseau*, I, 133, 171–177; II, 163. For interpretations which argue the impractical character of the *Social Contract*, see Starobinski, *Rousseau*, pp. 33–42, 123–124, 219–221, 279–297, 330–332; Starobinski, "Du *Discours de l'inégalité* au *Contrat social*," pp. 97–110; Starobinski, "La Pensée politique de Rousseau," pp. 83–84, 92–94, 97–98; Hoffmann, "Du *Contrat social*," pp. 303–310; Jouvenel, "Essai," pp. 38, 88–92; Weil, "Rousseau et sa politique," pp. 17–18, 26; Derathé, *Rousseau et la science politique*, pp. 23–25; Eméry, "Le *Contrat social* et la genèse des cités," *Le Contrat social*, VI (May–June 1962), 155–158.

Rousseau conceded that "it is impossible to make an Emile." Instead of a "true treatise on education," *Emile* is a "somewhat philosophical work on that principle advanced by the author in other writings, namely *that man is naturally good*." Letter to Cramer (Oct. 8, 1764; CC, XXI, 248). See also *Rousseau juge de Jean-Jacques* (P, I, 934); *Confessions* (P, I, 56–57). Elsewhere, noting that he never intended to provide an instructional "method for fathers and mothers," Rousseau explained his habit of addressing contemporary parents as a device which assures brevity and clarity. *Letters from the Mountain* (P, III, 783). See also *Favre Manuscript* (P, IV, 104); *Emile*, pp. 242, 264, 549–550. A similar disavowal of interest in practical reform for the larger society is in *Social Contract* (P, III, 351). See also *ibid.*, p. 470; *Geneva Manuscript* (P, III, 281); *Fragments on Laws* (P, IV, 500); letter to Mirabeau (July 26, 1767; CG, XVII, 155–157).

Furthermore, the effects upon Emile of Rousseau's guidance duplicate the transition from private to public self accomplished by the lawgiver in the *Social Contract*: the society in *Emile* is a miniature republic of citizen and lawgiver. At the conclusion of his education Emile does join a numerically larger, contemporary political society. But, owing to the corruption of European life from which Emile heretofore has been shielded, this membership is only a formality. Rousseau summarizes for Emile's benefit the "principles of political right" in the *Social Contract*, for every social relationship, first permitting self-recognition and appropriately ending with virtuous citizenship, is a public matter involving mutual instruction or "education."[5] Although Rousseau rejected the view that a true republic could derive historically from a deliberate contract, he employed the idea of a contract in both writings to define that convention which affirms the natural equality of men. Similarly, the Savoyard vicar's "natural religion" in *Emile* and the "civil religion" in the *Social Contract* are conclusive, essential lessons of identical political purpose for their respective citizens.[6]

The companion forms of common life exhibited in the *Social*

5. Rousseau frequently employed *education* as a synonym for *nurture* and to refer to cumulative social transformations. See *Discourse on Inequality*, p. 133; *Emile*, pp. 247, 252, 550–551; *Confessions*, pp. 10, 205; *Rousseau juge de Jean-Jacques*, p. 799.

6. Wolmar's autarky might appear more similar than the society of *Emile* to that of the *Social Contract*. In addition to the sudden autobiographical twists of the story [see F. C. Green, *Jean-Jacques Rousseau: A Critical Study of His Life and Writings* (Cambridge, 1955), pp. 184–213], there are two general reasons for distinguishing *La Nouvelle Héloise* from the *Social Contract* and *Emile*. First, Clarens is a partially restored society, at best analogous to Rousseau's Poland. The partial recovery of the main characters—and constant reference is made in *La Nouvelle Héloise* to the rebirth of Julie and Saint-Preux especially— follows that life of self-contradiction and hypocrisy which begins when the wish of Julie and Saint-Preux to marry collides with contemporary *moeurs*. In contrast, the imaginary societies of the *Social Contract* and

Contract and *Emile* supply a kind of sustained snapshot of Rousseau's political imagination. Changes in the common life either of the citizens in the *Social Contract* or of Emile after Rousseau has completed his education herald the irreversible slavery which concludes the *Discourse on Inequality*. Citizens in the *Social Contract* are subjects, but they obey only themselves. Emile is temporarily Rousseau's "subject,"[7] but he never obeys Rousseau. And, perhaps because of its advantageous scale, *Emile* is less curdled than the *Social Contract*.[8] Many

---

Emile involve simple *moeurs* faithful to man's original liberty and goodness.

More important, Clarens itself is an extended family. It has rulers and ruled in the fashion that Rousseau permitted within familial society. As a benevolent paternal despot, Wolmar rules servants and laborers as his children, as his "subjects" or simply "good subjects." Like relationships among "members of a family," there is "authority" in Clarens, for their common life is a "concord of equals" joined to the "subordination of inferiors." To be sure, those who command are "moderate" and those who obey are "zealous." But ruler and ruled are distinct. Only during annual grape harvests and music festivals is there that "reunion of different estates" which briefly restores the "natural order" of "sweet equality" or "liberty." *La Nouvelle Héloïse* (P, II, 445, 452, 460, 468–469, 548, 604–611). Thus, Rousseau's anarchistic imperative governs only the society of the novel's protagonists: Julie, Saint-Preux, Bomston, Wolmar and especially Claire are constantly curing, restoring, guiding, instructing, and testing one another, as equals. Perhaps these reasons explain why Rousseau repeatedly refused to place on the title page of *La Nouvelle Héloïse* the "Citizen of Geneva" motto which adorned all other writings published between 1750 and 1763, the year of his formal renunciation of Genevan citizenship. Rousseau also judged *La Nouvelle Héloïse* an "insipid and flat romance." See letter to Vernet (Nov. 29, 1760; CC, VII, 330); letter to Lenieps (Dec. 11, 1760; *ibid.*, p. 350). We need not share this judgment, but it does contrast with his pride in *Emile*. For similar interpretations of *La Nouvelle Héloïse* as a familial society that is inegalitarian, see Starobinski, *Rousseau*, pp. 102–139; Berman, *Politics of Authenticity*, pp. 231–264. For contrasting views of the significance of Clarens, see Broome, *Rousseau*, pp. 125–147; Shklar, *Men and Citizens*, pp. 57–74, 85–91, 119–184.

7. *Emile*, pp. 242, 465.

8. Rousseau called *Emile* his "best" and "most important" writing. See

years after the publication of the *Social Contract*, Rousseau was reported to have remarked that it "is a book to be rewritten, but I have neither the strength nor the time."[9] With *Emile* he had already rewritten, in the form of a replica, the *Social Contract*. As Rousseau himself said, the two writings "together form a complete whole."[10]

A True Republic

The *Social Contract* is divided into four books, but more fundamental is the division, with occasional overlap, between book one and the three succeeding books. Book one describes the effects of a contractual transition from the state of natural isolation to political society. The contract, however, is only the philosophical origin of this political society, an idea of right which defines those "essential conditions" responsible for man's transformation from private, self-governing individual to public, self-governing individual. It does not refer to an event that either has occurred or might have occurred in historical space and time, even though Rousseau referred to it as an act undertaken by men.[11] Hence the full title of this work is *Of the Social Contract; or, Principles of Political Right*: Rousseau was concerned with "not what is but with what is

Confessions, pp. 566, 573; *Rousseau juge de Jean-Jacques*, p. 687. See also *Letter to Beaumont* (P, IV, 935). For a view which argues that *Emile* is the major synthesis of Rousseau's political thought and that Emile's marriage to Sophie represents a "coexistence" of the two ideals of nature and society, see Peter D. Jimack, *La Genèse et la rédaction de l'*Emile *de J.-J. Rousseau*, in *Studies on Voltaire and the Eighteenth Century*, vol. 13 (1960), pp. 94–125.

9. Dusaulx, *De mes rapports avec J. J. Rousseau* (1789), p. 102; quoted in P, III, ciii.

10. Letter to Duchesne (May 23, 1762; CC, X, 281). Rousseau also wanted the works to be published simultaneously and said that the *Social Contract* is a "kind of appendix" to *Emile*.

11. *Social Contract*, pp. 360–361, 359, 378.

appropriate and just."[12] And he often referred elsewhere to his *Principles of Political Right*.[13]

The "events" of the succeeding three books, however, are conceivable in an imaginary time and space. In general, book two concerns the foundation of a true republic by a lawgiver and the character of popular sovereignty. Book three covers the subsequent establishment and operation of legitimate government. Book four discusses additional institutional devices designed to preserve the unity and discipline of common life first provided by the lawgiver.[14]

12. *Geneva Manuscript*, p. 305. Rousseau claimed in letters to his publisher that the *Social Contract* is "a book for all times," a "republican's" statement of those "principles" by which contemporary societies can be judged. Letters to Rey (Nov. 7, 1761; *CC*, IX, 221; and May 29, 1762; *CC*, X, 306–308). For Rousseau's defense of "general and abstract truth" as "the most valuable of all goods," see *Rêveries* (P, I, 1026–1031).

13. See letter to Rey (Aug. 9, 1761; *CC*, IX, 90); *Emile*, p. 311n. See also P, III, 1410.

14. Rousseau later asserted, after its condemnation by Genevan officials, that the *Social Contract* had described the "history of the government of Geneva," its "image from its birth to this day," and that the Genevan constitution had been his "model of political institutions." *Letters from the Mountain*, p. 809. Even this carefully qualified defense cannot be taken seriously, for Rousseau went on to distinguish the "legitimate" state which makes Genevans free from the "actual" state which makes them slaves. The Genevan government, "charged with the execution of laws" in the "ancient" constitution (which Rousseau called a "democracy" on four occasions), was at that time above the laws and had destroyed the "common equality." *Ibid.*, pp. 813–816, 824, 832, 837, 866–867. Further, Rousseau hurriedly summarized the *Social Contract* in the *Letters*. He used the phrase "will of all" instead of "general will" when defining inalienable popular sovereignty, concluding that sovereignty "resides essentially" in all members of the body politic. *Ibid.*, pp. 807–809. (But compare *ibid.*, p. 850.) The ninth and last *Letter* contains praise for some contemporary Genevans, but Rousseau clarified his position by asserting that Romans, Spartans, and "even Athenians" were far superior to Genevans. Most Genevans were like other modern men. They were "tradesmen, artisans, and bourgeois who are always concerned with their private interests, work, commerce, and profits." Liberty for men who "do not think of the public interest until their own interest is threatened" means the power to acquire property. *Ibid.*,

Thus, the free society imagined in the *Social Contract* has both philosophical and historical origins: the consequences of the lawgiver's foundation are identical with those which "follow" the nonevent of a social contract. While it is no more possible for us than it was for Rousseau to avoid discussing the social contract as if it refers or could refer to a historical event, the only comprehensible foundation of a true republic involves a lawgiver. For this reason Rousseau rejected contractual origin. Both natural men and early social men are incapable of the reason and foresight such contracts assume. In a contractual foundation, the efficient "cause" of common life would itself be the "effect" of common life: "The social spirit which must be the product of social institutions would have to preside over the setting up of those institutions; men would have to have already become before the advent of law that which they become as a result of law." Because Rousseau's social contract is a nonevent, he did not describe the intervening historical stages between the presocial state of nature and the foundation of a true republic. He merely assumed that the "primitive condition cannot endure," that "men reach a point where the obstacles to their preservation in a state of nature prove greater than the strength that each man has to preserve himself in the state." The ideas that all men are born "free and equal" and that "common liberty is a consequence of man's nature" require some intellectual bridge between natural independence and a free society. The idea of a social contract provides this bridge: "Since no man has any natural authority over his fellows, and since force alone bestows no right, all legitimate authority among men must be based on covenants."[15]

---

p. 881. There is a brief summary of the major interpretations regarding the Genevan "inspiration" of the *Social Contract* in P, III, 1664–1665. For Rousseau's "incontestable distortion of the Genevan past," see Jean-Daniel Candaux, introduction to the *Letters from the Mountain* (*ibid.*, pp. cxcvi–cxcvii).

15. *Social Contract*, pp. 383, 360, 352, 355. See also *ibid.*, p. 380; *Geneva Manuscript*, pp. 281–282; *Fragments on the State of Nature* (**P,**

The beginning of the first book of the *Social Contract* is familiar: "Man was born free, and he is everywhere in chains. Those who think themselves the masters of others are indeed greater slaves than they. How did this transformation come about? I do not know. What can make it legitimate? That question I believe I can answer." The social contract establishes the legitimacy of some "chains" of common life, specifically those bonds which make citizens self-governing. True citizens remain "perfectly independent of all [their] fellow citizens." Thus, in every true republic there exists, in fact, a social bond of reciprocal obligations and mutual trust: "My purpose is to consider if, in political society, there can be any legitimate and sure principle of government, taking men as they are [by nature] and laws as they might be. In this inquiry I shall try always to bring together what right permits with what interest prescribes so that justice and utility are in no way divided."[16]

Through this inconceivable "act by which people become *a* people," the creators of political society are themselves new creatures of common life. Every member is incorporated "as an indivisible part of the whole." The whole itself is not a contractual aggregation of unchanged partners because "in place of the individual person" there is created an "artificial [*moral*] and collective body" which receives, from the social contract, "its unity, its common *ego*, its life and its will." And "passing from the state of nature to the civil society produces a truly remarkable change in man; it puts justice as a rule of conduct in the place of instinct, and gives his actions the moral quality they previously lacked." Rousseau's social contract also conveys his anarchistic imperative. A citizen's "civil" or

---

III, 479). For a similar understanding of the contract as a nonevent that defines political right, see Pierre Burgelin, *Jean-Jacques Rousseau et la religion de Genève* (Geneva, 1962), pp. 31–32, and Leigh, "Liberté et autorité dans le *Contrat social*," p. 258. For a contrasting view, see Starobinski, "La Pensée politique de Rousseau," pp. 94–95.

16. *Social Contract*, pp. 351, 391.

"moral" liberty is "limited" only by the general will, by his own most comprehensive will. The social contract is a "reciprocal commitment between society and the individual, so that each person, in making a contract, as it were, with himself" is obligated only to the compassionate fellowship of which he is a creature.[17]

More specifically, this contract defines the conditions essential for social men's literal self-government: the unrepresentable general will of civic virtue and the inalienable sovereignty of the corporate whole. The general will is the united power of all citizens, their "single motive." It is the "social bond" common to particular wills because "if there were no point on which separate interests coincided, then society could not conceivably exist": the general will derives its generality not from the number of voices on any occasion but "from the common interest which unites them." The general will, as "the moral self" of a determinate whole, is "always rightful and always tends toward the public good." It is the "indestructible" or "constant" will of every member, so that even if an ignoble citizen sells his vote for money, "he does not extinguish the general will in himself; he evades it." Once again, the actual decisions of citizens might err. When citizens are not virtuous, when the "social bond is broken in every heart," a great discrepancy exists between the given general will and a "will of all," the sum of expressed desires. But even in such circumstances, the general will has not been "annihilated or corrupted." The general will itself is "always unchanging, incorruptible and pure."[18]

17. *Ibid.*, pp. 359, 361, 364, 362.
18. *Ibid.*, pp. 360, 368, 374, 371, 438, 440. Rousseau stated that the general will is the sum of the differences when all the pluses and minuses of contending particular wills have canceled each other. *Ibid.*, p. 371. This means that the *effects* of cancellation can leave an accurate *declaration* of the general will. This declaration is what is left after, not what results from, such cancellation. See also *ibid.*, pp. 368, 371n. For a similar view of this passage, see Plamenatz, *Man and Society*, I, 393.

Sovereignty, in turn, is "nothing other than the exercise of the general will." Sovereignty gives the whole its "movement and will," so that only "authentic acts" of the general will yield true laws. Because all members are entitled to participate directly in the affairs of common life, the sovereignty of a people must not be divided or transferred: "Just as nature gives each man an absolute power over all his own limbs, the social contract gives the body politic an absolute power over all its members; and it is this same power which, directed by the general will, bears . . . the name of sovereignty."[19] Any division or representation of sovereignty transfers liberty to particular men and enslaves all men by dismembering common life: the circumference of membership has narrowed to include only those who would claim the sovereign power of the original whole as their own.[20]

Like the infallible general will, "the sovereign by the mere fact that it is, is always all that it ought to be." No "fundamental law" can bind the sovereign, not even the original contract itself: it would contradict "the very nature of a political body" for the sovereign, "bearing only one single and identical aspect" of a "single person," to make a binding contract with itself. Nor, because no one is unjust to himself, can true laws be unjust. A sovereign people is always at liberty to alter its laws, even its best laws. As a matter of expediency only ancient laws obtain continuous respect. But a true republic always exists and endures through the legislative will of a sovereign people.[21]

Rousseau's contract is unique because it precludes any contractual relationship involving the responsibilities of rulers and the rights of the ruled. He used two curious expressions, "total

19. *Social Contract*, pp. 368–371, 378–379, 425, 372.
20. *Ibid.*, pp. 369–370, 421–422, 426–427, 429–433. For a different understanding of the significance of indivisible sovereignty, see Derathé, *Rousseau et la science politique*, pp. 280–294.
21. *Social Contract*, pp. 362–363, 394, 424. See also Ronald Grimsley, *The Philosophy of Rousseau* (London, 1973), pp. 99–104.

alienation" and "forcing men to be free," to characterize this historically inconceivable contract, phrases which are perhaps murky but which suggest suppression of liberty only if taken out of context.

Rousseau maintained that the "articles of association, rightly understood, are reducible to a single one, namely the total alienation by each associate of himself and all his rights to the whole community." To alienate is "to give or sell." And "total alienation" simply refers to an individual's contracting with the corporate whole. By total alienation each individual exchanges natural independence for the civil or moral liberty of the self-governing citizen.

Immediately after reducing all the articles of the contract to total alienation, Rousseau elaborated on this formulation. If interest is to become united with civic duty, if the social bond is to be "as perfect as possible," everyone's total alienation "to the whole community" is necessary: "The conditions [of association] are the same for all, and precisely because they are the same for all, it is in no one's interest to make the conditions onerous for others." If members make exclusive claims unsanctioned by the entire society, there would be no "higher authority to judge between them and the public," and the general will would be inapplicable in some cases or for some members. In the resulting tumult of particular wills, "each individual, being his own judge in some causes, would soon demand to be his judge in all; and in this way the state of nature would be kept in being, and the association [would] inevitably become either tyrannical or void." Consequently, only total alienation of every member assures absolute liberty: "Since each man gives himself to all, he gives himself to no one; and since there is no associate over whom he does not gain the same rights as others gain over him, each man recovers the equivalent of everything he loses, and in the bargain he acquires more power to preserve what he has." It is, then, "manifestly false to assert that individuals make any real renunciation [of liberty] by the social contract." Because of the contract, "they find themselves in a situation truly preferable in real terms to that which prevailed before; instead of an alienation, they have profitably exchanged an uncertain and precarious life for a better and more secure one; they have exchanged natural independence for freedom, the power to destroy others for the enjoyment of their own security."[22]

Rousseau concluded the first book of the *Social Contract* "with an observation which might serve as a basis" for this society based on total alienation: "The social pact, far from destroying natural equality, substitutes, on the contrary, a moral and lawful equality for whatever physical inequality that nature may have imposed upon mankind; so that however unequal in strength or intelligence, men become equal by covenant and by right." This moral equality means that every citizen is "perfectly independent of all his fellow citizens and excessively dependent on the republic" of which he is a creature.[23]

The salutary effect of total alienation is specific in the instance of property. Before the social contract or, in other words, before political society existed, exclusive ownership was mere "possession" that could not be justified by appeals to natural appetite or to private right, whether of the strongest or the first occupant. After the social contract, and only because of total alienation of all the goods of all associates, the same possession has become "property," and it is now defended by "legal right" or a "legal title" respected by fellow citizens.

Before political society, a first occupant's claim "to any piece of land whatever" was a better, though still inadequate, claim than the right of the strongest. For it to be legitimate, how-

22. *Social Contract*, pp. 360–361, 355, 375.
23. *Ibid.*, pp. 367, 394. For similar understandings of total alienation, see Derathé, *Rousseau et la science politique*, pp. 171, 201, 227–236, 240, 243–247, 350–358, 365–374; Leigh, "Liberté et autorité dans le *Contrat social*," pp. 252–253.

ever, certain conditions had to obtain: the land could not already be inhabited by others; a claimant could occupy no more land than he needed for self-preservation; and a claimant would take possession "not by an idle ceremony, but by actually working and cultivating the soil—the only sign of ownership which need be respected by other people in the absence of a legal title." These conditions could never obtain in a state of nature because all land is given and used in common. Even the claim by an industrious first occupant would be invalid, because man, entitled only to "what he needs" for preservation, does not need exclusive possession of any land.

Total alienation of all the goods of all associates, however, can render possession a "true right," a legal or civil right of property. In the social contract, all possessions are "alienated" to the sovereign and become "public territory." But the same possessions are simultaneously returned by the community to its members as property. The existence of a political society thus justifies possessions that would otherwise inspire endless conflicts among men asserting exclusive claims, for the transformed claim "compels in political society the respect of all men." This "positive act" of contract has made each citizen the legal proprietor of his land because it simultaneously excludes him from the property of fellow citizens: "His share having once been settled, he must confine himself to it, and he has no further right against the community . . . What this [legal] right makes one aware of is less what belongs to others than what does *not* belong to oneself." Because the united strength of the whole is "incomparably greater than [that] of an individual, public possession is in simple fact more secure and more irrevocable" than private claims. In short, "men have, by a surrender which is advantageous to the public and still more to themselves, acquired, so to speak, all that they have given up."[24]

24. *Social Contract*, pp. 364–367.

Thus, the meaning of "total alienation" is very different from what it might appear to be. The same holds true for the meaning of the phrase "forcing men to be free," by which Rousseau warned of the danger to liberty if citizens listen to the voice of "particular interest" rather than to the "common interest" of their general will. Thinking whatever they owe the common cause a "gratuitous contribution," such citizens demand the rights of membership without acknowledging those corresponding civic duties which alone guarantee the identical rights of other citizens. This exclusiveness denies the very possibility of common life or, if common life has been established already, proves ruinous to it: "Hence, in order that the social pact shall not be an empty formula, it is tacitly implied in that commitment—which alone can give force to all other engagements—that whoever refuses to obey the general will shall be constrained to do so by the whole body, which means nothing other than he shall be forced to be free."[25]

This does not mean that an alien or superior group, particularly magistrates, may command recalcitrant citizens. "Legitimate government" has not yet been established and its institution does not permit any division of popular sovereignty or representation of the general will. Moreover, to translate *"forcer d'être libre"* as "to force to be free" brings with it a quite unwarranted suggestion of actual force. A clearer sense comes from Rousseau's definition of virtue as *force de l'âme*, properly translated *strength* of soul.[26] Hence a better translation of *forcer d'être libre* would be "to strengthen to be free." When "the whole body strengthens men to be free," then their general will, which is a given will in the composite personality of every public creature, requires that every man become and remain a self-governing member of the whole. Every citizen must respect the social bond and obey the laws of the corporate whole. That men are "strengthened to be free" merely

25. *Ibid.*, pp. 363–364.
26. *Emile*, pp. 820, 817.

defines the mythological foundation of a true republic, the transitional nonevent of a social contract.[27]

The difficulty that arises from the contractual basis of political society—that of effect becoming cause—recurs in the conception of men "strengthening themselves to be free." Once the political society has been founded by a lawgiver, however, virtuous citizens are indeed required by their highest will, the general will of the corporate whole, to remain independent of the will of others: "For this [strengthening men to be free] is the condition which, by giving each citizen to the [fatherland], secures him against all personal dependence; it is the condition which shapes both the design and the working of the political machine, and which alone bestows justice on civil contracts [*engagements*]. Without it, such contracts would be absurd, tyrannical and liable to the grossest abuse."[28]

Men who are not strengthened to be free, who do not participate in the social contract, are "foreigners among the citizens." The social contract is, by definition, unanimous: "There is only one law which by its very nature requires unanimous assent. This is the social pact: for the civil association is the most voluntary act in the world; every man, having been born free and master of himself, no one else may under any pretext whatever subject him without his consent." Rousseau's nonevent, because it requires "total alienation" and involves the "strengthening of men to be free," is intended to solve the "fundamental problem" of finding " 'a form of association which will defend the person and goods of each member with the collective [strength] of all, and under which each indi-

27. See also *ibid.*, p. 467.

28. *Social Contract*, p. 364. For contrasting interpretations which examine "force to be free" in terms of positive liberty or moral perfectibility, see Hendel, *Rousseau*, II, 187–188; John Plamenatz, "Ce qui ne signifie pas autre chose, sinon qu'on le forcera d'être libre," in *Rousseau et la philosophie politique*, pp. 137–152; Masters, *Political Philosophy of Rousseau*, pp. 329–334. See also Launay, *Rousseau*, pp. 134–137; Hall, *Rousseau*, pp. 94–97.

vidual, while uniting himself with the others, obeys no one but himself, and remains as free as before.' "[29]

All members of a true republic are "as free as before," but their liberty cannot be exhibited in the indolent and lawless manner of presocial natural men. A citizen is also a subject: "Those who are associated in [the state] take collectively the name of *a people*, and call themselves individually *citizens*, in so far as they share in the sovereign power, and *subjects* in so far as they put themselves under the laws of the state. . . . This formula shows that . . . each person, in making a contract, as it were, with himself, finds himself doubly committed, first, as a member of the sovereign body in relation to individuals, and secondly as a member of the state in relation to the sovereign." Because this "dual relationship" of citizen-subject characterizes every member, Rousseau could assert without contradiction that subjects' liberty is "limited by the general will," that citizens' power is absolute and the sovereign need give no guarantees to subjects, and that, when voting in a legislative assembly, a citizen is obligated to ask himself whether a proposal is advantageous to the state, not to a man or group of men. Subjects' obedience to the sovereign's laws is literal self-government for citizens: "The essence of the political body lies in the union of freedom and obedience so that the words 'sovereign' and 'subject' are identical correlatives, the meaning of which is brought together in the single word 'citizen'."[30]

This dual citizen-subject character of every member also explains what might appear to be a retreat from the idea of popular sovereignty or total alienation: each associate "alienates by the social pact only that part of his power, his goods and his liberty which is the concern of the community," for

---

29. *Social Contract*, pp. 440, 360. See also *Letters from the Mountain*, p. 807. Although he skirted the term *general will* throughout the *Letters*, Rousseau still referred to men who remain "as free as before."

30. *Social Contract*, pp. 362, 365, 365, 438, 427.

the sovereign "may not impose on the subjects any burden which is not necessary to the community." This means that a member in his capacity as subject cannot be obligated by rules which he, in his capacity as citizen, had not previously imposed upon himself and all other subjects. "Every man can do what he pleases with such goods and such freedom" as are left him by the original convention of total alienation. But the "sovereign alone," not man in his capacity as subject, judges what is necessary to the community.[31]

The citizen-subject character of every member is also essential to understanding both the necessity and character of "legitimate government." Self-governing citizens are subject to rules, but they are never the subjects of rulers.

Historical Foundation: A Lawgiver

The second, third, and fourth books of the *Social Contract* concern the historical origin and preservation of a true republic, beginning with its foundation by a lawgiver. These "events" comprise an imaginary but conceivable realization of the original contract. A lawgiver like Moses, Lycurgus, or Numa has always been the temporary educator of a people who cannot contract in order to form a people.[32] The lawgiver of the *Social Contract* "frames the laws" of a small, peaceful society of good men, a society which corresponds to the third historical period of simple *moeurs* described in the *Discourse on Inequality*. Just as this period in the *Discourse on Inequality*

31. *Ibid.*, pp. 373, 375.
32. For Rousseau's discussion of these founders, see *Geneva Manuscript*, p. 317; *Discourse on the Sciences and Arts* (P, III, 24n); *Discourse on Inequality*, pp. 187–188; *Government of Poland* (P, III, 956–958); *Fragments on Laws*, pp. 498–500. See also Hendel, *Rousseau*, II, 163, and Raymond Polin, "La Fonction du législateur chez J.-J. Rousseau," in *Jean-Jacques Rousseau et son oeuvre*, pp. 231–247. Both see the lawgiver as an "educator," and Polin specifies similarities between the lawgiver's foundation in the *Social Contract* and Rousseau's task in *Emile*. Polin also sees a permanent lawgiver making an earlier, historical contract secure and enduring through a second "denaturing" of man.

represents a "golden mean between the indolence of the primitive state and the petulent activity of our vanity," so the lawgiver accomplishes his task in conditions which combine "the simplicity of nature together with the needs that society creates." Peoples, "like men, are teachable only in their youth." A people is "fit to receive laws" only when it is "without deep-rooted customs or superstitions." It must be "a people in which every member may be known to all; . . . one which is neither rich nor poor, but has enough to keep itself; and lastly one which combines the cohesion of an ancient people with the malleability of a new one. What makes the task of the lawgiver so difficult is less what has to be established than what has to be destroyed." A lawgiver's wisdom is practical reason: "Just as an architect who puts up a large building first surveys and tests the ground to see if it can bear the weight, so the wise lawgiver begins not by laying down laws good in themselves, but by finding out whether the people for whom the laws are intended is able to support them." Any other course of action spells self-contradiction: "If the lawgiver mistakes his object and builds on principles that differ from what is demanded by the circumstances; if his principle tends towards servitude while circumstances tend towards liberty, the one towards wealth and the other towards increased population, the one towards peace and the other towards conquest, then . . . the state will continue to be disturbed until it is finally destroyed or transformed, and invincible nature regains her empire."

Rousseau also considered exceptional opportunities. Some "violent epochs and revolutions" so cleanse men's memories of a corrupt past that "the state, after being consumed by civil war, is born again, so to speak, from its own ashes, and leaps from the arms of death to regain the vigour of its youth." But this opportunity could not happen twice to the same people: "Although a people can make itself free while it is still uncivilized, it cannot do so when its civil energies are worn out.

Disturbances may well destroy a civil society without a revolution being able to restore it, so that as soon as the chains are broken, the state falls apart and exists no longer; then what is needed is a master, not a liberator." Civil peace, then, is a prerequisite "which no other can replace and without which all the rest are unavailing." The man of wealth in the *Discourse on Inequality* requires civil war and foreign conflict to persuade corrupt men to accept legal slavery; a true lawgiver requires peace to establish liberty.[33]

The effects of a lawgiver's foundation precisely duplicate the social transformation of the original contract. Men derive their new public being from their organic relationship to one another: "Whoever ventures on the enterprise of setting up a people must be ready, shall we say, to change human nature, to transform each individual, who by himself is entirely complete and solitary, into a part of a much greater whole, from which that same individual will then receive, in a sense, his life and his being. The founder of nations must weaken the structure of man in order to fortify it." When "each citizen can do nothing except through cooperation with others, . . . [the] law-making has reached the highest point of perfection." Because simple men cannot share their lawgiver's vision, "the founders of nations throughout history . . . appeal to divine intervention and . . . attribute their own wisdom to the Gods." The lawgiver is entitled to deceive men so that they, "feeling subject to the laws of the state as they are to those of nature, and detecting the same hand in the creation of both man and the nation, obey freely and bear with docility the yoke of the public welfare."[34]

Clearly this historical origin violates the imperative of literal self-government.[35] Rousseau attempted, without success, to

---

33. *Social Contract*, pp. 383, 391, 384–385, 390–391, 393; *Discourse on Inequality*, p. 171.

34. *Social Contract*, pp. 381–383.

35. For another interpretation of the awkward necessity of a law-

deny the authoritative character of the lawgiver's task. Popular sovereignty is not delegated or divided by a legislator, he argued, because the foundation of a political society is an exceptional and unrepeatable event designed to institute inalienable popular sovereignty. Similarly, a true lawgiver is an exceptional man. He does not resemble any magistrate, especially a monarch, whose designation can occur only after the lawgiver completes his task and withdraws. A magistrate, as mere "mechanic," has only to follow the constitutional model which the lawgiver has already provided. A magistrate is concerned with civil laws. A lawgiver is concerned chiefly with the fourth kind of law, the *moeurs* of a people that "form the true constitution of the state." On these laws "the great lawgiver bestows his secret care, for though he seems to confine himself to detailed legal enactments, which are really only the arching of the vault, he knows that [*moeurs*], which develop more slowly, ultimately become its immovable keystone."

A lawgiver is also a man of exceptional intelligence and virtue. He understands the passions of men without experiencing them. He understands thoroughly but does not share the nature of man. Although his own happiness is independent of other men's, he is able to make their happiness his concern. Presumably, the uniqueness of the lawgiver and the foundation prevents even temporary infringement of absolute liberty: "The lawgiver is, in every respect, an extraordinary man in the state. Extraordinary not only because of his genius, but equally because of his office, which is neither that of the government nor that of the sovereign. This office, which gives the

---

giver, see Lionel Gossman, "Rousseau's Idealism," *Romanic Review*, LII (Oct. 1961), 174–177. Rousseau's summary of the *Social Contract* in the *Letters* does not mention the lawgiver's foundation and calls "lawgiver" a sovereign people. *Letters from the Mountain*, pp. 845, 894–895. Perhaps the reason for this omission is Rousseau's condemnation of the Genevan constitution: Calvin, praised for his "codification of our wise edicts" in the *Social Contract* (p. 382n), is again a mere "theologian" (and imperious ruler) in the *Letters* (pp. 715, 726n).

republic its constitution, has no place in that constitution. It is a special and superior function which has nothing to do with empire over men; for just as he who has command over men must not have command over laws, neither must he who has command over laws have command over men." Indeed, Rousseau claimed that a lawgiver does not truly legislate: "The man who frames the laws ought not to have any legislative right, and the people itself cannot, even should it wish, strip itself of this untransferable right; for, according to the fundamental compact, it is only the general will which compels individuals, and there can be no assurance that an individual will is in conformity with the general will until it has been submitted to the free suffrage of the people—I have said this already, but it is worth repeating."

And what Rousseau has said is worth rereading: a simple people is incapable of creating itself, but its founder does not represent the people when he frames fundamental laws on its behalf which it merely ratifies. Rousseau persisted in denying the authoritative character of the lawgiver's task, as if his readers were its credulous beneficiaries. By contrast, Rousseau's explanation of his task as lawgiver to Emile is more candid: only Emile is deceived. In the *Social Contract* Rousseau concluded that because a lawgiver can employ "neither force nor argument," he compels "by divine authority persons who cannot be moved by human prudence." A true lawgiver reverts to "an authority of another order" when he invokes the gods: "But it is not for every man to make the Gods speak, or to gain credence if he pretends to be an interpreter of the divine word. The lawgiver's great soul is the true miracle which must vindicate his mission." In founding a republic two matters are joined "which look contradictory—a task which is beyond human powers and a nonexistent authority [*une autorité qui n'est rien*] for its execution." Rousseau's anarchism dictates this bluff.

Still, every true lawgiver works to preserve absolute liberty.

A lawgiver must adapt a constitution to the "chief object," the "genius" of a simple people. But a lawgiver cannot ignore those "principles common to all [free] peoples"—liberty and equality. A people now has a worthy past and a civic consciousness, with the lawgiver their proudest memory and most noble inspiration.[36]

Nongoverning Government

In the first version of the *Social Contract* and, at least ten years later, in a defense of the final version, Rousseau reproved Montesquieu for using the substantive forms *exécutrice* and *législateur* instead of the adjectival forms of *exécutive* and *législative*, or *puissance exécutive* and *puissance législative*.[37] Rousseau was not interested in Montesquieu's grammar, at least not for its own sake. For Rousseau's unusual understanding of government depends upon a distinction between powers exercised in a free society, and precludes a distinction between kinds of social members: every division between ruling magistrates and obedient subjects is slavery to Rousseau. More specifically, the existence of government often composed of fewer citizens than the membership of the whole does not contradict Rousseau's insistence upon literal self-government for all citizens. What Rousseau called "legitimate government" in the *Social Contract* is not government in the conventional sense. Magistrates of legitimate government, whatever their number, never command because the responsibility of those who compose this "new body within the state"[38] is only executive administration of laws legislated by sovereign citizens

36. *Social Contract*, pp. 381, 394, 382, 383–384, 391–393.
37. *Geneva Manuscript*, pp. 334n–335n; *Letters from the Mountain*, p. 833n. For an examination of Rousseau's sometimes careless use of government, see Jean-Jacques Chevallier, "Le Mot et la notion de gouvernement chez Rousseau," in *Etudes sur le* Contrat social, pp. 291–313.
38. *Social Contract*, p. 399.

themselves. Indeed, in both its noncontractual establishment and operation, Rousseau's legitimate government prevents division of the body politic between rulers and ruled. Rousseau occasionally referred in the *Social Contract* to the orders or commands of magistrates. But this sanctions governmental authority only if read outside the entire context in which legitimate government operates.[39]

Rousseau's government is based upon his distinction between the unrepresentable, legislative general will of a sovereign people, which results in laws of a general character, and the executive or administrative power of legitimate government, which results in decrees of a particular character. For Rousseau, theorists who do not distinguish sovereignty from government defend slavery. Rousseau's distinction is not between legislative and executive powers of government, that is, mixed government of the sort Montesquieu defended, but between a sovereign people that always legislates directly for itself and an executive which only applies these laws. Legitimate government does not govern, not because magistrates are subject to law (which they are), or responsible to the citizenry (which they are), or restricted to considerations of actions by subjects (which they are), but because the only task of government is the execution of laws.[40]

39. For a contrasting view, which sees Rousseau's ideal as the absence of government itself, see Weil, "Rousseau et sa politique," pp. 23, 26–28.

40. *Social Contract*, pp. 395–396. For a contrasting view, which attributes the distinction between sovereign and government to Rousseau's desire for "better" or professionally "qualified" administration, rather than "individual liberty," see Krafft, *La Politique de Rousseau*, pp. 86–91. See also *Letters from the Mountain*, pp. 806–809; *Emile*, pp. 842–844. Rousseau's dedication to the "republic of Geneva" of the *Discourse on Inequality* had suggested his distinction between sovereign and government and, with Rousseau's differing salutations to the republic and its magistrates, had implicitly criticized the Genevan constitution for that transfer of popular sovereignty which establishes representative government. *Discourse on Inequality*, pp. 111–115, 117–118, 121.

For "every free action," Rousseau began, there are two distinguishable, concurrent causes—a moral cause, the legislative will which determines the act to be performed, and a physical cause, the power which executes the will: "When I walk towards an object, it is necessary first that I should resolve to go that way and secondly that my feet should carry me. When a paralytic resolves to run and when a fit man resolves not to move, both stay where they are. The body politic has the same two motive powers—and we can make the same distinction between will and strength: the former is *legislative power* and the latter *executive power*. Nothing can be, or should be, done in the body politic without the concurrence of both." Thus, legislative sovereignty exercised through the unrepresentable general will is a "declaration of will" by the corporate whole. When such declarations are made, they constitute binding, self-imposed law. The contribution by magistrates, the "application" of this law, is "only a declaration of a particular will or an act of administration." It is "at best a mere decree." The sovereign is thus "essentially different" and "naturally separate" from the government: law and political right must be distinguished from decrees and political fact. Legitimate government, as only the "trustee of the executive power" of the whole, does not "dismember the social body" between contending particular wills. Rousseau sought to capture the unity of distinguishable responsibilities in an organic metaphor: "The principle of political life dwells in the sovereign authority. The legislative power is the heart of the state, the executive power is the brain, which sets all the parts in motion. The brain may become paralyzed and the individual still live. A man can be an imbecile and survive, but as soon as his heart stops functioning, the creature is dead." If any magistrates usurp a sovereign's legislative power, if any magistrates represent the general will, then the state is destroyed. A smaller state, whose membership is confined to governing magistrates, has formed within and replaced the larger body politic. This new state has "no significance for the rest of the people except that of a master and a tyrant."[41]

In a democratic form of legitimate government, executive administration would be the permanent concern of all or most members of the state. There is, however, no requirement that every member exercise executive power, precisely because magistrates cannot legislate. Executive administration is always exercised only "by virtue of the authority and law" of the sovereign. Magistrates are merely the "agents," "ministers" or "deputies" of a sovereign people. They are the "officers" not the "masters" of a people. When legitimate magistrates speak to the people, it is always "in the name of the people itself."[42]

Legitimate government is a necessary "intermediary body" that unites the body politic by mediating between members in their capacity as citizens and in their capacity as subjects: "The public force needs its own agent to call it together and put it into action in accordance with the instructions of the general will, to serve also as a means of communication between the state and the sovereign, and in a sense to do for the public person what is done for the individual by the union of soul and body." Because legitimate government only "receives from the sovereign the orders which it gives to the people," all members of the whole simultaneously command and obey themselves. The only relationship established is "between the entire body seen from one perspective and the same entire body seen from another, without any division whatever." Nor is there a contradiction between the idea of citizens being free and being subject to law, "for the laws are but registers of what we ourselves desire," the general will of civic virtue.[43]

The operation of this citizens-magistrates-subjects relation-

41. *Social Contract*, pp. 394, 369–370, 432, 424, 422. See also *Letters from the Mountain*, p. 808.
42. *Social Contract*, pp. 396, 429, 434, 458, 406.
43. *Ibid.*, pp. 396, 379.

ship recapitulates the original contract guaranteeing absolute liberty. An "act of sovereignty" or lawmaking is "not a covenant between a superior and an inferior, but a covenant of the body with each of its members. . . . So long as the subjects submit to such covenants alone, they obey nobody but their own will." Governmental mediation completes this self-contract of all with all. Two powers, legislative and executive, are exercised within a true republic. But there are never two groups of members, ruling magistrates and obedient subjects. There exists also the corporate whole, for a sovereign citizenry is an active "single person." No magistrate-subject aspect of the entire relationship can be separated from the legislative contribution of sovereign citizens. The sovereign always exists "in itself." Legitimate government, which has "a kind of borrowed and subordinate life" and can act only "in accordance with the instructions of the general will," exists "only through the sovereign."[44]

Rousseau's requirement that citizens remain their own subjects explains his insistence that the unrepresentable general will be general in its object. That is to say, laws must apply to all subjects, so that the whole alone rules the whole. If citizens legislate for only some subjects, then the whole enslaves a part, and a part of the whole is excluded from obedience to its own laws. For "the general will, to be truly what it is, must . . . spring from all and apply to all; and it loses its natural rectitude when it is directed towards any particular and circumscribed object—for in judging what is foreign to us, we have no sound principle of equity to guide us." If legitimate government cannot divide common life between ruler and ruled, neither can the exercise of sovereignty.[45]

44. *Ibid.*, pp. 374–375, 399, 396.
45. *Ibid.*, p. 373. See also *ibid.*, pp. 374, 378–379; *Geneva Manuscript*, pp. 326–330. For the view that Rousseau retreated from the requirement of a general object, see Charles Eisenmann, "La Cité de Jean

Correspondingly, Rousseau's imperative of absolute liberty *requires* a nongoverning government to apply general laws to particular cases: "If the sovereign seeks to govern [i.e., to execute the laws], or if the magistrate seeks to legislate, or if the subjects refuse to obey, then order gives way to chaos, power and will cease to act in concert, and the state, disintegrating, will lapse into despotism or anarchy." True laws, general in both their object and their source, are the "things" of a free society, obedience to which assures that each citizen remains his own subject: "It is impossible for the government, so long as it acts only for the public good, to attack liberty because it only executes the general will; and no one can say he is enslaved when he obeys only his own will."[46] Magistrates no more govern subjects than the "foot power" of execution commands its walking body.

That Rousseau intended to assure the nongoverning character of government is also seen in difficult instances of executive mediation. We have noted that a self-governing citizen's civic duty includes military service and even risking death in defense of his fatherland. Similarly, criminal disobedience is a traitorous act of self-betrayal justifying death. Only magistrates can summon specific subjects for military service and punish or pardon specific criminals because particular objects are involved. But magistrates are not rulers in these instances because they merely apply the law previously imposed by sovereign citizens upon all subjects. Magistrates only execute the citizen's general will: "The purpose of the social treaty is the preservation of the contracting parties. Whoever wills the end wills also the means. . . . Whoever wishes to preserve his own life at the expense of others must give his life for them when

---

Jacques Rousseau," in *Etudes sur le* Contrat social, pp. 200–201; Charvet, *Social Problem in the Philosophy of Rousseau*, pp. 129–137.

46. *Social Contract*, p. 397; *Fragments on the Social Pact* (P, III, 484). See also *Fragments on Laws*, p. 492; *Letters from the Mountain*, pp. 841–842.

it is necessary. Now, as citizen, no man is judge any longer of the danger to which the law requires him to expose himself; and when the [magistracy] says to him: 'It is expedient for the state that you should die,' then he should die, because it is only on such terms that he has lived in security as long as he has and also because his life is no longer the bounty of nature but a gift he has received conditionally from the state." The death penalty for criminals "may be seen in much the same way." For "it is in order to avoid becoming the victim of a murderer that one consents to die if one becomes a murderer oneself."[47]

Similarly, Rousseau denied that during a divided vote in a legislative assembly a majority of citizens commands a minority. As an anarchist, he rejected the view that a unanimous original contract entitles a majority to bind all citizens, although the original convention may include a majority mechanism as a matter of convenience.[48] Rousseau could not defend or disallow, on intrinsic grounds, the superiority of numbers or the rights of a minority: a citizenry's general will is itself a given, common will, not that aggregative "will of all," of either a majority or a minority, which yields only a "declaration of the general will." Consequently, every vote in a legislative assembly need not and probably will not be unanimous. But every vote is nevertheless unanimous, regardless of its outcome. No member is enslaved when all citizens, including an opposed minority, "consent" to a law enacted by their general will: "The citizen consents to all the laws, even to those that are passed against his will [*malgré lui*], and even to those which punish him when he dares to break any one of them. The constant will of all the members of the state is the general will; it is through it that they are citizens and free." More specifically, when assembled citizens decide about a legislative proposal, "what is asked of them is not precisely whether they

47. *Social Contract*, p. 376.
48. *Ibid.*, pp. 359, 110.

approve of the proposition or reject it, but whether it is in conformity with the general will which is theirs." Each citizen, by voting, gives his opinion on this question; "and the counting of votes yields a declaration of the general will. When, therefore, the opinion contrary to my own prevails, this proves only that I have made a mistake, and that what I believed to be the general will was not so. If my particular opinion had prevailed against the general will, I should have done something other than what I had willed, and then I should not have been free." Rousseau immediately added that this explanation of a divided vote assumes that a majority "will of all" closely approximates the general will: "When these [characteristics of the general will] cease to be there, no matter what position men adopt, there is no longer any freedom."[49]

If the operation of legitimate government confirms Rousseau's anarchism in that such a government does not govern, there is nevertheless a paradox concerning the form of legitimate government: Rousseau's demand for literal self-government finds inexpedient a direct democracy and favors an aristocracy selected by lot.[50]

Rousseau claimed that we cannot say what is the best form of executive administration because the form of government must reflect a host of circumstances.[51] Moreover, he designated

49. *Ibid.,* pp. 440–441.

50. Rousseau often contrasted "republican" and "monarchical" government, or "free states" and "monarchies." *Ibid.,* pp. 410, 415. He conceded the appropriateness of monarchical government in some circumstances, namely contemporary, large states of enslaved and tranquil men who covet money and luxury. Every monarch sooner or later claims to embody popular sovereignty. *Ibid.,* pp. 370–371, 408–413. See also letter to George Keith (Aug. [18] 1762; *CC,* XII, 205–206). For a similar understanding of Rousseau's "republicanism" as it applies to monarchical government, see Robert Derathé, "Rousseau et la problème de la monarchie," *Le Contrat social,* VI (May–June 1962), 165–168.

51. These include number of citizens, climate, fertility of soil, wealth and its distribution, the *moeurs* of common life, the manner of tax collection, and the extent of territory. *Social Contract,* pp. 397–398,

as "republics" all states which have a legitimate government of whatever form, for the members of such states are "ruled by law." But with a democratic form of government, where there are more "citizen-magistrates" than ordinary citizens, sovereignty and government are not sufficiently distinguished. Such citizen-magistrates are apt to be corrupted by considering particular objects, with the entire state becoming "corrupted in its very substance." Indeed, a democratic government has never existed because citizens cannot be permanently assembled for the purpose of administering the laws.[52]

But the form of legitimate government in every free state must be temporarily democratic on two occasions, when government is first established and when magisterial tenure is reviewed. Only temporary democracy on these occasions assures that the object of the general will remains general, with the corporate whole alone ruling itself.

The original, noncontractual establishment of legitimate government is "complex, or composed of two [parts]." The first part determines the form of government. Because the object here is general, because the determination of the form of government does not speak to an exclusive or particular part of the citizenry, this decision can be made by sovereign citizens and is rightly called a law. The second part of this complex act is the designating of a limited number of specific citizens to be invested with executive power: "Since this nomination is a particular act, it is not a second law, but simply a sequel to the first and a function of government." Thus all citizens, "in

403–404, 414–419. For a working out of Rousseau's illustrative proportion involving the numerical size of sovereign and government, see Masters, *Political Philosophy of Rousseau*, pp. 340–348.

52. *Social Contract*, pp. 379–380, 403, 404–405. An aristocracy must be elective rather than "natural" (age) or hereditary; hereditary aristocracy is "the worst of all governments" or of all "legitimate administations." *Ibid.*, pp. 406, 422n; *Letters from the Mountain*, pp. 808–809. For Rousseau's "unfair" obliteration of Aristotle's distinctions between aristocracy, oligarchy, and polity, see *Social Contract*, p. 408.

a new relation of all to all," have in fact served as temporary magistrates in order that the designation of other magistrates can proceed: "It is not possible to institute the government in any other legitimate manner, without abandoning the principles established in earlier chapters." Rousseau's anarchism dictates this method of establishing government: men are enslaved if the object of the general will is particular, for then the whole is ruling a part.

Temporary democracy also occurs during assemblies of sovereign citizens, the purpose of which is "the maintenance of the social treaty." The opening of every assembly is marked by two motions "which may never be annulled and which must be voted separately: the first, 'Does it please the sovereign to maintain the present form of government?' The second, 'Does it please the people to leave the administration to those at present charged with it?'" Because of its particular character, the second question can be handled only if the sovereign people temporarily becomes a democratic magistracy. Thus, the moment a people is "lawfully assembled as a sovereign body," the entire jurisdiction of the government automatically ceases: "in the presence of the represented, there is no longer any representation [of executive power]." And a sovereign people is entitled to change the form of government and appoint and dismiss magistrates "as it pleases." A people can "limit, modify and resume at pleasure" executive power. The surrender of this right "would be incompatible with the nature of the social body and contrary to the purpose of the social union."[53]

Such changes are not prudent because of the danger of civil strife. But this absolute right to dismiss magistrates does not constitute a popular right to revolution either. It is scarcely a revolutionary act for citizens with no contractual obligations

53. *Social Contract*, pp. 433–436, 426, 427–428, 434, 396.

of obedience to magistrates to dismiss them and to reinstitute a government which cannot govern.

Virtuous Citizens

Earlier we saw how Rousseau's nonindividualism and an- archism converge in the conception of a united and disciplined common life composed of truly virtuous citizens. The *Social Contract* illustrates the same pattern, for the institutional de- vices Rousseau described in book four are designed to post- pone enslaving fratricide. Because absolute liberty always rests upon the *moeurs* and loyalties of citizens and the quality of their common life, no remedy to the decline of even a true republic can exist.

Government usurpation of legislative sovereignty is "the in- herent and inescapable defect which, from the birth of the political body, tends relentlessly to destroy it, just as old age and death destroy the body of a man." Accordingly, Rousseau recommended frequent assemblies of citizens. Unforeseen events may necessitate extraordinary assemblies; but there must also be "fixed and periodic assemblies which nothing can abolish or prorogue, so that on the appointed day the people is rightfully summoned by the law itself without a further formal convoca- tion being needed." Each assembly begins by asking whether to retain the form of government and the magistrates. No citi- zen may be denied the rights to speak and vote. Because con- temporary "slaves smile in mockery" at the word *liberty*, Rousseau devoted the second longest chapter of the *Social Contract* to considering the several methods of assembling and voting in the Roman comitia: frequent assemblies of sovereign citizens are practical.[54]

A "wisely tempered" tribunate is a negative, special magis- tracy separate from the regular magistracy and established to restore the balance of magistrates who mediate between citi-

54. *Ibid.*, pp. 421, 426, 425, 444–453.

zens and subjects. The tribunate can serve as "the guardian of the laws and of the legislative power," although it is not a "constitutive part of the republic." Its power "ought to be all the greater, for although it can do nothing, it can prevent anything from being done." Such a tribunate degenerates into tyranny as soon as it usurps the executive power, of which it is only the "moderator," or when it attempts to legislate, instead of only protecting existing laws. The best way of discouraging usurpation by tribunes is to require by law intervals during which this body must be suspended.[55]

But circumstances may also require sudden, decisive actions by magistrates which the inflexibility and slow procedures of formal law do not permit. Accordingly, "political institutions" may be "suspended" momentarily. Either a temporarily strengthened executive power or the establishment of a "dictatorship" is useful in "rare and obvious cases" of "greatest emergency" when citizens still affirm the indissolubility of their common life. When governmental power is concentrated in the hands of one or two consuls who are already magistrates, "it is not the authority of the laws which is being diminished, but only the form of the administration." When a "supreme" magistrate or "dictator" is appointed, this "suspension of the legislative authority does not abolish it. The magistrate who silences it cannot make it speak; he dominates it, without having the power to represent it. He can do everything, except make laws." Whichever irregular "commission" is used, "it is imperative to limit its duration to one short term that can never be prolonged."[56]

The effectiveness of these institutional devices depends upon virtuous *moeurs*. Accordingly, Rousseau required the early establishment of a permanent censorial tribunal of special magistrates. Its members apply to particular cases that "form of law" involving public opinion: "Far, then, from the cen-

55. *Ibid.*, pp. 453–455.
56. *Ibid.*, pp. 455–456, 458.

sorial tribunal being the arbiter of the people's opinion, it is only the spokesman; and as soon as it departs from this, its decisions are void and without effect." Censorship "may be useful in preserving [*moeurs*] but never in restoring [them]. Set up censors while the laws are still vigorous; for as soon as their vigour is lost, everything is hopeless; nothing legitimate has any force when the laws have force no longer."[57]

Ultimately, then, censorship by special magistrates can never be more than a temporary matter; the state ultimately rests on the self-censorship of virtuous citizens for the guarantee of absolute liberty. And it is to a religion of civic virtue that Rousseau turned in his last and longest chapter. By consecrating common life itself, this "civil religion" recapitulates the foundation of the republic by a lawgiver who had invoked the gods.[58]

Rousseau rejected three alternatives as dangerously inappropriate to virtuous citizenship. The first is the religion of "man," the religion of "true" Christianity. Without temples, altars, rituals, or priests, this pure religion of the Gospel is an inward devotion to the supreme God and the eternal obligations of morality. However, because this religion has "no particular connexion with the body politic," it "leaves the law with only the force the law itself possesses, adding nothing to it." True Christianity, "far from attaching the hearts of the citizens to the state, . . . detaches them from it as from all other things of this world; and I know of nothing more contrary to the social spirit." Indeed, the idea of a Christian republic is a con-

57. *Ibid.*, pp. 458–459.
58. For a similar understanding of the way a civil religion recapitulates the entire *Social Contract*, see Robert Derathé, "La Religion civile selon Rousseau," *Annales*, XXXV (1959–1962), 162–163; Strauss, "On the Intention of Rousseau," pp. 481–482. See also P, III, 1498–1500. For the view that the civil religion is not an "integral part" of the *Social Contract*, see Green, *Rousseau*, pp. 301–305. The references to the rejected religions and the civil religion are taken from *Social Contract*, pp. 462, 464–469.

tradiction in terms: "Christianity preaches only servitude and submission. Its spirit is too favourable to tyranny for tyranny not to take advantage of it. True Christians are made to be slaves; they know it and they hardly care; this short life has too little value in their eyes."[59]

The second is the religion of the "citizen," the religion of pagan peoples. It gives each nation exclusive deities. Its dogmas, rituals, and forms of worship are prescribed by law and foster social unity. But because everything outside the nation is judged "infidel, alien [and] barbarous," it makes a people "bloodthirsty and intolerant." Such men "breathe only murder and massacre, and believe they are doing a holy deed in killing those who do not accept their Gods." War among theocratic nations proves self-destructive.

A third, "more curious" kind of religion is the religion of the "priest." This religion dismembers common life by upholding "a kind of mixed and anti-social system of law which has no name." It gives citizens "two legislative orders, two rulers, two [fatherlands], puts them under two contradictory obligations, and prevents their being at the same time both churchmen and citizens." With this arrangement "men have never known whether they ought to obey the civil ruler or the priest." For Rousseau nothing could be worse than this arrangement: "Everything that destroys social unity is worthless, and all institutions that set man at odds with himself are worthless."[60]

Rousseau concluded by requiring the sovereign to establish articles of a "purely civil" profession of faith, "not strictly as religious dogmas, but as sentiments of sociability, without which it is impossible to be either a good citizen or a loyal subject." The articles of the civil religion "must be simple and few in number, expressed precisely and without explanations or commentaries. The existence of an omnipotent, intelligent,

59. See also letter to Usteri (July 18, 1763; CC, XVII, 63-65); Letters from the Mountain, pp. 705-707.

60. See also letter to Franquières (Jan. 15, 1769; P, IV, 1145-1147).

benevolent divinity that foresees and provides; the life to come; the happiness of the just; the punishment of sinners; the sanctity of the social contract and the law—these are the positive dogmas. As for the negative dogmas, I would limit them to a single one: no intolerance. Intolerance is something which belongs to the religions we have rejected." Rousseau also limited the substantive scope of this civil religion to "the boundaries of public utility," for subjects are not accountable to the sovereign for beliefs which are not "important to the community." Although "it is very important to the state that each citizen should have a religion which makes him love his duty," each subject, in addition, "may hold whatever opinions he pleases, without the sovereign having any business to take cognizance of them."

In vaguely suggesting this limit, however, Rousseau was not suddenly employing that distinction between private and public sectors characteristic of traditional liberalism. Religion itself is eminently a public matter, even if this might not include some additional and therefore insignificant religious beliefs. The possible limitation of scope also pertains to artificial individuals only in their capacities as subjects: a sovereign, once again, may effectively "limit" itself because its legislative power is absolute and inalienable. And whatever is beyond "the boundaries of public utility" is in fact beyond this world: "For the sovereign has not competence in the other world; whatever may be the fate of the subjects in the life to come, it is nothing to do with the sovereign, so long as they are good citizens in this life."[61]

Because new social men must remain absolutely free, they cannot tolerate religious beliefs which threaten the integrity

---

61. Rousseau later insisted that he was concerned in the *Social Contract* not with the truth of religious doctrines but with their "*rapports to political bodies.*" *Letters from the Mountain*, p. 703. He specified theological subtleties and mysteries inessential to civic virtue in *Emile*, pp. 728–729.

of common life. However tolerant of the beliefs of foreigners, who also constitute another world, self-governing citizens are characteristically serious about sedition and hypocrisy: "Without being able to oblige anyone to obey these articles [of a civil religion], the sovereign can banish from the state anyone who does not believe them." He is banished "not for impiety but as an antisocial being, as one unable sincerely to love law and justice, or to sacrifice, if need be, his life to his duty." If anyone publicly acknowledges the articles of the civil religion and acts "as if he did not believe in them, then let him be put to death, for he has committed the greatest crime, that of lying before the law."[62] Thus, Rousseau's single "negative dogma" was intended to prevent only the foreign and national strife of "bloodthirsty" sects and pagan theocracies.[63] Once again, if artificial individuals are to avoid enslavement, they must simply remain sincerely virtuous citizens: true citizens are subjects of themselves alone.

62. In his *Letter to Voltaire* of August 18, 1756, which first mentioned the importance of a "catechism of the citizen," Rousseau defended banishment "not for impiety but for seditiousness." See P, IV, 1073.

63. See also *Geneva Manuscript*, p. 341, where Rousseau argued that intense public watchfulness destroys genuinely virtuous sentiments. These two paragraphs do not appear in the *Social Contract*. See also *Letter to Beaumont*, pp. 970–980.

CHAPTER 10

From Subject to Citizen

A Miniature Republic: Lawgiver and Citizen

Rousseau's *Emile; or, Of Education* is the *Social Contract* writ small. Rousseau's education of his "imaginary pupil"[1] duplicates on a more manageable, temporally more extended scale the foundation of a true republic by a lawgiver in the *Social Contract*. In demonstrating the method and purpose of "natural education," Rousseau was founding in words a miniature republic: Emile is a free "subject" of his educator's "guidance." Isolated from European slavery, Emile is gradually transformed from presocial anonymity to virtuous citizenship. Three successive periods of common life involving Rousseau and this representative man form a "history of human nature" and exhibit "the natural development of the human heart." The periods correspond to the successive developments that the species undergoes through the first three historical periods described in the *Discourse on Inequality*.[2]

This political character of *Emile* is partially seen in the differences and similarities Rousseau drew between a state and a familial society. Rousseau denied that the state is an extension of the family. Agreeing with Sidney and Locke, Rousseau

1. *Emile* (P, IV, 264).
2. *Ibid.*, pp. 251, 265–267, 777. Thus, *Emile* cannot be identified with Rousseau's plans for tutoring M. de Mably's sons in 1740–41, or with his advice to friends and correspondents regarding the education of their children. For Rousseau's experiences as tutor and adviser, see Guéhenno, *Rousseau*, I, 93–95, 100–106, 132–134; II, 15–16, 121.

argued in the *Discourse on Inequality* that the "bonds" in a family differ from those in a political society. A father's gentle authority over his children bears no relationship to the "ferocious spirit of despotism" that imbues monarchial governments. Moreover, the family is not the earlier form of social dependence: "Instead of saying that civil society is derived from paternal power, it should be said on the contrary that it is from civil society that this power draws its principle force. An individual was not recognized as the father of many until they remained assembled around him." Elsewhere, Rousseau insisted that the rules of conduct in "domestic government" are not appropriate to "civil government," for the members of a state are "naturally equal."[3]

But there are also similarities between domestic society and civil society. In the *Social Contract*, Rousseau suggested that the family may perhaps be seen as the "first model of political societies." On other occasions he called the state a "great family" compared to the "little family" or "little society." Indeed, that intensity of compassionate unity among self-governing citizens which Rousseau demanded is familial in character. Outdoor festivals in Geneva would bring citizens together "not so much for a public entertainment as for the gathering of a big family." When advising Corsicans not to employ tax-farmers, Rousseau asserted that "it is better that the administration of the public treasury should be like that of the father of [a] family, and lose something, than for it to gain more and be like that of a usurer." Toward the conclusion of Emile's education Rousseau observed that it is "the good son, the good husband, and the good father who make the good citizen": devotion to the "great family" is impossible unless

3. *Discourse on Inequality* (P, III, 182); *Discourse on Political Economy* (P, III, 241–244); *Social Contract* (P, III, 352, 412). See also *Emile*, pp. 838–839.

virtuous passions are first nourished in "that miniature fatherland, the family."[4]

The small fatherland of *Emile* is a miniature republic of lawgiver and citizen, not a family. Rousseau explained in the opening pages of *Emile* that there are two kinds of education,
"public" or "common" education and "natural," "particular,"
or "domestic" education. Plato's *Republic* is an example of the
former: "This is not a work on politics, as those who judge
books only by their titles think. It is the finest treatise on education ever written." Such instruction is now ludicrous: "Where
there is no longer a fatherland, it is impossible to have citizens.
These two words, *fatherland* and *citizen*, ought to be stricken
from modern languages." Contemporary colleges are not true
"public institutions." They fashion hypocrites who profess to
care for others while thinking only for themselves: "Harmony
is impossible. Forced to combat nature or social institutions,
we must choose to fashion a man or a citizen. . . . The natural
man lives entirely for himself; he is a numerical unity, . . .
The value of a social man . . . is in his *rapport* to the whole,
which is the social body. Good social institutions are those
which best make a man unnatural, which replace an absolute
existence for oneself with a relative existence, which transform the *self* into a common unity." Educated in a miniature
republic, the mature Emile becomes both man and citizen: his
inclinations are his civic duties. Rousseau concluded his discussion of the insoluble contemporary dilemma: "But how will
a man come to live with others when he is educated only for
himself? If the two purposes could be reconciled into one by
removing man's inner contradictions, one great obstacle to his

4. *Social Contract*, p. 352; *Discourse on Political Economy*, pp. 241–
242; *Letter to d'Alembert*, p. 176; *Constitutional Project for Corsica*
(P, III, 933–934); *Emile*, p. 700. See also *La Nouvelle Héloise* (P, II,
81, 461); *Letters from the Mountain* (P, III, 832); *Discourse on Inequality*, p. 117.

happiness would be removed. To judge this you must see him fully educated; you must have observed his tendencies, seen his progress, followed his development. In a word, you must know the natural man. I think you will have made some progress in these matters when you have read this work."[5] Society and absolute liberty are perfectly reconciled in *Emile*, for Emile's transformation is the "common" education of a single citizen.

The idea of a "natural education," then, is not self-contradictory. On the one hand, modern society irreparably corrupts an infant's natural goodness and liberty: "In the present situation and among other men, a man left to himself from birth would be the most corrupted of all. Prejudices, authority, necessity, example—all the social institutions in which we find ourselves embedded would stifle nature in him and put nothing in her place." On the other hand, without society "everything would be still worse, and our species cannot be made by halves." Like the simple men of the *Social Contract*, who cannot found their own political society, Emile is incapable of unaided self-definition. He requires an educator. But Rousseau, because he neither commands nor obeys Emile, is "the minister of nature, never her foe." Emile himself is therefore "nature's pupil, not man's pupil." The mature Emile retains the integrity of pre-social life, for much "art" is required if education is to avoid "contradictions between the rights of nature and the laws of society," and to prevent "social man from being altogether artificial."[6]

The educational principles Rousseau endorsed and those he rejected presuppose that a naturally free man's perfection is virtuous citizenship. The contemporary mother who does not nurse her infant "disturbs the whole moral order and extinguishes nature in every heart." Infants shuffled off to wet-

5. *Emile*, pp. 248–251.
6. *Ibid.*, pp. 245, 639, 549, 361, 640. See also *ibid.*, pp. 242–243, 259–260, 279–281.

nurses are taught ingratitude and dishonesty, so that parents and children become strangers in their "gloomy solitude" and the state is deprived of citizens. Rousseau warned against permitting children to learn to speak in the timid, indistinct stammer of contemporary men: "A man who has learned to speak only in narrow streets could not make himself heard at the head of a battalion and would make little impression on the people during a riot." After the youthful Emile is no longer afraid of darkness, he "will be ready for a military expedition at any hour, with or without his troops." Rousseau emphasized that Emile "has not been fashioned into a savage to be exiled to the woods" and "has not been made to live alone." Emile is "a member of society and must fulfill these duties." He must perfect "the one art absolutely necessary to man and to citizen, the art of living among his fellow men."[7]

That the society of *Emile* is a miniature republic of lawgiver and citizen explains the discrepancy between the egalitarian principle underlying Rousseau's guidance and the inequality permitted in familial society. Children's temporary obedience to their father qualifies the anarchistic imperative of absolute liberty within Rousseau's thought. For Rousseau argued that the "natural" weakness of children compared to the strength, talent, and experience of their father justifies their obedience. With maturity only gratitude and respect may dictate voluntary obedience.[8]

Again and again Rousseau pointed to Emile's weakness during infancy and childhood.[9] However, because Emile and Rousseau constitute a miniature republic, not a family, because Rousseau is a lawgiver, not a foster father or ordinary tutor, Emile's weakness does not invite or permit Rousseau's commands. If other children recover their independence only when

7. *Ibid.*, pp. 257–258, 296, 388, 551, 654–655.
8. *Discourse on Political Economy*, pp. 242–243.
9. *Emile*, pp. 247, 273–274, 285–287.

they are grown,[10] Emile is always independent of the will of his educator. As an inseparable and compassionate equal, Rousseau shares Emile's games, his developing moods and talents, and his self-imposed tasks. Professionalism never disrupts their fellowship, for Rousseau never "instructs" Emile: "The tutor must never give precepts; he must let the pupil discover the duties of man for himself." As in the *Social Contract*, liberty is both the method and purpose of Emile's education, its "greatest good."[11]

Other considerations identify Rousseau with the lawgiver in the *Social Contract*. Both are attentive to favorable opportunity and circumstance. Just as a lawgiver cannot work among enslaved men of aged societies who seek merely to postpone death, so a pupil's physical survival does not warrant Rousseau's attention: "I would not burden myself with a sickly, feeble infant should he live to eighty years. I do not want a pupil who is always useless to himself and others. . . . What do I accomplish in vainly taking care of him, except to double the loss to society and to deprive it of two men instead of one? I do consent to let another take care of this sickly child, and I do approve of his charity. But that is not my own gift: I do not know how to teach someone to live who intends only to keep himself from dying." In contrast, a father "has no choice and must show no preference for the children God has given him; all his children are his alike, and he owes all of them the same care and tenderness." Accordingly, Rousseau selects an ordinary but "strong, well-formed, healthy" infant. Emile

10. *Discourse on Inequality*, p. 182; *Social Contract*, p. 352; *Emile*, p. 838.

11. *Emile*, pp. 265–266, 308–309, 538–539, 663–664. See also *Favre Manuscript* (P, IV, 88–89). For a similar view of the importance of liberty in Emile's education, see Wright, *Meaning of Rousseau*, pp. 45, 50–51. For a view that Emile is not free—morally free—because Rousseau's mediation and watchfulness deprive him of spontaneity, see Starobinski, *Rousseau*, pp. 268–272.

is actually an orphan from a wealthy family: "Let us choose our pupil from among the rich; we shall at least have made a better man." Like the lawgiver in the *Social Contract*, Rousseau requires "rustic simplicity" and fresh air: "Bodily infirmities, and the vices of the soul, are the infallible effect of crowdedness." Emile's education begins in the countryside at Montmorency, a lingering reminder of the golden age.[12]

More generally, Rousseau explained his task in terms that recall the lawgiver's architectonic contribution in the *Social Contract*. Guiding a pupil is a task for a "wise workman." The "capstone" of his work occurs when permanent sentiments of civic virtue have gradually succeeded the passions of natural goodness: "As great illnesses interrupt memory, so great passions threaten *moeurs*. Our tastes and inclinations change, but this change, though it may be rather sudden, is softened by our habits. In the succession of our inclinations, as in a good color scheme, the skillful artist must make the transitions imperceptible by blending and mixing his tints; and, so that there may be no sudden breaks, some colors cover his entire work."[13] Rousseau's task is itself a selfless, long-range civic duty performed by an exceptional man: "There are callings so noble that they cannot be undertaken for money without demonstrating our unworthiness for them; one such calling is that of the soldier; another is that of the instructor." Rousseau devotes his "own time, attention, affection and his very self" solely to Emile. And, like the lawgiver of the *Social Contract*, Rous-

12. *Emile*, pp. 267–269, 296, 276–277. See also *ibid.*, pp. 325–327. For a contrasting view, see Jean Starobinski, "The Illness of Rousseau," *Yale French Studies*, XXVIII (Fall–Winter, 1961–1962), 64. Starobinski interprets Rousseau's refusal to educate a sickly child to "tranquil indifference" or "a kind of approving admiration" of natural selection as pitiless as Spartan practice. For a discussion of the appropriateness of place and time throughout *Emile*, see Pierre Burgelin, "*L'Idée* de place dans l'*Emile*," *Revue de littérature comparée*, XXXV (Oct.–Dec. 1961), 529–537.

13. *Emile*, pp. 502, 317, 520, 787, 800.

seau's guidance is both "negative" and deceptive or manipula-
tive. In order to prepare for the triumph of civic virtue, it is
enough, especially when Emile is young, to take precautions
that his heart is preserved from vice. Rousseau's "art" is that
"of doing everything by doing nothing." As the lawgiver in
the *Social Contract* cleverly invokes the gods, so Rousseau
conceals his hand behind a "necessity in things."[14] Emile obeys
only this necessity, without detecting Rousseau's hand.

The language of "contract" and "agreement" appropriately
appears throughout *Emile*. Rousseau first used "contract"
when he assumes responsibility for Emile's education. Because
Emile is an orphan and because Rousseau did not introduce
Emile's natural parents, Rousseau was not referring to an actual
agreement with Emile's parents. Nor could the political society
of Rousseau and Emile derive from a tacit contract between
God and educator since Rousseau's task, in contrast to that of
a father, is a self-imposed civic duty. This nonevent involving a newborn infant and his lawgiver comprises several
"clauses" of an "agreement" (*traité*). Rousseau's "first and only
condition" is that Emile honor his parents but "obey" him.
Emile is certainly obedient, even "docile." But he never obeys
Rousseau or even confronts Rousseau's will. Rousseau immediately amends the agreement, thereby defining their unusual
equality: "We must never be separated except by mutual consent. This clause is essential; and I would even like pupil and
tutor to regard themselves as so inseparable that their destiny
is always a common object between them. As soon as they
envisage a future separation, as soon as they foresee a moment

14. *Ibid.*, pp. 263, 326, 323–324, 362, 321. See also *ibid.*, pp. 340, 363–
364, 424, 461; *Letter to Beaumont* (P, IV, 945–946). Some parallels
between Rousseau's task in *Emile* and the lawgiver's in the *Social Contract* are discussed in Burgelin, *Rousseau et la religion de Genève*, pp.
56–57, and in his introduction to *Emile* (P, III, cxxvii–cxxxii). See also
Meyer, "The Individual and Society in Rousseau's *Emile*," pp. 112–113.

which must render them strangers to each other, they are already strangers, . . . and they remain together only against their wishes."[15]

It would be a misreading of the title of *Emile* to assume that it presents an alternative to the *Social Contract*, that it is a practical treatise on private, familial education and moral duty as distinct from politics and civic duty. As Rousseau conceded, *Emile* is the "reverie of a dreamer," the vision of a lawgiver of the pen. Rousseau was concerned with abstract principles of political right, not their "applications": he has again forsaken the irredeemable facts of contemporary slavery.[16]

Nature and Society

Emile is divided into five books. Book one covers Emile's infancy, the time between birth and two years of age. Here Rousseau described his pupil and outlined his principle of "disciplined liberty." Childhood, Emile's life from the age of two to about twelve, is dealt with in book two, and concerns sensory and bodily training. Book three covers a brief period of early adolescence before puberty, between the years twelve and fifteen. Emile now acquires useful intellectual skills as his capacity for judging physical objects and relationships is developed. In book four Emile becomes knowledgeable about

15. *Emile*, pp. 267–268. This egalitarian contract contrasts with Rousseau's arrangements for tutoring M. de Mably's eldest son. Here questions of Rousseau's fitness for the task, and of his rights and responsibilities, occasion elaborate negotiations with M. de Mably: Rousseau's "authority" to rule derives from an actual contractual authorization involving a "naturally superior" father and Rousseau as a "depository" of his authority. M. de Mably's son would also become a gentleman by "developing his liking . . . for the [fashionable] society for which he is intended." *Projet pour l'éducation de M. de Sainte-Marie* (P, IV, 35–51). For a discussion of some similarities between the contracts of the *Social Contract* and *Emile*, and of parallels between the lawgiver's task in the *Social Contract* and Rousseau's in *Emile*, see Launay, *Rousseau*, pp. 372–381, 417–418, 454–456.

16. *Emile*, pp. 242–243, 548–550.

men. During this period, from fifteen years of age to twenty, Emile acquires that "virtue" or "reason" or "conscience" essential to the habitual mastery of vain passions. An important interlude, the "Profession of Faith of a Savoyard Priest," appears in book four. In book five, beginning with the section "Sophie; or, Of Woman," Emile is permanently attached to others through his formal declaration of citizenship and his courtship and marriage to Sophie. But the treatise is actually divided into three fundamental phases of Emile's social transformation. Book one or infancy is a presocial state of nature, and the last two books comprise a single conclusive period.[17]

Emile's infancy, or the "first state of man," corresponds to the static, purposeless contentedness of presocial nature described in the *Discourse on Inequality*. Although Emile is largely passive, or unconsciously mechanical in his reactions, Rousseau is already beginning to build the foundation for Emile's emergence as a virtuous citizen. As we have seen, in the *Discourse on Inequality* Rousseau dismissed philosophers who failed to go far enough backwards to reach the "true state of

17. The recurring dispute over the nature of the periods in *Emile* is abetted by Rousseau's inconsistencies in terminology. For similar interpretations, some of which also draw parallels between the early periods in the *Discourse on Inequality* and those in *Emile*, see Pierre Burgelin, "The Second Education of Emile," *Yale French Studies*, XXVIII (Fall-Winter, 1961), 106–111, and his introduction to *Emile* (P, III, cxiv–cxix); John S. Spink, introduction to the *Favre Manuscript* (P, III, lxxxiv); Starobinski, *Rousseau*, pp. 257–263; Martin Rang, "Le Dualisme anthropologique dans l'*Emile*," in *Rousseau et son oeuvre*, pp. 195–203; Broome, *Rousseau*, pp. 110, 115–116; Wallon, "*Emile; ou, de l'éducation*," pp. 130–135; Wright, *Meaning of Rousseau*, pp. 38–65. For a view which argues parallels between the stages of Emile's education and the entire evolution of the species in the *Discourse on Inequality*, see Lapassade, "L'Oeuvre de Rousseau," pp. 388–393. A discussion of often varying "ages" in manuscript versions, as well as contrasting interpretations of these variations, is in Jimack, *La Genèse et la rédaction de l'Emile*, pp. 152–178. Rousseau also suggested three cumulative periods in his plans for M. de Mably's sons. See *Mémoire à M. de Mably* (P, IV, 7, 11–12, 15–18, 25–28); *Projet pour l'éducation*, pp. 41–48.

nature," the actual infancy of the species. They ascribed to natural man the reason, memory, language, and foresight of later, artificial men. The confusing of the sequential "order of human life" elicits Rousseau's identical complaint in *Emile:* "We know nothing of infancy. . . . The wisest writers devote themselves to what is important for men to know, without considering what infants are capable of learning. . . . It is this study to which I have most directed myself." Rousseau frequently referred to his pupil and infancy as "natural man" and man's "natural" or "primitive" condition.[18]

18. *Emile,* pp. 286, 303, 241–242, 280–281, 304, 311, 407. Rousseau complained that the word *enfance* cannot distinguish between the presocial time of inarticulate gestures and cries and the period of articulate language. *Ibid.,* p. 299. See also *ibid.,* p. 426. I translate *enfance* as "infancy" or "childhood," depending on the context. One corollary of Rousseau's insistence upon the presocial character of infancy is his rejection of what he called Locke's "chief maxim" in *Thoughts on Education,* namely Locke's reliance upon reasoning with children. See *ibid.,* pp. 317–320, 324. Moreover, at many, sometimes crucial moments during Emile's education, Rousseau attacked Locke's views. The "wise Locke who had spent part of his life studying medicine" correctly cautioned against administering medicines to children; but Rousseau condemned all doctors and defended the importance of exercise and manual labor for both health and true citizenship. *Ibid.,* pp. 269–272. The "wise Locke" is later praised for appreciating the importance of exercise, only to be accused of "falling again into inconsistencies" for refusing to permit children to drink cold water when they are hot or to lie on damp grass. *Ibid.,* pp. 371, 374. These matters are no trifle. When Rousseau discussed the importance of a healthy, honest manual trade that "does not develop odious moral qualities incompatible with humanity," Locke's *Thoughts on Education* again supplied the contrast: "I would never want Emile to be an embroiderer, a gilder, or a varnisher like Locke's gentleman." *Ibid.,* p. 473. And Locke was further criticized for turning a child's introduction to the duties of generosity and gratitude into a lesson in contractual exchange that teaches greed to a deceitful usurer; for ignoring a child's motives of use or enjoyment when he learns to read; and for recommending "the method of superstition, prejudice and error" in religious training. *Ibid.,* pp. 338–339, 358, 551–552. The Savoyard even equates Locke's ideas with that materialist philosophy which, taking society to be an "aggregation of [sensitive] individuals," finds man incapable of noble sentiments and actions. *Ibid.,*

To be sure, an infant does not possess the physical strength of original man. But strength is always relative to desire and need: "What does one mean, 'Man is weak'? The word *weakness* suggests a relation, a relation of the creature to whom it is applied. One whose strength exceeds its needs, be it an insect or a worm, is strong. One whose needs exceed its strength, be it an elephant, a lion, a conqueror, a hero, or a god, is weak." Like the indolent, unimaginative, but healthy natural man in the *Discourse on Inequality*, Rousseau's infant is at peace with himself in his "primitive condition" because his strength is adequate to his natural desires. Because Emile's infancy is a presocial state of nature, he obtains, at the conclusion of book one, his first sustained awareness of his educator and therefore his first consciousness of self. He is entering "the first epoch of his life," his childhood: "Up to now, he is little more than he was in the womb of his mother; he has neither feeling nor ideas nor hardly any sensations; he is not even aware of his own existence."[19]

The remaining four books of *Emile* describe three periods. During childhood, the "first age" (book two), Emile is seeking agreeable experiences and avoiding unpleasant ones. He is now learning the "law of [physical] necessity" from contact with objects. During early adolescence or the "second period" of his education (book three), Emile uses physical objects for his own purposes. Emile's strength greatly exceeds his needs, making this an appropriate time "for work, instruction, and study"

p. 584. Yet immediately before lamenting that philosophers are ignorant of prerational infancy, Rousseau characteristically suggested that *Emile* is a mere elaboration on Locke's *Thoughts on Education. Ibid.*, p. 241.

19. *Ibid.*, pp. 305, 304, 298. See also *ibid.*, p. 284. The *Favre Manuscript* does not divide into books at this point but mentions the beginning of a "second stage of infancy which properly begins the life of man." *Favre Manuscript*, p. 81. For discussions of similarities between the presocial state of nature in the *Discourse on Inequality* and book one of *Emile*, see Groethuysen, *Rousseau*, pp. 22–26; Starobinski, *Rousseau*, pp. 28–31; and Château, *Rousseau*, pp. 114–129.

of the physical universe. During the last period (books four and five), Emile correctly judges men and their *moeurs* by means of "ideas of goodness or perfection which reason gives us." This is the "critical age" for Emile. His passions, aroused by attachments to others, are now in excess of his "strength" to satisfy them. Emile's first meeting with Sophie, "the most important and difficult" event of his education, is the "crisis which provides passage from infancy to manhood." Emile's marriage is the "closing scene" of the third and "last act of his youth." Thus, the structure of *Emile* corresponds to the growth of a presocial infant into a virtuous citizen.[20]

In his discussion of presocial infancy, Rousseau insisted that education not contradict man's natural liberty and goodness: he denounced the "chains" and "tortures" inflicted on infants by contemporary parents. Clothing an infant in caps and swaddling clothes, rubbing his head with oil to improve its shape, and hiring incompetent, "mercenary" nurses render him "more miserable than a criminal in irons." The requirement that contemporary infants "give or take orders" is responsible for their aggressive caprices. Thus Rousseau disputed, as he had disputed at the identical prehistorical moment in the *Discourse on Inequality*, Hobbes' assertion that man is naturally wicked. Infants do "good or evil without knowing it and there is no morality in their actions." When an infant overturns or breaks an object, he does not express "pride, the spirit of domination, vanity, wickedness" or even "consciousness of his own weakness." It is simply the "overflowing activity" of nature. Only when taught by others to "consider people around them as instruments to be used," do infants become "troublesome, tyrannical, imperious, wicked, unmanageable." Because "the first

20. *Emile*, pp. 316, 321, 426, 428–429, 517, 630, 777, 692. In terms of Emile's physical development, however, there is a second, biological calendar. Rousseau called the first period of social dependence the "second term of life," just as he later calls the second stage of common life a "third age of human life." *Ibid.*, pp. 299, 494.

impulses of nature are always right," a gentle love of self (*amour de soi*) is man's only natural passion. Since "an infant has no necessary relations to other people, he is, in this respect, naturally indifferent to them; his love of self becomes good or bad only by the use made of it and the relationships that one gives him."

For a pupil not enslaved to others, love of self turns into gratitude to persons who contribute to his welfare. As "the consciousness of his relationships to others is awakened," he acquires a conscientious sense of duties and moral preferences. But if education inspires the insatiable, unnatural passion of self-love (*amour-propre*), of invidiously "comparing oneself with others," then man becomes imperious and deceitful. This contrast between natural love of self and self-love born of corrupt society is identical to that in the *Discourse on Inequality*.[21]

Education itself is the cumulative social transformation which fashions a new public creature: "We are born weak, destitute of everything, and dull; we need strength, aid, and judgment. All that we lack at birth, all that we need when grown, is given us through education." As in the *Discourse on Inequality*, three causes of this transformation are nature, men, and things: "The internal growth of our faculties and our organs is the education of nature; the use we learn to make of this growth is the education by men; and what we acquire from our own experience of objects which surround us is education by things." Rousseau coordinates and controls this edu-

---

21. *Ibid.*, pp. 253–258, 364, 288–290, 322, 492–493. See also *ibid.*, pp. 314–316, 511–516. In the *Discourse on Inequality* Rousseau argued that pity is natural to man. In *Emile* he did not make this claim, but there is no inconsistency because love of self, in *Emile*, is understood in a wider sense than mere self-preservation: love of self is later "extended" into compassionate identification with the sufferings of others (*ibid.*, p. 547), so that social man's virtues are all "modifications" of natural love of self. For a similar view of "pity" in *Emile*, see Wright, *Meaning of Rousseau*, pp. 12–13; Masters, *Political Philosophy of Rousseau*, pp. 138–139. See also *Emile*, pp. 286, 329, 500–505, 517, 564.

cation by isolating the young Emile from contemporary men and by carefully arranging and censoring the objects he encounters. He accustoms Emile to cold water by progressively lowering the temperature: many simple peoples bathe newborn infants in rivers or the sea. By using a thermometer Rousseau avoids risks and assures that temperature changes are "gradual and imperceptible" to Emile; soon Emile can tolerate ice-cold water in winter as well as summer. Emile must also become fearless: "Infants raised in clean houses, where there are no spiders, are afraid of spiders; and their fear often remains throughout life. I never saw peasants, neither men, women, nor children, who were afraid of spiders." And because a citizen must often drill to the sound of a gun, Rousseau fires a pistol with a very small charge in Emile's presence, an event whose sudden flash of lightning delights every infant. The exercise is repeated with gradually larger charges so that Emile becomes accustomed "to the sound of a gun, fireworks, a cannon and the most terrible explosions." This training will make him "fit for every human situation." Now, we never see the mature Emile drilling to the sound of guns, but the identity of a pupil who becomes fearless, resilient, and versatile is unmistakable; and we know that virtuous citizenship is the only trade of one who is by nature free and good.[22]

To summon aid and to express frustration, an infant uses crying and gesturing, which is the only "natural language" common to mankind. Like presocial man's "cry of nature" in the *Discourse on Inequality*, an infant "speaks before knowing how to speak." But contemporary parents ignore the language of infancy: "The use of our languages has led us to neglect their language to the point of forgetting it entirely. Let us study infants and soon we will relearn it from them." A failure to understand the language of infancy has the disastrous consequence of imparting ideas of "rule and tyranny," for an in-

22. *Emile*, pp. 247, 277 278, 283 284, 267.

fant's tears "forge the first link in that long chain which forms the social order." When a tutor relearns the language of infancy, he is able to distinguish those "desires which come immediately from nature" and require his attention from those "which arise from opinion" and should be ignored. He can even learn to anticipate natural desires "so that infants need not proclaim their needs by crying." Nor does Rousseau ever subject Emile to an extensive vocabulary, hurry his ability to speak, or attempt to understand him when he stammers—there is time enough to acquire social man's "unhappy facility" with words. An infant who "always expects to be listened to is exercising a kind of rule."[23]

In the *Discourse on Inequality*, apologizing for "forgetting [variations of] times and places," Rousseau had exhorted worthy observers to study and report on simple peoples living in historical proximity to the presocial state of nature.[24] A comparable invitation is extended in *Emile* when he implores his readers to become knowledgeable about infancy, for Rousseau is reporting in the first book of *Emile* on his own imaginary voyage back to the state of nature. Rousseau sees the infant or original man as he might appear to himself, if he were capable or interested in seeing himself. And Rousseau's preliminary lessons, from prohibiting swaddling clothes to properly responding to Emile's cries to exposing Emile to spiders, illustrate the lawgiver's method of deceptive manipulation: "disciplined" or "well-regulated liberty" (*la liberté bien réglée*), liberty regulated only by a "necessity in things." Referring the reader to his discussion of law and the general will in the *Social Contract*, where he had "proved that no particular will can command in the social system," Rousseau elaborates on this method. Dependence upon the will of men "comes from society." Such dependence is prohibited. It "en-

23. *Ibid.*, pp. 285–286, 290, 293, 296–298. See also *ibid.*, pp. 341–342.
24. *Discourse on Inequality*, p. 133.

genders all vices, and through this dependence master and slave become mutually depraved." But "dependence on things" is natural. This dependence "can do no injury to liberty and can engender no vices." With natural liberty uncorrupted, it can be said that Emile "remains as free as before": Rousseau "absolutely never commands anything," and "the words *obey* and *command* are proscribed from Emile's vocabulary."[25] One can even say that Emile is "strengthened to be free," that is, required by circumstances to become a sincerely virtuous citizen. As self-governing citizens of the *Social Contract* obey only laws, so Emile obeys only the things he encounters.[26]

Stages of Common Life

In the first period of social dependence in the *Discourse on Inequality*, "nascent man" lives in a nonobligatory "free association" or herd to obtain food and safety. Having been compelled by natural disasters to surrender a repetitive life of indolence and "pure sensation," men become "agile, fleet in running, vigorous in combat." All of their senses are fully developed and they exhibit "mechanical prudence" in overcoming the height of trees and the ferocity of other animals. By noticing and remembering their relative strengths, men become conscious of themselves as distinctive members of a single species. As a result men experience "the first stirring of pride" in their limited accomplishments; and, their language unrefined but honest, they "acquire some crude idea of mutual engagements and of the advantages of fulfilling them, but only insofar as present and perceptible interest could require." Foresight still means nothing to them; and "far from being

25. *Emile*, pp. 320–321, 311, 316.
26. For a contrasting view of the significance of unmediated encounters with things, see the discussion of Rousseau's understanding of language in Starobinski, *Rousseau*, pp. 172–207, 239–241, 244–245, 279–281. See also Bretonneau, *Valeurs humaines de Rousseau*, pp. 91–115.

concerned about a distant future," they do not even think of "the next day."[27]

The form of social evolution in *Emile* cannot correspond exactly to those of the *Discourse on Inequality*, for only a single citizen is being educated, and the miniature republic does not change. But like this period in the history of the species, Emile's childhood involves his physical growth, the perfection of his bodily senses, and that first recognition of self which means that "the life of an individual properly begins." When "memory extends this feeling of identity to every moment of his existence, he becomes truly a person, always the same and consequently already capable of happiness or misery. It is important therefore to begin to consider him a moral being."[28]

Emile, too, is incapable of unaided self-improvement. He is not the liberal theorists' genius. His natural perfectibility is only potential: "We are born capable of learning, but aware of nothing and knowing nothing." Without other men we would have remained forever in or near "the state of original ignorance and stupidity natural to man." Passive experience of an external environment, resulting from the "natural and mechanical use of the senses," is not a sufficient basis for either memory or reason. A single man merely senses, without being conscious of the significance of perceived objects. He obtains only separate and inert "images" of external objects. Reason, "the active principle which judges," makes it possible to acquire and use true "ideas" about the relations of objects; and this reason is itself a consequence of education. Therefore, because they are appropriate to the limited needs of childhood, Rousseau employs various devices involving games, bodily exercises, and prearranged encounters with things: "To exercise

27. *Discourse on Inequality*, pp. 164–167.
28. *Emile*, p. 301. Accordingly, Rousseau first referred to his pupil by name toward the end of book one. *Ibid.*, pp. 296–297.

the senses, it is not enough merely to make use of them; we must learn to judge by their means; we must learn, so to speak, to perceive, because we cannot touch, see or hear except as we have been taught." Rousseau's manipulation of things initiates for Emile the same escape from presocial ignorance that environmental accidents provide the species in the *Discourse on Inequality*.[29]

Unlike that of contemporary pupils "subjected to an intolerable yoke and condemned to endless tasks like galley slaves," Emile's childhood is an "age of gaiety," without "tears, punishments, threats, and slavery." Wearing "little or nothing on his

29. *Ibid.*, pp. 279, 280–281, 344–345, 380. For the exercises and games which develop the senses, see *ibid.*, pp. 380–390 (touch), 396–401 (sight), 404–407 (hearing), 407–411 (taste), 416–417 (smell). However, the sequential appearance and relative importance of a child's senses are not identical to original man's in the *Discourse on Inequality*. In a note accompanying his discussion of an infant's inability to reason, Rousseau complained about the poverty of available terminology. And he did use "reason" in two very different senses throughout *Emile*. Reason during childhood is a crude, sensory intelligence which becomes, in adolescence, a practical or instrumental facility with and about things. In the last period, however, reason is a matter of passionate but accurate moral judgment of men and of one's duties, what the Savoyard calls "conscience." See *ibid.*, pp. 359–360, 417–418, 430–432, 481–486, 551–552, 570–572. This last citation contains the Savoyard's rejection of individualist sensationalism and repeats, in almost identical language, the surviving notes of Rousseau's abandoned refutation of Helvétius' *De l'esprit*. See Pierre-Maurice Masson, "Rousseau contra Helvétius," *Revue d'histoire littéraire de la France*, XVIII (1911), 105–113. See also *Favre Manuscript*, pp. 113–114, where Rousseau referred to his disagreements with "the author of *De l'esprit*." For interpretations which identify, in varying degrees and manners, Emile's earliest education and the Savoyard's epistemology with the sensationalism of Locke, Condillac, and Helvétius, see Mornet, *Rousseau*, pp. 136–138; Jimack, *La Genèse et la rédaction de l'Emile*, pp. 88–93, 129–130, 228–233; Yvon Belaval, "La Théorie du jugement dans l'Emile," in *Jean-Jacques Rousseau et son oeuvre*, pp. 149–157; Masters, *Political Philosophy of Rousseau*, pp. 27–39, 52n, 58–66; Shklar, *Men and Citizens*, pp. 33–41, 53–54, 82–83, 140, 222. For a contrasting view, see Gouhier, *Les Méditations métaphysiques de Rousseau*, pp. 67–75.

head" in all seasons, Emile runs about barefooted in a meadow, falls down frequently, jumps and leaps, shouts, climbs trees and walls. He does not distinguish work from play in his activities, many of which continue earlier lessons which accustomed him to hardship. Rousseau removes only harmful objects. But he "absolutely" refuses to "order anything" of Emile. He has "relinquished all rights to exhortations, promises, threats, emulation or the desire to show off" before others.[30]

The story of Emile's learning to run fast illustrates the manipulation of things during childhood. One day, when Emile and Rousseau are planning their usual walk, Rousseau puts in his pocket an extra cake of the sort Emile especially likes. When Emile, "who could eat six," asks for this cake Rousseau suggests instead a race with two boys nearby. He places the cake on a rock at the end of a marked course as a prize. Emile decides to compete but loses. And he loses subsequent races that week as Rousseau adds more competitors and lengthens the course. Soon neighbors stop to watch and cheer; the boys' excitement quickens each day at what are for them "Olympian games." Some of Emile's friends, but not Emile, get in the way of one another or place stones in a competitor's path. Rousseau then separates the runners, having each start simultaneously from different directions equidistant from the prize. This new arrangement furnishes additional opportunities for Emile's physical and sensory development.

Emile soon begins to appreciate the importance of strength and speed. On the sly, he practices alone. Soon he is winning many races. As he gets used to winning, he shares the prize with his friends. But now, to instruct Emile in the coordination of his senses, "to teach him to see," Rousseau marks off courses of varying distances. Ignoring distance Emile chooses the smoothest path and begins to lose again. When Emile finally

30. *Emile*, pp. 300–302, 312, 344, 390, 421, 423, 393.

realizes what is happening Rousseau dismisses his anger: "What is your complaint? Am I not the master of the conditions of a gift which I give? Who forces you to run? Did I promise you I would make the courses equal? Don't you have a choice of courses?" At first Emile attempts to pace off the different courses, but several races a day make this a slow, inaccurate means of measurement. Later Emile, by practicing from several vantage points when no races are scheduled, has educated himself to judge distances accurately by sight: "As sight, of all the senses, is least separable from mental judgments, it takes a long time to learn to see; it takes a long time to compare sight and touch, in order to train the former to give us a faithful report of shapes and distances. Without touch, without constant motion, the sharpest eyes in the world could not give us any sense of space. The whole universe must seem a mere point to an oyster." After several months of practice testing and races, Emile's visual judgment of distances is so certain that "his glance is nearly as accurate as a surveyor's chain." No doubt by this time he can also run extraordinarily fast.[31]

This awakening and training of Emile's senses, however, remains rudimentary during childhood. As long as he becomes strong and healthy by the age of twelve, it does not matter if he cannot tell his right hand from his left. Premature efforts at formal instruction designed to develop a child's reason entail coercion and threats, which impart prejudice and servile habit. Because childhood has its "own ways of seeing, thinking and feeling," Emile remains incapable of sustained foresight and ignorant of obligations. And the limited education possible and desirable during childhood is always best obtained from simple, immediate experience, not books. Emile scarcely knows what a book is until he is twelve. He finally learns to read when reading becomes, for him, related to "actual and present advantage, either of enjoyment or use." When Emile is not able

31. *Ibid.*, pp. 393-398. See also *ibid.*, pp. 410-411, 806-807.

to find someone to read friends' invitations, he asks Rousseau to teach him to read.[32]

At the age of twelve Emile has reached the "perfection" or "maturity" of childhood. Because Rousseau has remained "his friend and comrade," because they "never depend on each other," Emile's "quick but certain movements express the liveliness of his age, the firmness of independence, and the experience of many activities." He has an "open and free manner, not insolent or vain. . . . Question him and you do not fear importunity, chatter, or indiscreet questions. . . . He knows nothing of routine, custom or habit. . . . He never follows a rule, concedes anything to authority or example, and he acts or speaks only as he pleases. . . . If he needs some assistance, he will seek it readily of the first person he meets. He will seek assistance of a king or of his lackey: all men are still equal in his eyes." Because Emile "knows he is free" and "master of himself," he never acts thoughtlessly toward others. In his voice and demeanor one detects neither the "servile submission of a slave nor the imperious tone of a master."[33]

During the second period of common life in the *Discourse on Inequality*, men for the first time control physical objects in a foresighted and routine manner. They use crude implements of hard, sharp stones to cut wood, spoon out the earth, and fashion huts. Families divide labor; a husband works out of doors at his original occupation while his wife confines herself to housekeeping and caring for their children.[34]

Emile's development during the period of early adolescence parallels these events. He begins to train for an occupation, distinguishing this work from play. Moving beyond the crude notions of "sensory reason," he makes "active judgments" and acquires "intellectual reason," that "sixth sense, called common

32. *Ibid.*, pp. 317–319, 323–324, 333–341, 357–358.
33. *Ibid.*, pp. 419–423.
34. *Discourse on Inequality*, pp. 167–168.

sense, . . . because it results from the well-regulated use of the other senses and informs us about the nature of things through the concurrence of all their appearances." Because Emile's strength now exceeds his desires, he is able to "get outside himself" during this short, "peaceful age of intelligence." Emile is largely isolated from other adolescents now: "There should be no comparisons with other children, no rivalries, no contests, even in running races, as soon as he begins to reason. I would much prefer that he learn nothing than have him learn through jealousy or vanity." Rousseau's prohibition of books excepts only *Robinson Crusoe*, "the best treatise on natural education." With *Crusoe* Emile can measure his intellectual progress and begin to acquire a faint understanding of his natural origin. Crusoe's "condition, I admit, is not that of a social man; nor is it Emile's own condition. But it is from this condition alone that he must judge all others. The surest way to raise oneself above prejudice and to order judgments about the true relations of things is to put oneself in the position of an isolated man, and to judge all things as they would be judged by such a man—in relation to his own utility."[35]

A tutor's commands remain even more dangerous than those of authors: "If ever you substitute authority for reason he will reason no longer; he will be merely a victim of the opinions of others." A pupil's attention "should never be forced"; he must find pleasure and utility in knowing the relations of things. Emile is "told" and "taught" nothing by Rousseau but rather permitted and encouraged to "discover" and "understand" objects himself. For "the conceptions of things one teaches oneself are much clearer and more certain" than the conceptions others teach us; and "we develop greater ingenuity in finding relations, in connecting ideas, and in inventing instruments,"

35. *Emile*, pp. 417, 466, 436, 453–455. See also *ibid.*, pp. 426–430, 444–445, 465–466.

than when we "submit servilely to authority." Nor is Emile permitted to command. Rousseau's answers are designed only to whet his curiosity: "Above all, when you see that a pupil rambles and overwhelms you with silly questions, instead of seeking self-instruction, refuse to answer at once; for it is clear that he no longer cares about a matter and wants only to enslave you to his questions."[36]

An early instance of cunning self-instruction about and through things concerns geography and astronomy. Like Crusoe, and with Rousseau's aid and by correcting his own mistakes, Emile makes a map of his neighborhood and learns to tell time by the sun. Rousseau casually remarks one afternoon that the forest is north of Montmorency. Emile questions the utility of this information. Rousseau, concurring, agrees to resume other activities. The next morning, when Rousseau announces that he is taking a walk before breakfast, Emile, who still likes to run about, asks to accompany him. Soon they are lost in the forest. As noon approaches, Emile, hot, tired, hungry, and not knowing that only a thicket hides Montmorency from his view, begins to cry. When Rousseau reminds Emile that the day before they had observed that the forest was north of Montmorency, Emile realizes that Montmorency must be south of the forest. After interpreting midday shadows, Emile, "clapping his hands and with a cry of joy," proudly leads Rousseau out of the woods: "Oh, I see Montmorency! There it is right in front of us. . . . Come to breakfast, come to dinner, run quickly. Astronomy is useful."

Similar lessons follow. After Emile's prearranged encounters with a conjurer at a local fair introduce him to the phenomenon of magnetism (and intellectual pride), Emile fashions his own compass by floating a toy magnetic duck in a bowl of water. Learning the properties of air by submerging an inverted glass in water and by comparing the bounces of differ-

36. *Ibid.*, pp. 430, 433, 442, 436.

ent balls leads Emile to discover the laws of hydrostatics and to understand a barometer, siphon, and air pump. Mechanics is introduced by pivoting a stick on the back of a chair. And what Emile learns he always retains because his motives reveal nothing of reputation or fashion.[37]

Now capable of foresight and adaptable to self-imposed routine, Emile is ready to enter the contemporary world. Working at his future occupation will "imperceptibly awaken a taste for thought and reflection and counteract the sluggishness that would result from his indifference to the judgment of men and the calm of his passions." After Rousseau and Emile work at the "natural arts which may be carried on by one man alone," Emile is introduced to the "industrial arts which call for the cooperation of many hands." Through this first experience of "mutual dependence" Emile becomes somewhat aware of its "moral side." He is still too young to understand that modern man has made himself "the chief instrument of man," but he can judge various trades with reference to their utility. He prefers a shoemaker to a poet, and he finds it curious that men appear to be more polite in a jeweler's shop than at a blacksmith's. Emile also begins to realize that "man is the same in all estates," that "a rich man's stomach is no larger and digests food no better than the stomach of a poor man . . . and, as natural needs are the same for all, that the means of satisfying them should be equal."

A lawgiver does not impose his occupational preference: "The child must be everything, and you must devote yourself completely to him." In order to live in "liberty, health, truth, industry and justice," Emile will choose a manual trade: "Of all the occupations which furnish sustenance to man, that which is nearest to the state of nature is working with one's hands." Farming may be "the earliest, the most honest, useful and consequently the most noble" of manual trades, but a

37. *Ibid.*, pp. 434, 447–450, 437–442.

contemporary farmer is harassed and finally ruined by "an enemy, a prince, a powerful neighbor, or a lawsuit." An artisan, however, simply packs his tools and moves: "The artisan . . . is as free as the farmer is enslaved." Emile resolves to learn carpentry, "for it is clean and useful; it may be done at home; it keeps his body sufficiently exercised; it requires skill and industry; and elegance and taste are not excluded from objects fashioned for their usefulness." Rousseau and Emile serve as apprentice carpenters once or twice a week in a craftsman's shop. They do not spend the entire week at the workshop because they are "apprentice men," not merely "apprentice workmen."[38]

At fifteen Emile's education has been largely confined to things and the relations between men and things, not "the moral relations among men." If Emile "does not even know the word *history*, nor *metaphysics*, nor *morals*," he still exhibits the integrity of his natural self: "It only remains, to achieve manhood, to make a being loving and compassionate, that is to say to perfect reason through feeling."[39] Emile's apprenticeship to life in the final two books corresponds to the third period of common life in the *Discourse on Inequality*. Families are united in small, simple societies. Still confining themselves "to tasks that a single person could do and to arts that did not require the cooperation of several hands," men enjoy "free, healthy, good, and happy" lives and "the sweetness of independent intercourse." Comparisons in "public esteem" are frequent, so that the passions of natural goodness can no longer cement their "nascent society." The "first duties of civility" are soon succeeded by "the first rules of justice" essential to a new life of self-mastery.[40]

38. *Ibid.*, pp. 480, 459–463, 468, 470, 478. See also *La Nouvelle Héloise*, pp. 536, 546.
39. *Emile*, pp. 487, 481.
40. *Discourse on Inequality*, pp. 169–173.

"We are born, so to speak, twice," Rousseau observed of Emile's last epoch. We are "born into existence as a member of the species and born into life as a man." Emile is now in- flamed by passions which are "relative" or "imaginative" be- cause they arise from comparison and preference. Rousseau will help Emile impose a habitual "order and rule" on his pas- sions. When Emile makes his interest his duty, when his "strength" is once again adequate to his desires, he will have become a true citizen for whom "justice and goodness are . . . true affections of the heart, clarified by reason, an orderly outcome of our primitive affections."

The basis for Emile's discipline is natural goodness, which has already sown the "first seeds of humanity" in the heart of a grateful pupil. As a "bond of affection" with other men, Emile now shares the "common sufferings" of mankind: "He begins to perceive himself in his fellow men, to be moved by their cries, to suffer their pains." The uninterrupted sight of contemporary misery would only inure Emile's heart, so the time has come for Emile to enlarge his library by studying history. This undertaking carries the advantage that when done properly "the experience and authority of a teacher" can- not be substituted for Emile's "own experience and the devel- opment of his reason." As their judge but never their accuser or accomplice, Emile comes to understand men, "to read the hearts of men without the lessons of philosophy."

The study of the past presents difficulties. History, Rousseau explained, is largely silent about men's virtuous deeds and about small, peaceful, self-sufficient nations: "Only the wicked become famous; the good are forgotten or twisted by ridicule. This is how history, like philosophy, endlessly slanders man- kind." Moreover, ignorance and partiality transform the past "in the head of a historian." By expanding or contracting cir- cumstances but "without altering a single historical deed," or by inventing the cause of a battle's outcome when the battle might have been decided by "a tree more or less, a boulder to the right or left, or a cloud of dust raised by the wind," or by embellishing an event with fanciful portraits, a historian ceases to be a trustworthy guide. Accuracy may be less important than "conveying the truth of *moeurs* and character," but "one falls again into the very error one intended to avoid, by giving to historians the authority taken from the tutor." Accordingly, Emile will be supplied with specific facts.

Rousseau censors modern historians. Thucydides, in contrast, is the "true model" for all historians. He "relates facts without judging them; and he omits no circumstances essential to our forming our own judgments. . . . Far from interposing himself between the events and his readers, he hides himself; we seem not to read but to see." Unforunately, Thucydides speaks constantly of war, "the least instructive thing of the world." So Emile will first study Plutarch, then Herodotus and Livy. Ancient conquerors and usurpers may not have failed in their plans. But because Emile has "preserved right judgment and a compassionate heart," he cannot avoid recognizing the misery of vicious men: "Brought up in the most absolute liberty, the greatest wrong he can imagine is servitude. He pities these miserable kings, the slaves of all who obey them; he pities false prophets chained to their empty reputation; he pities rich fools, martyrs to their magnificence."[41]

At the age of eighteen, Emile does not know what is meant by a soul and has never heard the name of God. As his thoughts turn to religion, Rousseau provides Emile with an instructive historical portrait of his own composition, "The Profession of Faith of a Savoyard Priest." He relates the life and beliefs of an unusual man who had "opened his heart" to Rousseau thirty

41. *Emile*, pp. 489, 500, 522–523, 502–504, 526–529, 536. See also *Fragments on Sparta and Rome* (P, III, 538–539); *Fragments on Moeurs* (P, III, 558); *Confessions* (P, I, 8–9); *La Nouvelle Héloise*, pp. 57–60. M. de Mably's sons would instead study modern history, especially that of their own "country." *Mémoire à M. de Mably*, pp. 8, 29–30.

years before. The Savoyard had inspired a "young fugitive," as Rousseau described himself, to realize that virtue was not vanity and that he himself, though a poor, exiled, and formerly defrocked Catholic priest, was a happy man at peace with himself.[42] Like the "civil religion" of the *Social Contract*, the "Profession of Faith" is the conclusive lesson in Emile's transformation from presocial infancy to self-governing citizenship. Everything that follows is an application of the Savoyard's beliefs.

The details of the Savoyard's life, and his reason for believing in metaphysical dualism, need not detain us. Neither the Savoyard when talking to the young Rousseau nor Rousseau in relating the Savoyard's profession to Emile seeks to persuade his pupil of the intrinsic truth of specific religious dogmas.[43] Each seeks to arouse and strengthen the "conscience" of his listener, to encourage him to "perfect reason through feeling" so that he may judge men for himself: "So long as we yield nothing to human authority nor to the prejudices of our native country, the light of reason alone, in the pattern of nature, can lead us no farther than natural religion; and this is as far as I go with my Emile. If he must have another religion, I no longer have the right to be his guide; he alone must choose it."[44]

42. *Emile*, pp. 549, 560–561, 565.
43. *Ibid.*, pp. 556–558, 565–566, 582, 630–631.
44. *Ibid.*, pp. 630, 635–636. See also *Letters from the Mountain*, p. 749. Rousseau frequently asserted that the tenets of the Savoyard's faith comprise his personal faith and are consistent with everything he has written on the subject of religion, including Julie's deathbed profession of faith. See letters to Moultou (Dec. 23, 1761; *CC*, IX, 341–342; Jan. 18, 1762; *CC*, X, 40–41; and April 30, 1763; *CC*, XVI, 125); *Letters from the Mountain*, p. 694; *Confessions*, p. 407; *Rêveries* (P, I, 1018–1020). For Rousseau's earlier assertion of metaphysical dualism and his "proof of sentiment" for the immortality of the soul, see *Letter to Voltaire* (Aug. 18, 1756; P, IV, 1070–1073). In his letter to Franquières (Jan. 15, 1769; P, IV, 1137–1139) Rousseau stressed the social utility of correct religious beliefs, of those "internal sentiments" which form a mean

Like Crusoe, the Savoyard starts from the certainty of his own existence, the "self-evident" notions that he is conscious of sensations from objects outside himself and that he possesses the capacity of an "intelligent and active being" for judging and comparing sensations. After explaining his reasons for thinking that matter is naturally at rest, the Savoyard is led to the first of three "plain, clear and strikingly obvious" articles of his creed, that "there is will behind the movements of the universe and the animation of nature." The Savoyard's judgment that the motion of the physical universe proceeds "according to definite laws" suggests the existence of "a supreme intelligence," the second article of his faith: "This being who wills and who is able to will, this being active through his own power, this being, whoever he may be, who moves the universe and orders all things, I call God." Man's limited reason cannot discern the nature of God except for His attributes of supreme intelligence and will and, what follows necessarily, His goodness and justice. Then the Savoyard "returns to himself" to seek to discover his place "in that order of things which He governs and which I can examine." He first discovers his species: man alone appears free to carry out his own will. Only man can observe, measure, control, and forecast the movements of other beasts and objects. Only man can "unite, so to speak, the sentiment of a common existence with that of his individual existence." Yet contemporary men are at war: "Harmony reigns among the elements; men are in chaos. Animals are happy; their king alone is miserable." From these reflections, "the sublime idea of man's soul" is grasped. Modern man is a self at war with himself; he is divided by particular and general loyalties.[45]

The "indisputable feeling" that man alone is "active" or

---

between brute instinct and the sectarian vanity of contemporary philosophers.

45. *Emile*, pp. 570–573, 614, 576, 578–583.

"free" persuades the Savoyard of the third article of his faith, "the principle of all action is in the will of a free being." Except for the freedom not to desire his own welfare or to desire his own harm, man is by nature his own master. His misery is "no part of the system ordered by Providence." Then the Savoyard "deduces" a number of subsidiary tenets: death, as the cessation of worldly suffering, is not to be feared; the soul survives at the death of the body and is perhaps immortal; rewards or punishments await the good and wicked in the life to come, although the Savoyard's pity for his fellow men and his faith in the goodness and justice of God lead him to think that the punishment of the wicked is not eternal.[46]

The Savoyard's "opinions" form the appropriate "civil religion" for a single citizen—for a fugitive from modern society —and not merely because the tenets of his "natural religion" are nearly identical to the few, simple "sentiments of sociability" of the civil religion in the *Social Contract*. Only the social utility of religious belief concerns the Savoyard.[47] The tone of his natural religion is admittedly more cosmopolitan than that of the civil religion in the *Social Contract*, but this is because he, like Emile, is in, not of, contemporary society. His natural religion especially does not correspond to the religion of "man" rejected in the *Social Contract*: "true" Christianity distinguishes man from citizen. As the civil religion assures the integrity of an entire body politic in the *Social Contract*, the Savoyard's natural religion promises peace of soul to an orphaned "natural man" educated within a miniature republic. As the civil religion in the *Social Contract* recapitulates a true

46. *Ibid.*, pp. 585–592. See also *La Nouvelle Héloïse*, pp. 726–729; letter to Vernes (Feb. 18, 1758; *CC*, V, 32–33).

47. See also *Letters from the Mountain*, pp. 694–695, 700–707, 790–792, 798–801; letter to Néaulme (Feb. 22, 1762 [?]; *CC*, X, 113); *La Nouvelle Héloïse*, pp. 692–699, 714–715. Rousseau's concern for the social utility of religious beliefs is apparent in his earliest letters. Letter to Esther Giraud (May–June 1731; *CC*, I, 9); letter to Isaac Rousseau (Spring, 1735 [?]; *CC*, I, 24 25), letter to Conzié (Jan. 17, 1742, *CC*, I, 132–139).

republic's foundation, the Savoyard's natural religion recapitulates Rousseau's guidance of Emile toward civic virtue. The Savoyard's adoration of the physical universe is the equivalent of an entire society's gratitude and fervor for its own divine order in the Social Contract. In a miniature republic of two self-governing persons, death and banishment are not conceivable penalties for sedition and hypocrisy. Yet, as the Savoyard observes, every man, watched by God and himself, judges his own deeds so that the wicked do not escape in this life the self-inflicted punishment of remorse as a penalty for their amour-propre.[48]

Rousseau introduces Emile to the Savoyard's "Profession" because religion is essential to civic virtue. It is essential for the "rule of particular passions," for the "harmony" and "completeness" of Emile: "The neglect of all religion leads to the neglect of the duties of man." Emile must "find his true interest in being good, in doing right when he is not watched by men and when he is not forced by law." Similarly, the Savoyard decides "to remain in profound ignorance" of matters which do not concern his duties. He seeks those simple maxims that must guide his conduct and the rules he must prescribe to himself not in the "principles of a philosophy" but in the depths of his heart, "engraved by nature in characters nothing can erase." Recently granted permission to say Mass again, the Savoyard welcomes all men to his services, where he exhorts them with reverence to "love peace and equality," to "love one another, to consider themselves brothers, to respect

48. *Emile*, pp. 592, 597. For statements of the substantive compatibility between the Savoyard's natural religion and the civil religion in the *Social Contract*, and of Rousseau's concern for social utility, see Pierre-Maurice Masson, *La Religion de Jean-Jacques Rousseau*, 3 vols. (Paris, 1916), II, 257–258 and *passim;* Wright, *Meaning of Rousseau*, pp. 88–90; Starobinski, *Rousseau*, pp. 83–85; Burgelin, *La Philosophie de l'existence de Rousseau*, pp. 435–446, 553–554; Henri Gouhier, "La Religion du vicaire savoyard dans la cité du *Contrat social*," in *Etudes sur le* Contrat social, pp. 263–275.

all religions and to let each live peaceably in his own religion."
He does not attempt to persuade anyone to abandon his
father's faith: "I will always preach virtue to men and exhort
them to good deeds, and so far as I can I will provide them
a good example. I will try . . . to strengthen men's faith in
those dogmas which are truly useful and which every man
must believe."[49]

Virtuous passions are both possible and necessary because
man is by nature free and good. More specifically, the Savoyard's "Profession" contains Rousseau's most sustained attack
upon the liberal's notion of "interest." "It is said that we are indifferent to everything except our interest," the Savoyard observes, "yet the charms of friendship and humanity console us
in our pains; and, even in our pleasures, we would be too
lonely and too miserable if we had no one with whom to share
them." If there is "no morality in man's heart, what is the
source of his enthusiastic admiration for heroic deeds and his
rapturous love of great men? What connection is there between this enthusiasm for virtue and our private interest? Why
should I choose to be Cato dying by his own hand, rather than
Caesar triumphant?" A man who, "having concentrated everything in himself, comes in the end to love only himself—this
man feels no raptures, his cold heart no longer throbs with joy,
a tender compassion never moistens his eyes; he no longer delights in anything; a miserable man, he neither feels nor lives;
he is already dead." Nor can the nobility of many men's sentiments be disputed: "Injustice pleases only so long as we profit
from it; in all other instances, we want the innocent to be protected. If we see . . . some act of violence or injustice, then
anger and indignation at once arise in the depths of our heart
and carry us to the defense of the oppressed. . . . If we see
some act of clemency or generosity, what admiration, what

49. *Emile*, pp. 557, 561, 636, 569, 627, 594, 628–629. See also *Letter to
Beaumont*, pp. 960–965, 986–990.

love does it inspire!" Even when we cannot personally profit
or lose, we are not indifferent: "It is certainly of very little
interest to us that, two thousand years ago, a man was wicked
or just; and yet we show the same concern for ancient history,
as if everything happened today. What are the crimes of Cati-
line to me? Do I fear becoming his victim? Why therefore do
I have the same horror of him as if he were my contemporary?
We hate the wicked not only because they harm us, but because they are wicked." No man is consistently self-interested:
"Everyone has, whatever his desires, pity for the unfortunate;
when we witness their suffering, we suffer too. The most depraved men cannot entirely corrupt this sentiment; often it
puts them in contradiction with themselves. The thief who
plunders travelers still covers the nakedness of the poor; the
most ferocious murderer supports a faltering man."[50] There is,
the Savoyard concludes, "an innate principle of justice and
virtue, by which, in spite of our current maxims, we judge our
actions and those of others good or wicked; and it is this principle I call conscience." Man's conscience, his "interior voice"
of pity, is "the voice of his soul." Man is obligated to "fulfill
his duties on earth, for it is by forgetting ourselves that we are
really working for ourselves." The true interest of a free being
is identical with his duty because only a virtuous man is at
peace with himself.[51]

After Emile has been inspired by the Savoyard's "Profes-

50. *Emile*, pp. 596–597. See also *Rousseau juge de Jean-Jacques*, pp.
970–972.

51. *Emile*, pp. 598, 594–595, 635, 602. See also *Moral Letters* (P, IV,
1106–1110); *La Nouvelle Héloise*, pp. 682–684. Recourse to "conscience,"
as a form of protective withdrawal for one living in a corrupt society,
is discussed in Grimsley, *Rousseau and the Religious Quest*, pp. 60–67,
71–72, 83–86, and in Grimsley, *Rousseau*, pp. 138–139, 157–159. For a
discussion of the Savoyard's entire "Profession" as that "masterpiece of
Rousseau's pen" which refutes the mechanistic "rationalism" of eighteenth-century philosophes, see Wright, *Meaning of Rousseau*, pp. 126–
164.

sion," he can understand another historical lesson, that of his own education. Through talks over several months, Rousseau explains to him "how his time and mine have been spent; what he is and what I am; what I have done and what he has done, what we owe one another." Emile then approaches Rousseau with a proposal to renew the original contract. He asks Rousseau to protect his "work" by continuing his "authority"; and he promises that his "constant will" is to obey Rousseau's "laws." Rousseau hesitates, explaining to Emile that he must understand the burden of obligation: "Do you not see that when you are obligated to obey me, you oblige me to guide you, to forget myself in my devotion to you, to hear neither your complaints nor your murmurs, to combat incessantly your desires and my own. You impose a heavier yoke on me than on yourself." Later, "when Emile has, so to speak, signed the contract" and Rousseau's "authority" has been authorized, Rousseau's "first care" is "to avoid the necessity of using it." Even a visit to Paris with Rousseau does not corrupt Emile. Though always polite in his disbelief, Emile is an "amiable foreigner" among men who are ignorant of the meaning of citizenship. During this visit Rousseau begins to describe a "Sophie" to Emile.[52]

Meanwhile Sophie, to guarantee her own "constant will," is making an "agreement" (*accord*) with her parents. Her father explains that, in contemporary marriages "arranged by the authority of fathers," only custom and opinion are consulted: "It is not two persons who are united, but positions and properties." In contrast, reciprocated affection will commend Sophie's husband: "That is the right of nature, which nothing can abrogate; those who have obstructed this right with so many civil laws have shown more concern for apparent order

---

52. *Emile*, pp. 641, 651–653, 670. Burgelin, who notes that Rousseau in *Emile* acts "like an ancient lawgiver," characterizes Emile's proposal as an "oath of allegiance." Introduction to *Emile*, p. cxxxi.

than for the happiness of marriage and the *moeurs* of citizens." But Sophie must wisely employ this "absolute liberty" of choice her parents are granting her. Her parents reserve the right to judge if Sophie is mistaken, to veto her choice if, without knowing it, she is "doing something other than she wants to do."[53] This unusual contract is the first suggestion in Sophie's otherwise conventional education by her parents that the union of Sophie and Emile will itself constitute a miniature republic, not a family.

A Miniature Republic: Virtuous Citizens

As we have seen, a father's temporary rule of his children bears no comparison to Emile's education: Rousseau is a lawgiver to a single citizen, not a foster parent or ordinary tutor in a plan of familial education. He never rules Emile. Rousseau's other instance of familial inequality concerns a husband's rule of his wife. We must briefly examine this surprising blind spot of Rousseau's for the two reasons. First, Rousseau believed that a husband's rule of his wife is a defensible exception to the rule of literal self-government. He examined the "original" or "natural" relationship between the sexes, and he concluded that women are disqualified from participating directly in that common life of virtuous citizenship which alone assures absolute liberty. Rousseau did not explain why the nature of woman is to be discovered in relationship to man. Nor did he explain how citizens can be self-governing when they also rule their wives and when citizenship itself is exclusive. True, he continued to insist upon the ways that those who obey effectively command their rulers, and he welcomed the fact that women "govern us" in the family.[54] But a wife's devices for

53. *Emile*, pp. 755–758.
54. *Ibid.*, p. 730. See also Rousseau's discussion of the indirect contribution women have made to restorations of virtue and simplicity. *Ibid.*, pp. 742–744. The contemporary ascendency of women within the

preventing the relationship from becoming enslaving are precisely those devices of contemporary slaves Rousseau condemned as beneath human dignity and as exhibiting the servitude of both ruler and ruled. Second, the marriage of Emile and Sophie institutes a miniature republic of self-governing citizens. We can better appreciate this unusual equality of Emile and Sophie in their marriage through its contrast with the inequality of a family.

In *Emile*, to determine woman's "place in the physical and moral order," Rousseau returned to presocial nature. He elaborated on his discussion in the *Discourse on Inequality* of presocial sexual encounters and later "moral" love born of society. Some needs and faculties of a woman are characteristic of the species, but there are also "natural differences" between the sexes: "These resemblances and differences must influence moral matters; this inference is sensible, conforms to experience, and shows the vanity of disputes about the superiority or equality of the sexes." When copulating, man and woman "cooperate alike in the common object" but not in the same manner: "Man must be active and strong, woman weak and passive; the one must have the will and the power, while it suffices that the other offers little resistance." Rousseau inferred a difference in "moral relations": "If a woman is made to please and to be subjected to a man, she must render herself pleasing to man and not anger him; her strength is in her charms, and it is by their means that she should compel him to discover and use his strength. The surest way of stimulating his strength is to make it necessary by resistance." Woman's timidity, modesty, and shame are the weapons "with which nature has armed the weak for the conquest of the strong."

household might contribute to an improvement of *moeurs* among citizens. *Discourse on the Sciences and Arts* (P, III, 21n), *Discourse on Inequality*, pp. 119–120. See also *Fragments on Women* (P, II, 1253–1259); *Letter to d'Alembert*, pp. 62–76, 110–122, 134–144.

The actual "reign of women" within familial society is sanctioned by nature.

There is, however, no "parity" in the consequences of this inequality, for "a woman is a wife all her life, or at least all her youth." She needs attention during pregnancy, leisure when her child is born and nursed. The woman must also sustain familial unity, because "she alone can win a father's love for his children and convince him that they are his own." Nor is it enough for a wife to be faithful: "her husband, her neighbors, everyone" must accept her fidelity, for "opinion is the grave of a man's virtue and the throne of a woman's."

For these reasons, Rousseau asserted that women should not share the duties of citizenship: "Will she be a wet-nurse today and a soldier tomorrow? Will she change her inclinations and her tastes as a chameleon changes his color? Will she pass suddenly from the shadow of seclusion and of domestic cares to the buffeting of the winds, the toil, the fatigue, and the perils of war? Will she now be fearful, now brave, now fragile, now robust?" Rousseau acknowledged that Plato had assigned the same duties to men and women in the *Republic*. He countered that Plato, having eliminated the family and not knowing what to do with women, was compelled to "turn them into men." Plato's "civil promiscuity" could produce only "the most intolerable abuses."[55]

Thus, the object of a young girl's physical training should be grace. The Greeks provide a useful model for this training, although Rousseau rejected the Spartan practice of having girls take part in military games: "It is not necessary that mothers carry muskets and exercise in the Prussian manner in order to give soldiers to the state." While boys prefer movement and noise in their games and toys, girls "prefer things which ap-

55. *Emile*, pp. 693–703. See also *La Nouvelle Héloise*, pp. 127–128; letter to Lenieps (Nov. 8, 1758; *CC*, V, 213).

peal to the eye and can be used for adornment," such as mirrors, jewelry, finery, and dolls: "The doll is the girl's special plaything; this obviously demonstrates her taste fixed by her destiny." Cutting out fabrics, embroidery, and drawing "follow naturally." As a young girl shares these activities with her mother, she becomes conscious of her "natural" dependence upon the aid and kindness of others: "The first and most important quality of a woman is gentleness. Made to obey a being so imperfect as man, a being often vicious and always faulty, she should immediately learn to endure even injustice, to bear the wrongs of her husband without complaint." As long as her husband is not monstrous, "the gentleness of a wife will tame her husband so that she triumphs over him sooner or later." Her triumph is assured by cultivating her "natural talent" of cunning. Without cunning "a woman would be a man's slave rather than his partner: it is through this superiority of talent that she maintains her equality and governs him while obeying him." A woman must also perfect the "pleasing arts" of singing, dancing, and speaking attractively and politely.[56]

Although a woman's mind is "naturally" more suited to practical matters of detail than discovering abstract principles of conduct, Rousseau would not leave woman's education entirely to contemporary conventions. Her "conscience" must be developed to give her some means of judging contemporary opinion. She must also cultivate "the faculty of reason" to serve as arbiter between her "two guides" of conscience and opinion. This development of a woman's reason includes some instruction in the practical details of current social institutions and beliefs, "the source of human judgments and the passions by which they are determined." As a result, a woman becomes especially adept at applying that "experimental" science of

56. *Emile*, pp. 704–712, 715–717. Kite-flying is also a sport for young girls. *Ibid.*, pp. 401–402.

modesty, restraint, and good taste which compensates for her natural weakness.[57]

Sophie has been educated as a representative woman. She has a pleasing disposition. She is not truly beautiful, but men are delighted by her presence. She is meticulous in her appearance. With "no singing teacher except her father and no dancing mistress except her mother" and with a few lessons from a neighbor organist, Sophie has become a tasteful if amateur musician. She likes the "feminine arts" of needle work and dressmaking. She has benefited from the experience of occasionally managing her mother's household. Her mind is pleasing and thorough, rather than brilliant or profound. She recovers her composure quickly when intemperate or impatient. Spared tiresome religious sermons by her parents but with their worthy example "engraved on her heart," Sophie "knows the essential practice of right conduct." She judges, quietly and modestly, the faults and virtues of men, becoming distressed when she does not meet a worthy suitor while spending the winter with her aunt in a nearby town.[58]

Emile, too, is impatient. He reproves Rousseau because he did not find "the bride of his heart" in Paris. But having fled Paris, Emile and Rousseau are now wandering on foot through the countryside toward Montmorency. After losing their way they stumble upon the cottage of a peasant who shares his meager lunch with them. Noting the tiredness and hunger of his visitors, the peasant remarks that they would have been more comfortable at a neighbor's house: "They are not more generous than I, but they have greater means, even though it is said that they used to be wealthy. Still, they do not suffer, and the whole countryside is grateful for their presence." Emile immediately decides to visit this house "whose owners are a blessing to the neighborhood." After losing their way and be-

57. *Ibid.*, pp. 730–731, 736–737.
58. *Ibid.*, pp. 747–748, 751–752, 759–760.

ing delayed by a storm, Emile and Rousseau are welcomed by a kindly man and his wife. The preparation of dinner is hurried on their account. A fifth place at the dinner table is taken by their daughter. Her name is Sophie.[59]

The details of the courtship, in which Rousseau serves as "the confidant of these two good persons and the mediator of their affection,"[60] need not be repeated here. For it is the political character of their marriage and Emile's mastery of "imaginary" passions which are significant: Emile's marriage completes his education to virtuous citizenship.

Upon first meeting Sophie, Emile is "blinded" by desires of an unfamiliar kind and intensity. In three months, as Sophie becomes adept at reassuring Emile and at failing to notice his expressions of affection, Emile's "desire for exclusive possession" becomes a consuming passion. He exhibits the "distrustful and sorrowful fantasy called jealousy." One day Rousseau enters Emile's room clutching a letter: "What would you do if someone informed you that Sophie is dead?" When Rousseau repeats his question, Emile can only reply that he "would never speak to the person who brought me such news." Rousseau hastily assures Emile that Sophie is well and that they are expected for dinner. Rousseau suggests they first go for a walk to talk things over. This "terrible preamble," Rousseau informed his reader, had been necessary to obtain Emile's attention.

During their walk Rousseau applies the Savoyard's lesson. With his second birth, Emile must not prepare for himself a "second death," Rousseau tells him: "You still have not learned to impose a law on the desires of your heart; and the difficulty of life arises more from our affections than from our needs. . . . My son, there is no happiness without courage, nor virtue without struggle." The virtue to which Rousseau refers is that

59. *Ibid.*, pp. 770, 773–775.
60. *Ibid.*, p. 788.

of the citizen, for Rousseau tells Emile that he must temporarily leave Sophie. He must travel in Europe to select a state of which he will become a member: "You hope to be a husband and a father. Have you considered these duties? In becoming head of a family you will become a member of the state. And do you know what it means to be a member of the state?" Emile hesitates. He cannot understand why he cannot leave Sophie as her husband. Because Emile is blind to duty, Rousseau invokes their recently renewed contract. Throughout Emile's education, this is the only time Rousseau commands Emile. Emile asks when they are to leave. Rousseau suggests a week to prepare Sophie for his absence. Rousseau consoles Sophie. Sophie's father reminds Rousseau "that your pupil has signed his contract of marriage on my daughter's lips."[61]

Their voyages comprise a section of book five of *Emile* entitled "Of Travel." For two years Emile completes his historical studies by becoming familiar with contemporary *moeurs*. Emile comes to know "man in general" through his experience and judgment of national diversity: "I maintain as an incontestable maxim that whoever has seen only one people does not know mankind." As the "original characteristics" of European peoples are dissolving, Rousseau and Emile concentrate on "remote provinces" where they can observe men "in the simplicity of their original genius." To add to Emile's experience of "what is" the essential dimension of "what ought to be" Rousseau summarizes the *Social Contract*: "He who wishes to judge existing governments must combine" the "positive laws of established governments" with "the principles of political right."[62]

The abyss between the principles of political right and mod-

61. *Ibid.*, pp. 796, 814–817, 823–825.
62. *Ibid.*, pp. 827, 850–852, 836–837. M. de Mably's son would study instead Grotius and Pufendorf. *Projet pour l'éducation*, pp. 50–51.

ern states accounts for the hesitancy and formality of Emile's decision. With some prodding from Rousseau, Emile decides to remain in France. But the slavery and corruption of contemporary common life make patriotic fervor of questionable worth and dictate that Emile's significant membership will be within the miniature republic he and Sophie are about to institute. Emile's decision regarding citizenship represents a narrowing of the circumference of common life from formal membership in a modern "country" to locality and miniature republic.

Emile responds to Rousseau's request for his decision: "The more I examine the work of men in their institutions, the more I see that, in their efforts to become independent, men make themselves slaves and waste their very liberty in futile attempts to secure it." So Emile announces that if he inherits his father's land, he will keep it. If he loses it, then sobeit: "Rich or poor, I will be free. I shall not be free merely in this country or that; I shall be free in any part of the world." Rousseau is gratified to hear the "discourse of a man" but disputes Emile's assertion that the place he chooses to live is of no importance: "If I spoke to you about the duties of a citizen, you would perhaps ask me, 'where is my fatherland?' And you would think you had confounded me. Yet you would be mistaken, dear Emile, for he who does not have a fatherland has at least a country." To be sure, "the social contract has not been respected" and "particular interest has not protected him as the general will would have done." But a "semblance of laws" has given Emile some security. And every man is indebted to his native land: "Whatever country it may be, he owes to it the thing most precious to man, the morality of his actions and the love of virtue. Born in the depths of a forest, he would have lived in greater happiness and liberty; but having nothing to combat in following his inclinations, there would have been no merit in his goodness; he would not have been virtuous as he now may be in spite of his passions." Someone like Rousseau himself "is more useful to his fellow citizens outside his fatherland than if he lived within it. Then he must listen only to his own zeal and must bear his exile without a murmur; that exile is itself one of his duties." But Emile has "not undertaken the sad task of telling the truth to men."[63]

Emile's declaration of membership is of only symbolic significance because he has been fulfilling civic duties for years: "Most often he hurries through the nearby countryside learning natural history; he observes and studies the soil, its products, and methods of cultivation; he compares the methods he sees with those with which he is familiar. He seeks the reasons for differences; when he judges other methods preferable to local ones, he tells farmers. If he thinks of a better form of plough, he has one made from his drawings; if he finds a lime pit, he teaches farmers how to use lime in the soil; often he assists in this work himself." True citizenship is not an occasional matter: "For one neighbor he has a falling roof repaired or replaced; for another he has an abandoned piece of land cleared; to another he provides a cow, a horse or stock of any kind to replace a loss. Two neighbors are ready to go to court; he wins their confidence and conciliates them. A peasant falls ill and he arranges care for him, looking after him himself. Another peasant is harassed by a powerful neighbor; he protects him and speaks in his behalf. Poor young people are planning

63. *Emile*, pp. 855–859. Rousseau frequently claimed that he could best fulfill in exile the duties of a Genevan citizen: he could warn his fellow citizens of dangerous innovations and uphold the maxims of his fatherland (or country) in foreign lands. He also conceived his secluded life at Montmorency, helping peasants and warning them of fatal opinions, as an exemplary life. See letter to Rey (Mar. 23, 1755; *CC*, III, 113); letter to marquise de Créqui (Sept. 8 [?], 1755; *CC*, III, 170–172); *Confessions*, p. 406; *Letters to Malesherbes* (Jan. 1762; *P*, I, 1143); *Letters from the Mountain*, p. 801. For a view of Rousseau's character as considerably less forthright and courageous, see Starobinski, *Rousseau*, pp. 287–296.

to marry; he helps them to do so. A good woman has lost her beloved child; he goes to see her and consoles her." Always, in becoming "the benefactor of some and the friend of others, Emile does not cease to be their equal."[64]

The concluding incident of Emile and Sophie's courtship reveals the complementary character of the duties of man and citizen in *Emile*, because it demonstrates the way in which, as Rousseau observed in the *Social Contract*, a competing particular identity can remind a citizen of his greater responsibility to the whole.[65] One evening Emile and Rousseau, expected for dinner, do not appear. Sophie cries all night fearful for their safety. Her tears turn to apparent indifference and then anger when she receives a message indicating only that they are well and when, the next day, Emile and Rousseau arrive. Rousseau explains to Sophie that they had started for her house the afternoon before but stopped to assist a peasant who, having had too much wine, had fallen off his horse and broken his leg. They carried him to his cottage where, overcome at the sight of her husband's misfortune, his pregnant wife began her labor. Emile walked to town to bring a surgeon and a nurse. Neither Rousseau nor Emile could return to their lodgings until two o'clock in the morning. Before Sophie can respond, Emile adds: "Sophie, you are the arbiter of my fate, as you well know. You may condemn me to die of sorrow. But do not hope to make me forget the rights of humanity: they are more sacred to me than your rights. I will never renounce them for you." Sophie kisses Emile shyly: "Emile, take this hand; it is yours. When you want, you will be my husband and my teacher [*maître*]; I shall try to be worthy of that honor." After dinner Sophie asks if it is too far to visit the recovering peasant whom Emile has already provided with an extra bed and nurses. Soon Sophie

64. *Emile*, pp. 804–805.
65. *Social Contract*, p. 371n. This incident appears in *Emile*, pp. 810–814.

is helping to change linens and clean the peasant's house. Later Emile and Sophie are godparents to the newly born infant. And the peasant with the mending leg? He is the man who shared his lunch with Rousseau and Emile after they had fled Paris and suggested Emile might want to visit his neighbor's house!

Sophie's sharing of Emile's civic duties on this occasion anticipates the unusual equality of their marriage.[66] Although Sophie will not remember everything, Emile eagerly gives her lessons in philosophy, physics, mathematics, and history— "everything he knows." And as they prepare to be "united in the indissoluble chain" of marriage, Rousseau observed that their union does not contradict a husband's authority: "There is a great difference between claiming the right to command and guiding [gouverner] him who commands. . . . The woman must reign in the home like a minister in the state, by con- triving to be ordered to do what she wants." Indeed, as non- governing government in the Social Contract assures citizens' literal self-government, Emile does not even attempt to com- mand Sophie. Each retains the right to judge the other, and their mutual affection assures that there is no "constraint" or "complaisance" or hypocrisy in their marriage: "The social relations of the sexes is admirable. From this society there re- sults a moral person of which the woman is the eye and the man the hand; but the two are so dependent on one another that the husband teaches his wife what to see while she teaches him what to do. . . . In the harmony which reigns between them, eveything tends toward the common end; no one knows who contributes more; each follows the lead of the other; each obeys and both are masters [maîtres]."[67]

66. For a contrasting view of Sophie, see Jost, Rousseau, II, 134–174.
67. Emile, pp. 791, 860, 766, 862–864, 720. For a discussion of similarities between this marriage and a social contract of total alienation, see Pierre Burgelin, "L'Education de Sophie," Annales, XXV (1959–1962), 124– 128.

Emile's marriage to Sophie completes the third stage of his education. For Rousseau, who had arranged their first meeting, their marriage is "the crown of my work": marriage itself is "the most inviolable and the most sacred of all contracts" and establishes "the sweetest form of society."[68] Emile is again at peace with himself for he has obtained the self-mastery of the whole man. He has become a self-governing citizen. Together, as equals, Emile and Sophie might revive that gaiety and simplicity of the golden age: "While dreaming, I see how Emile and Sophie, from their simple retreat, may spread their blessings about themselves, restore life to the countryside and revive the extinguished zeal of unfortunate villagers. I believe I see the population increasing, the land restored, the earth clothed with fresh beauty. I see numerous men and bountiful crops transforming work into festivals; and I hear shouts of joy arising from the midst of rustic games which this lovely couple has revived."[69]

A few months after his marriage, Emile returns to Rousseau's rooms and embraces him. Emile is to become a father and asks Rousseau to remain the "teacher of young teachers," to advise him and Sophie about the education of their child.[70] The lawgiver in exile from his own fatherland withdraws, his civic responsibility completed. He resumes his exile, the "sad task of telling the truth to men."

In the *Social Contract*, Rousseau had described the true lawgiver as one who serves as the catalyst for self-government but who, with the nonindividualist bonds of society established, does not attempt to govern. In *Emile*, he himself assumed the lawgiver's task with respect to a single citizen. Once again, having brought Emile to the point of self-government, the lawgiver must withdraw and self-government must take its

68. *Emile*, pp. 860, 650.
69. *Ibid.*, p. 859.
70. *Ibid.*, pp. 867–868.

own course. The departure of Rousseau into truth-telling exile provides a fitting moment at which to leave him, for the conclusion of Rousseau's political thought is the beginning of the virtuous citizen's obligation to govern himself. Because the purpose of common life is liberty, Rousseau must leave Emile, and us, free even of himself.

Bibliography

A nearly complete list of editions, translations, and interpretative studies of Rousseau can be found in the *Annales de la Société Jean-Jacques Rousseau*. See also John W. Chapman, "Jean-Jacques Rousseau," *A Critical Bibliography of French Literature*, Vol. IV (Supplement), *The Eighteenth Century*, edited by Richard A. Brooks (Syracuse, New York: Syracuse University Press, 1968), pages 142–164; and Michel Launay, *Jean-Jacques Rousseau: Ecrivain politique (1712–1762)* (Grenoble: L'A.C.E.R., 1971), pages 477–496. I list here (1) French editions and (2) English translations used in this study, many of which include cited interpretative essays, introductions, and notes, and (3) interpretations which are exclusively or largely about Rousseau's philosophy and which also have been cited in this study.

1. French Editions

Du contrat social de Jean-Jacques Rousseau. Ed. Bertrand de Jouvenel. Geneva: Editions du Cheval Ailé, 1947. [Includes Jouvenel's "Essai sur la politique de Rousseau."]

Correspondance complète de Jean Jacques Rousseau. Ed. R. A. Leigh. 21 vols. Geneva: Institut et Musée Voltaire; Madison: The University of Wisconsin Press; Banbury, Oxfordshire: The Voltaire Foundation, 1965——.

Correspondance générale de J.-J. Rousseau. Ed. Théophile Dufour and P.-P. Plan. 24 vols. Paris: Armand Colin, 1924–1934.

Jean-Jacques Rousseau: Discours sur les sciences et les arts. Ed. George R. Havens. New York: Modern Language Association of America, 1946.

J.-J. Rousseau: Lettre à M. d'Alembert sur les spectacles. Ed. M. Fuchs. Lille: Librairie Giard, 1948.

Jean-Jacques entre Socrate et Caton: Textes inédits de Jean-Jacques

319

320 / Bibliography

Rousseau (1750–1753). Ed. Claude Pichois and René Pintard. Paris: Librairie José Corti, 1972.

Jean-Jacques Rousseau: Oeuvres complètes. Ed. Bernard Gagnebin and Marcel Raymond. 4 vols. Paris: Bibliothèque de la Pléiade, Gallimard, 1959.

Oeuvres complètes de J. J. Rousseau. 13 vols. Paris: Librairie Hachette, 1865–1873.

The Political Writings of Jean Jacques Rousseau. Ed. C. E. Vaughan. 2 vols. 1915. Reprint. Oxford: Basil Blackwell, 1962.

2. English Translations

Jean-Jacques Rousseau: The First and Second Discourses. Ed. Roger D. Masters; trans. Roger D. and Judith R. Masters. New York: St. Martin's Press, 1964.

Jean-Jacques Rousseau: Essay on the Origin of Languages. Trans. John H. Moran. In On the Origin of Language. New York: Frederick Ungar Publishing Co., 1966.

Politics and the Arts: Letter to M. d'Alembert on the Theater, by Jean-Jacques Rousseau. Trans. and ed. Allan Bloom. Glencoe, Illinois: The Free Press, 1960.

Rousseau: Political Writings. Trans. and ed. Frederick Watkins. Edinburgh: Thomas Nelson, 1953.

The Social Contract: Jean-Jacques Rousseau. Trans. Maurice Cranston. Baltimore, Maryland: Penguin Books, 1968.

3. Interpretations

Adam, Antoine. "De quelques sources de Rousseau dans la littérature philosophique, 1700–1750." In Jean-Jacques Rousseau et son oeuvre: Problèmes et recherches, pp. 125–132. Paris: C. Klincksieck, 1964.

——. "Rousseau et Diderot." Revue des sciences humaines, n.s. LIII (Jan.–Mar. 1949), 21–34.

Allen, Glen O. "La Volonté de tous and la volonté générale: A Distinction and Its Significance." Ethics, LXXI–LXXII (July 1961), 263–275.

Allers, Ulrich S. "Rousseau's Second Discourse." Review of Politics, XX (Jan. 1958), 91–120.

Amiel, Henri-Frederic. Jean Jacques Rousseau. Trans. Van Wyck Brooks. New York: B. W. Huebsch, 1922.

Baczko, Bronislaw. "Rousseau et l'aliénation sociale." Annales de la Société Jean-Jacques Rousseau, XXXV (1959–1962), 223–233.

Barth, Hans. "Volonté générale et volonté particulière." In *Rousseau et la philosophie politique*, pp. 35–50. Annales de philosophie politique, vol. 5. Paris: Presses Universitaires de France, 1965.

Belaval, Yvon. "La Théorie du jugement dans l'*Emile*." In *Jean-Jacques Rousseau et son oeuvre: Problèmes et recherches*, pp. 149–157. Paris: C. Klincksieck, 1964.

Benda, Harry J. "Rousseau's Early Discourses." *Political Science* (Wellington, New Zealand), V (Sept. 1953), 13–20; VI (Mar. 1954), 17–27.

Berman, Marshall. *The Politics of Authenticity: Radical Individualism and the Emergence of Modern Society*. New York: Atheneum, 1973.

Bonnard, Roger. "Les Idées politiques de Jean-Jacques Rousseau." *Revue du droit politique et de la science politique en France et à l'étranger*, XXVII (Oct.–Nov. 1907), 784–794.

Bretonneau, Gisèle. *Valeurs humaines de J.-J. Rousseau*. Paris: La Colombe, 1961.

Broome, Jack Howard. *Rousseau: A Study of his Thought*. New York: Barnes & Noble, 1963.

Burgelin, Pierre. "L'Education de Sophie." *Annales de la Société Jean-Jacques Rousseau*, XXXV (1959–1962), 113–130.

——. "L'Idée de place dans l'*Emile*." *Revue de littérature comparée*, XXXV (Oct.–Dec. 1961), 529–537.

——. *Jean-Jacques Rousseau et la religion de Genève*. Geneva: Editions Labor et Fides, 1962.

——. *La Philosophie de l'existence de J.-J. Rousseau*. Paris: Presses Universitaires de France, 1952.

——. "The Second Education of Emile." *Yale French Studies*, XXVIII (Fall–Winter, 1961), 106–111.

Cameron, David. *The Social Thought of Rousseau and Burke*. London: Weidenfeld and Nicolson, 1973.

Cassirer, Ernst. *The Question of Jean-Jacques Rousseau*. Trans. and ed. Peter Gay. Bloomington, Indiana: Indiana University Press, 1963.

——. *Rousseau, Kant, and Goethe: Two Essays*. Trans. James Gutmann, Paul Oskar Kristeller, and John Herman Randall, Jr. New York: Harper and Row, 1963.

Chapman, John W. *Rousseau—Totalitarian or Liberal?* New York: Columbia University Press, 1956.

Charvet, John. *The Social Problem in the Philosophy of Rousseau*. London: Cambridge University Press, 1974.

Château, Jean. *Jean-Jacques Rousseau: Sa philosophie de l'éducation.* Paris: Vrin, 1962.

Chevallier, Jean-Jacques. "Jean-Jacques Rousseau ou l'absolutisme de la volonté générale." *Revue française de science politique*, III (Jan.–Mar. 1953), 5–30.

——. "Le Mot et la notion de gouvernement chez Rousseau." In *Etudes sur le* Contrat social *de Jean-Jacques Rousseau*, pp. 291–313. Paris: Société les Belles Lettres, 1964.

Cobban, Alfred. *Rousseau and the Modern State.* 2d rev. ed. London: George Allen & Unwin, 1964.

Colletti, Lucio. *From Rousseau to Lenin: Studies in Ideology and Society.* Trans. John Merrington and Judith White. London: NLB, 1972.

Collinet, Michel. "L'Homme de la nature et la nature de l'homme." *Le Contrat social*, VI (May–June 1962), 147–154.

Cotta, Sergio. "La Position du problème de la politique chez Rousseau." In *Etudes sur le* Contrat social *de Jean-Jacques Rousseau*, pp. 177–190. Paris: Société les Belles Lettres, 1964.

Crocker, Lester G. "The Priority of Justice or Law." *Yale French Studies*, XXVIII (Fall–Winter, 1961–1962), 34–42.

——. "The Relation of Rousseau's Second *Discours* and the *Contrat social*." *Romanic Review*, LI (Feb. 1960), 33–44.

——. "Rousseau et la voie du totalitarisme." In *Rousseau et la philosophie politique*, pp. 99–136. Annales de philosophie politique, vol. 5. Paris: Presses Universitaires de France, 1965.

——. *Rousseau's Social Contract: An Interpretive Essay.* Cleveland: The Press of Case Western Reserve University, 1968.

Deaver, Jack W. "La Liberté individuelle dans *Emile et Sophie*." In Michel Launay *et al.*, *Jean-Jacques Rousseau et son temps*, pp. 151–158. Paris: Librairie A.-G. Nizet, 1969.

Dehaussey, Jacques. "La Dialectique de la souveraine liberté dans le *Contrat social*." In *Etudes sur le* Contrat social *de Jean-Jacques Rousseau*, pp. 119–141. Paris: Société les Belles Lettres, 1964.

Derathé, Robert. "Jean-Jacques Rousseau et le christianisme." *Revue de métaphysique et de morale*, LIII (Oct. 1948), 379–414.

——. *Jean-Jacques Rousseau et la science politique de son temps.* Paris: Presses Universitaires de France, 1950.

——. *Le Rationalisme de J.-J. Rousseau.* Paris: Presses Universitaires de France, 1948.

——. "La Religion civile selon Rousseau." *Annales de la Société Jean-Jacques Rousseau*, XXXV (1959–1962), 161–170.

——. "Rousseau et le problème de la monarchie." *Le Contrat social,* VI (May–June 1962), 165–168.

——. "L'Unité de la pensée de Jean-Jacques Rousseau." In *Jean-Jacques Rousseau,* pp. 203–218. Neuchâtel: La Baconnière, 1962.

Durkheim, Émile. "Le *Contrat social* de Rousseau." *Revue de métaphysique et de morale,* XXV (1918), 1–23; XXVI (1919), 129–161.

——. *Montesquieu and Rousseau: Forerunners of Sociology.* Trans. Ralph Manheim. Ann Arbor: The University of Michigan Press, 1960.

Einaudi, Mario. *The Early Rousseau.* Ithaca, New York: Cornell University Press, 1967.

Eisenmann, Charles. "La Cité de Jean-Jacques Rousseau." In *Etudes sur le* Contrat social *de Jean-Jacques Rousseau,* pp. 191–201. Paris: Société les Belles Lettres, 1964.

Eméry, Léon. "Le *Contrat social* et la genèse des cités." *Le Contrat social,* VI (May–June 1962), 155–158.

——. *Rousseau l'annonciateur.* Lyon: Audin, 1954.

Fabre, Jean. "Réalité et utopie dans la pensée politique de Rousseau." *Annales de la Société Jean-Jacques Rousseau,* XXXV (1959–1962), 181–216.

Fetscher, Iring. "Rousseau, auteur d'intention conservatrice et d'action révolutionnaire." In *Rousseau et la philosophie politique,* pp. 51–75. Annales de philosophie politique, vol. 5. Paris: Presses Universitaires de France, 1965.

——. "Rousseau's Concept of Freedom in the Light of His Philosophy of History." In *Liberty (Nomos IV),* Yearbook of the American Society for Political and Legal Philosophy, pp. 29–56. Ed. Carl J. Friedrich. New York: Atherton Press, 1962.

Friedrich, Carl J. "Law and Dictatorship in the *Contrat social.*" In *Rousseau et la philosophie politique,* pp. 77–97. Annales de philosophie politique, vol. 5. Paris: Presses Universitaires de France, 1965.

Gilliard, François. "Etat de nature et liberté dans la pensée de J.-J. Rousseau." In *Etudes sur le* Contrat social *de Jean-Jacques Rousseau,* pp. 111–118. Paris: Société les Belles Lettres, 1964.

Gossman, Lionel. "Rousseau's Idealism." *Romanic Review,* LII (Oct. 1961), 173–182.

——. "Time and history in Rousseau." In *Studies on Voltaire and the Eighteenth Century,* ed. Theodore Besterman. Vol. 30, pp. 311–349. Geneva: Institut et Musée Voltaire, 1964.

Gouhier, Henri. *Les Méditations metaphysiques de Jean-Jacques Rousseau*. Paris: J. Vrin, 1970.

——. "Nature et histoire dans la pensée de Rousseau." *Annales de la Société Jean-Jacques Rousseau*, XXXIII (1953–1955), 7–48.

——. "La Religion du vicaire savoyard dans la cité du *Contrat social*." In *Etudes sur le Contrat social de Jean-Jacques Rousseau*, pp. 263–275. Paris: Société les Belles Lettres, 1964.

Green, F. C. *Jean-Jacques Rousseau: A Critical Study of His Life and Writings*. Cambridge: Cambridge University Press, 1955.

Grimsley, Ronald. *Jean-Jacques Rousseau: A Study in Self-Awareness*. Cardiff: University of Wales Press, 1961.

——. *The Philosophy of Rousseau*. London: Oxford University Press, 1973.

——. *Rousseau and the Religious Quest*. London: Clarendon Press, Oxford, 1968.

Groethuysen, Bernard. *J. J. Rousseau*. Paris: Gallimard, 1949.

——. "La Liberté selon Rousseau." *La NEF*, IV (Aug. 1947), 3–17.

Guéhenno, Jean. *Jean-Jacques Rousseau*. 2 vols. Trans. John and Doreen Weightman. London: Routledge and Kegan Paul, 1966.

Hall, John C. *Rousseau: An Introduction to His Political Philosophy*. London: Macmillan, 1973.

Havens, George R. "Diderot, Rousseau, and the *Discours sur l'inégalité*." In *Diderot Studies*, vol. 3, ed. Otis Fellows and Gita May, pp. 219–262. Geneva: Librairie E. Droz, 1961.

Haymann, Franz. "La Loi naturelle dans la philosophie politique de J. J. Rousseau." *Annales de la Société Jean-Jacques Rousseau*, XXX (1943–1945), 65–110.

Hendel, Charles W. *Jean-Jacques Rousseau: Moralist*. 2 vols. in 1, 2d ed. New York: Bobbs-Merrill Co., 1962.

Hoffmann, Stanley. "Du *Contrat social*, ou le mirage de la volonté générale." *Revue internationale d'histoire politique et constitutionnelle*, n.s. IV (Oct.–Dec. 1954), 288–315.

Hubert, René. *Rousseau et l'Encyclopédie: Essai sur la formation des idées politiques de Rousseau (1742–1756)*. Paris: Librairie Universitaire, 1928.

Jedryka, Zygmunt. "Du gouvernement de la liberté selon Rousseau." *Le Contrat social*, VI (Nov.–Dec. 1962), 356–364.

Jimack, Peter D. *La Genèse et la rédaction de l'Emile de J.-J. Rousseau. Studies on Voltaire and the Eighteenth Century*, ed.

Theodore Besterman. Vol. 13. Geneva: Institut et Musée Vol
taire, 1960.
Jost, François. *Jean-Jacques Rousseau, Swisse.* 2 vols. Fribourg:
Editions Universitaires, 1961.
Jouvenel, Bertrand de. "Rousseau, évolutionniste et pessimiste." In
Rousseau et la philosophie politique, pp. 1–19. Annales de philos-
ophie politique, vol. 5. Paris: Presses Universitaires de France,
1965.
———. "Rousseau the Pessimistic Evolutionist." *Yale French Studies*,
XXVIII (Fall–Winter, 1961), 83–96.
———. "Théorie des formes de gouvernement chez Rousseau." *Le
Contrat social*, VI (Nov.–Dec. 1962), 343–351.
Kateb, George. "Aspects of Rousseau's Political Thought." *Political
Science Quarterly*, LXVI (1961), 519–543.
Krafft, Olivier. *La Politique de Jean-Jacques Rousseau: Aspects
méconnus.* Paris: Librairie Générale de Droit et de Jurisprudence,
1958.
Lanson, Gustave. "L'Unité de la pensée de Jean-Jacques Rousseau."
Annales de la Société Jean-Jacques Rousseau, VIII (1912), 1–31.
Lapassade, Georges. "L'Oeuvre de J.-J. Rousseau: Structure et
unité." *Revue de métaphysique et de morale*, LXI (July–Dec.
1956), 386–402.
Launay, Michel. *Jean Jacques Rousseau: Ecrivain politique (1712–
1762).* Grenoble: L'A.C.E.R., 1971.
Leigh, R. A. "Liberté et autorité dans le *Contrat social.*" In *Jean-
Jacques Rousseau et son oeuvre: Problèmes et recherches*, pp.
249–262. Paris: C. Klincksieck, 1964.
Léon, Paul. "Rousseau et les fondements de l'état moderne."
Archives de philosophie du droit et de sociologie juridique, III–
IV (1934), 197–238.
Lévi-Strauss, Claude. "Jean-Jacques Rousseau, fondateur des sciences
de l'homme." In *Jean-Jacques Rousseau*, pp. 239–248. Neuchâtel:
La Baconnière, 1962.
Lovejoy, Arthur O. "The Supposed Primitivism of Rousseau's *Dis-
course on Inequality.*" *Modern Philology*, XXI (1923), 165–186.
McAdam, James I. "Rousseau and the Friends of Despotism."
Ethics, LXXIV (Oct. 1963), 34–43.
Masson, Pierre-Maurice. *La Religion de Jean-Jacques Rousseau.* 3
vols. Paris: Librairie Hachette, 1916.
———. "Rousseau contre Helvétius." *Revue d'histoire littéraire de la
France*, XVIII (1911), 103–124.

Masters, Roger D. *The Political Philosophy of Rousseau.* Princeton: Princeton University Press, 1968.

Meyer, Paul H. "The Individual and Society in Rousseau's *Emile.*" *Modern Language Quarterly,* XIX (June 1958), 99–114.

Morel, Jean. "Recherches sur les sources du *Discours de l'inégalité.*" *Annales de la Société Jean-Jacques Rousseau,* V (1909), 119–198.

Mornet, Daniel. *Rousseau: l'Homme et l'oeuvre.* Paris: Boivin, 1950.

Munteano, Basil. "Les 'contradictions' de J.-J. Rousseau: Leur sens expérimental." In *Jean-Jacques Rousseau et son oeuvre: Problèmes et recherches,* pp. 95–111. Paris: C. Klincksieck, 1964.

Osborn, Annie Marion. *Rousseau and Burke: A Study of the Idea of Liberty in Eighteenth Century Political Thought.* 1940. Reprint. New York: Russell & Russell, 1964.

Pétrement, Simone. "Rousseau et la liberté." *Le Contrat social,* VI (Nov.–Dec. 1962), 340–342.

Pickles, William. "The Notion of Time in Rousseau's Political Thought." In *Hobbes and Rousseau: A Collection of Critical Essays,* ed. Maurice Cranston and Richard S. Peters, pp. 366–400. Garden City, N.Y.: Doubleday, 1972.

Plamenatz, John. "Ce qui ne signifie pas autre chose, sinon qu'on le forcera d'être libre." In *Rousseau et la philosophie politique,* pp. 137–152. Annales de philosophie politique, vol. 5. Paris: Presses Universitaires de France, 1965.

Polin, Raymond. "La Fonction du législateur chez J.-J. Rousseau." In *Jean-Jacques Rousseau et son oeuvre: Problèmes et recherches,* pp. 231–247. Paris: C. Klincksieck, 1964.

——. *La Politique de la solitude: Essai sur la philosophie politique de Jean-Jacques Rousseau.* Paris: Sirey, 1971.

Rang, Martin. "Le Dualisme anthropologique dans l'*Emile.*" In *Jean-Jacques Rousseau et son oeuvre: Problèmes et recherches,* pp. 195–203. Paris: C. Klincksieck, 1964.

——. "L'Education publique et la formation des citoyens chez J.-J. Rousseau." In *Etudes sur le* Contrat social *de Jean-Jacques Rousseau,* pp. 253–262. Paris: Société les Belles Lettres, 1964.

Raymond, Marcel. "J.-J. Rousseau: Deux aspects de sa vie intérieure." *Annales de la Société Jean-Jacques Rousseau,* XXIX (1941–1942), 5–57.

Shklar, Judith N. *Men and Citizens: A Study of Rousseau's Social Theory.* Cambridge: Cambridge University Press, 1969.

Soto, Jean de. "La Liberté et ses garanties." In *Etudes sur le* Contrat social *de Jean-Jacques Rousseau*, pp. 227–252. Paris: Société les Belles Lettres, 1964.

Starobinski, Jean. "Du *Discours de l'inégalité* au *Contrat social.*" In *Etudes sur le Contrat social de Jean Jaoquos Rousseau*, pp. 97–110. Paris: Société les Belles Lettres, 1964.

——. "The Illness of Rousseau." *Yale French Studies*, XXVIII (Fall-Winter, 1961–1962), 64–74.

——. *Jean-Jacques Rousseau: La Transparence et l'obstacle*. Paris: Plon, 1958.

——. "La Pensée politique de Jean-Jacques Rousseau." In *Jean-Jacques Rousseau*, pp. 81–99. Neuchâtel: La Baconnière, 1962.

——. "Rousseau et Buffon." In *Jean-Jacques Rousseau et son oeuvre: Problèmes et recherches*, pp. 135–146. Paris: C. Klincksieck, 1964.

——. "Tout le mal vient de l'inégalité." *Europe* (Nov.–Dec. 1961), pp. 135–149.

Stelling-Michaud, Sven. "Rousseau et l'injustice sociale." In *Jean-Jacques Rousseau*, pp. 171–186. Neuchâtel: La Baconnière, 1962.

Strauss, Leo. "On the Intention of Rousseau." *Social Research*, XIV (Dec. 1947), 455–487.

Wahl, Jean. "La Bipolarité de Rousseau." *Annales de la Société Jean-Jacques Rousseau*, XXXIII (1953–1955), 49–55.

Wallon, Henri, "*Emile; ou, de l'éducation.*" *Europe* (Nov.–Dec. 1961), pp. 128–135.

Weil, Eric. "J. J. Rousseau et sa politique." *Critique*, IX (Jan. 1952), 3–28.

Wright, Ernest Hunter. *The Meaning of Rousseau.* 1929. Reprint. New York: Russell & Russell, 1963.

Index

Library of Congress Cataloging in Publication Data
(For library cataloging purposes only)

Ellenburg, Stephen.
  Rousseau's political philosophy.

  Bibliography: p.
  Includes index.
  1. Rousseau, Jean Jacques, 1712-1778—Political
science.   I. Title.
JC179.R9E55   1976   320.5'092'4   75-30481
ISBN 0-8014-0960-8